"Favaro's refreshing book synthesizes lessons from his four-decade career as one of the great strategy advisors. He gives these lessons in the form of questions a CEO might be wondering about, and he answers every question clearly, concisely, and in plain English. His down-to-earth style delivers a karate chop to the solar plexus of most of the high-minded writing on strategy. The result is a highly readable guide—a major contribution to practical management advice on this crucial, much obfuscated subject. Every business leader should keep this book within reach!"

—**Shumeet Banerji** Board Director, HP Inc., BBC, and Reliance
Industries Limited, Founder and Managing Partner, Condorcet, LP,
Former CEO, Booz & Company (now Strategy& PwC)

"I personally experienced (and learned from) much of what Favaro writes about in *Real Strategy*. Following what he has to say will benefit the strategy of any business."

—**Sir Jonathan Symonds** Chairman of the Board, GSK
(GlaxoSmithKline), Deputy Group Chairman, HSBC, Board member
of Genomics England, Former CFO, Novartis

"In *Real Strategy* Favaro offers a roadmap for a transformative journey into the essence of strategy. His guidance proved instrumental in aligning my company's board and team, setting the stage for our business to take flight."

—**Nan-Wei Gong** Founder and CEO, FIGUR8

"*Real Strategy* is a must-have handbook for leaders of any type of organization. Favaro's practical guidance answers many of the questions leaders must master to create a great strategy, keep it great, and get the most of out of it."

—**Valerie Redford** Former Head, Prudential Insurance's Retirement
Retail Solutions, Former Chief Strategy Officer, TIAA Direct to
Consumer Business, Former Head, TIAA Strategic Consulting

"There are lots of books on strategy, but it is still a misunderstood—and hence underleveraged—concept. Favaro's book cuts through it all and provides a clear, practical, and hopeful guide to growing your business. As a former CMO—and now CEO and board director—I recommend *Real Strategy* to any marketer who has aspirations to rise above being a "functional leader" to become a true business leader."

—**Jim Stengel** CEO, The Jim Stengel Company, Host, The CMO Podcast, Former Global Marketing Officer, Procter & Gamble

"No business leader or MBA student should miss what Favaro has to say in *Real Strategy*. His experience working with CEOs comes through loud and clear, with compelling answers to the most important questions about strategy."

—**Glenn Hubbard** Professor of Finance and Economics and former Dean, Columbia University Graduate School of Business, Former Chair, Council of Economic Advisors, Board Director, MetLife, KKR, and ADP

"A strategy is worthless without genuine alignment in your team and board. Even an OK strategy with alignment is invaluable. I've seen the advice in *Real Strategy* help CEOs achieve outstanding results for their companies."

—**Andrew Thompson** Managing Director and Co-Founder, Spring Ridge Ventures, Co-founder and former CEO, Proteus Digital Health, Co-founder and former CEO, FemRx (acquired by J&J)

"In *Real Strategy* Favaro provides a sharp and clear definition of what strategy is and what makes one great. Drawing from his unparalleled experience and wisdom, he offers practical, actionable advice and guidance to business leaders and MBA students."

—**Stefanos Zenios** Professor of Entrepreneurship and Operations, Information, and Technology, Stanford University Graduate School of Business (the GSB), Architect, Startup Garage at the GSB, Faculty co-director, Center for Entrepreneurial Studies at the GSB

REAL
STRATEGY

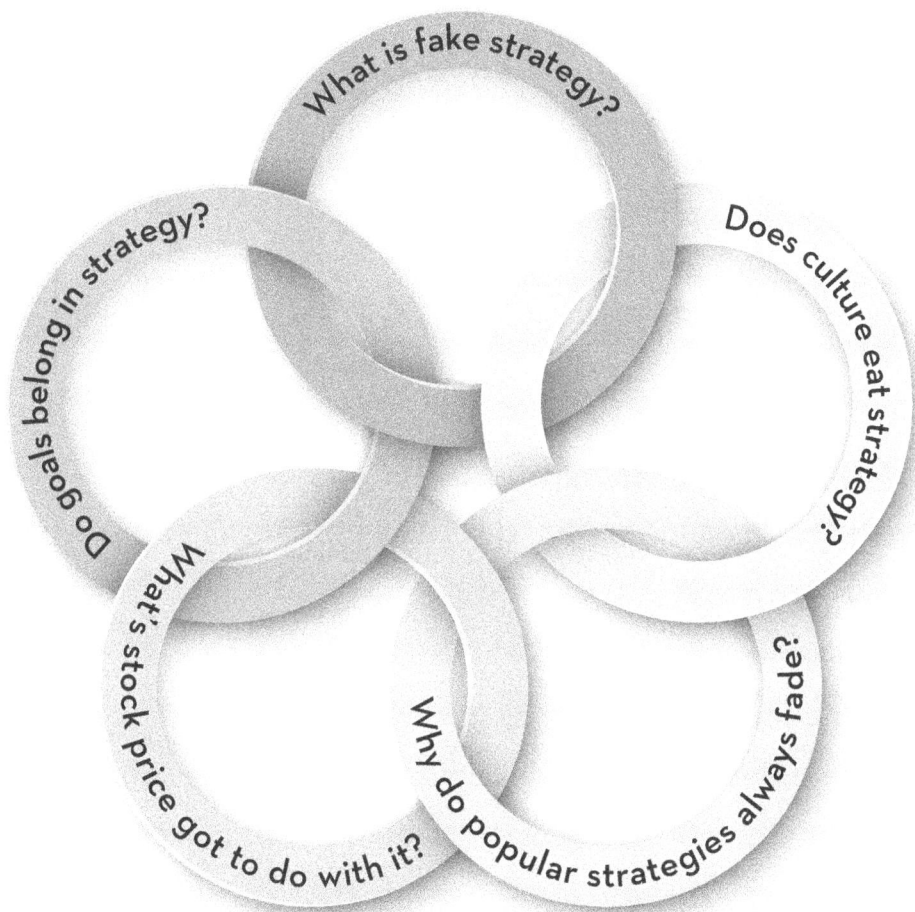

What is fake strategy?

Do goals belong in strategy?

Does culture eat strategy?

What's stock price got to do with it?

Why do popular strategies always fade?

A no-nonsense guide for leaders with 65 questions
and answers you won't find anywhere else

KEN FAVARO

Softcover: 979-8-9902880-0-3

Ebook: 979-8-9902880-1-0

Copyeditor: Mark Woodworth, Mark Woodworth Editorial Services

Cover and interior design: Vicky Vaughn Shea, Ponderosa Pine Design

Publishing Strategist: Holly Brady, Brady New Media Publishing

act2

Bronxville, New York

act2advice@gmail.com

Printed in the United States of America

*To the many potholes, cul-de-sacs, and detours
that are on the road to learning.*

Contents

Why this book

I asked ChatGPT—the chatbot developed by OpenAI—to write a table of contents for a book on strategy. Here's the reply:[1]

Chapter 1: Understanding Business Strategy 1.1 The Essence of Business Strategy 1.2 Types of Business Strategies

Chapter 2: Vision, Mission, and Core Values 2.1 Crafting a Clear Vision Statement 2.2 Defining Your Mission and Purpose

Chapter 3: Environmental Analysis and Market Research 3.1 Conducting a PESTEL Analysis 3.2 Unraveling Industry Dynamics

Chapter 4: SWOT Analysis and Competitive Advantage 4.1 Leveraging SWOT Analysis for Strategic Decision-making 4.2 Uncovering Your Competitive Advantage 4.3 Sustaining Competitive Advantage

Chapter 5: Strategic Goal Setting and KPIs 5.1 Establishing SMART Goals 5.2 Key Performance Indicators (KPIs) for Measuring Success 5.3 Cascading Goals Throughout the Organization

Chapter 6: Strategic Planning Process 6.1 Creating a Strategic Planning Framework 6.2 The Role of Scenario Planning in Strategy Development 6.3 Integrating Risk Management in Strategic Plans

Chapter 7: Innovation and Disruptive Strategies 7.1 Embracing a Culture of Innovation 7.2 Identifying and Responding to Disruptive Forces

7.3 Collaborative Strategies for Open Innovation

Chapter 8: Market Segmentation and Targeting 8.1 Understanding Market Segmentation 8.2 Selecting the Right Target Market 8.3 Personalization and Customization in Targeting

Chapter 9: Branding and Competitive Positioning 9.1 Building a Strong Brand Identity 9.2 Crafting a Unique Value Proposition 9.3 Positioning Strategies for Market Leadership

Chapter 10: Strategic Alliances and Partnerships 10.1 The Power of Strategic Alliances 10.2 Evaluating and Selecting the Right Partners

Chapter 11: Mergers, Acquisitions, and Diversification 11.1 Assessing Merger and Acquisition Opportunities 11.2 Successful Integration of Merged Entities 11.3 Diversification Strategies for Sustainable Growth

Chapter 12: Implementing and Executing Strategy 12.1 Overcoming Implementation Challenges 12.2 Effective Resource Allocation and Budgeting 12.3 Monitoring and Adapting the Strategy

ChatGPT's outline is essentially a synthesis of everything that's ever been published on business strategy. And it neatly captures a drawback that all books on strategy have: none do a very good job of answering the many tricky questions that headline the chapters in this book. These questions bedevil the understanding and utility of strategy as one of the most powerful tools leaders have to build their companies and lead their organizations. Answering these questions is one of my primary motivations for writing this book. You won't find them—or their answers—anywhere else. Together, the answers in this book add up to a practical, coherent guide to help leaders harness the power of strategy as a leadership tool.

My second motivation for writing this book is equally important. The concept of business strategy took off about 50 years ago. The graphic below illustrates the point.

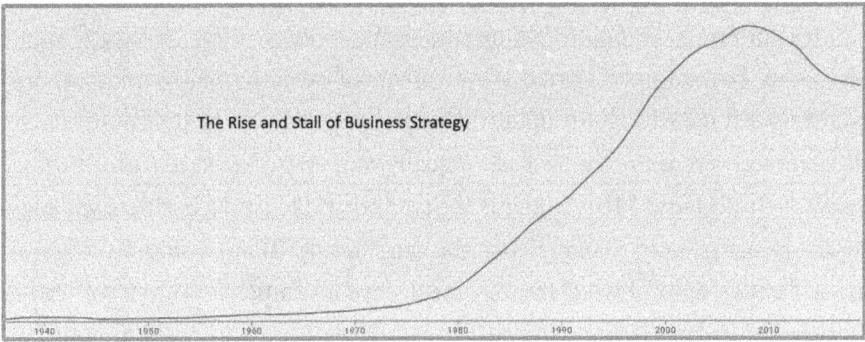

The Rise and Stall of Business Strategy

This image comes from Google's Ngram Viewer, which measures the popularity of words based on their usage in publications. It's a way to visualize the life cycle of fads, fashion, ideas, concepts, movements, and more. The curve above vividly depicts the Cambrian explosion of books and other publications on business strategy that began in the 1970s and accelerated over the following two decades.

Today, it seems as if everything is "strategy." For example, see the table below for a partial list.

50 Shades of Strategy

• Competitive strategy	• Sales strategy	• R&D strategy
• Portfolio strategy	• Product strategy	• Manufacturing strategy
• Global strategy	• Customer strategy	• Supplier/Sourcing
• Growth strategy	• Market entry strategy	strategy
• Local strategy	• Operational strategy	• Marketing strategy
• Cost strategy	• Value chain strategy	• People strategy
• Margin strategy	• China strategy	• Financial strategy
• Risk strategy	• Pricing strategy	• Technology strategy
• M&A strategy	• Partner strategy	• IT strategy
• Diversification strategy	• Commercial strategy	• Digital strategy
• Divestment strategy	• Channel/Distribution strategy	• Data strategy
• Innovation strategy	• Communications strategy	• IoT strategy
• Go-to-market strategy	• Government relations strategy	• Web3.0 strategy
• Ecosystem strategy	• Public relations strategy	• e-Commerce strategy
• Shareholder value strategy	• Investor relations strategy	• Blockchain strategy
• Social value strategy	• DEI strategy	• Metaverse strategy
• Stakeholder value strategy	• ESG/Net zero/Climate strategy	• AI/Generative AI strategy

It's gotten to the point that no one seems to know what "strategy" means any more. For example, I often ask members of executive teams and corporate boards to tell me what it means at their company. I always hear almost as many different answers as the people I ask. Equally worrying, I've asked future business leaders—fresh-faced MBA students at Stanford and Harvard business schools—to do the same, only to experience the same result. That's a shame. When we lose collective sight of what strategy means, we lose a powerful tool for leading companies. Perhaps that is why the curve in the earlier image peaks around 2010 and stalls from there. Changing this picture—by helping business leaders reclaim the power of strategy—inspired me to tackle the questions I pose in this book.

This brings me to a third reason for writing the book. Strategy is strongest when it's simple. It doesn't require fancy formulas, busy charts, complex matrices, or elaborate frameworks. But there's a fine line between simple and simplistic. I wrote this book to help business leaders stay on the simple side of that line. To guide me, I've used a saying often attributed to Einstein that "Everything must be made as simple as possible, but not one bit simpler."

Finally, I thought it was time to bring together into a single place the many pieces I've written on strategy for *Harvard Business Review, Forbes.com, Strategy+Business*, and other publications. These are listed in appendix 2.

ABOUT THIS BOOK

Part I establishes the definition of strategy used throughout this book. "Strategy" can mean very different things to different people, and I'm often amazed by how often people opine on strategy without giving us their definition of it. We'll explore this in chapters 1–3.

Parts II through V expand on what strategy is by spelling out what it's not, what a great one is, and what it takes to create a great strategy and keep it great. These lay a foundation for the rest of the book.

Part VI tackles head-on the role of strategy in running a business well, including execution, culture, and organizational effectiveness.

Parts VII through IX cover the most common questions that I've come across in my long-in-the-tooth career concerning the scope of strategy, guideposts to keep a strategy on track, and the role of various agents who have a stake in their company's strategy.

The book's final chapters explore what leaders can learn by looking at the range of strategy challenges that different types of enterprises and industries face. These can be found in Parts X and XI, respectively.

Finally, appendix 1 covers the great shareholder–stakeholder debate. Though not about strategy per se, the debate creates an ever-present, boisterous backdrop that can confuse leaders in their efforts to have and hold great strategies. Here, leaders will find a framework and pertinent advice to help them form their own views and find the best language to express them.

HOW TO READ THIS BOOK

You can read this book as an integrated whole or as a collection of individual topics that can be sampled. The chapters stand on their own and are bite-sized in length, with an average word count of less than 1,300, which is about a third of the typical article in *Harvard Business Review*. The time to read a single chapter is about five minutes, or less than six hours for the whole book.

In every chapter, I call out other chapters that are relevant to what you are reading. You can safely ignore these if you wish, or you can use them to learn more if you want.

You can dip in and out of this book wherever you like. But also, the chapters build on previous ones and often set up later ones. Thus, you can read the book from start to finish and experience a logical flow that adds up to a multifaceted, comprehensive guide to strategy.

Alternatively, if you haven't the time or interest to read yet another book on strategy, no matter how great it might be (and this one is great!), you can get the gist by reading "This book in three minutes" and "A final word."

WHEN TO READ THIS BOOK

A good time to pick up this book is when you are about to embark on a strategy project with your team, your board, or your client. Or when you've been asked by your boss or board to facilitate a strategy process or to build (or rebuild) a strategy function. Or when you have a great idea for starting a new business and want to build a strategy around that idea. Or when you as a business leader feel frustrated by poor execution in your team or organization. Or when you want to arm yourself for a strategy class at business school, or perhaps a career in management consulting, or even a new job with responsibilities that include strategy. Or when you have a particular question that can be found in the Contents.

GROUND RULES FOR THIS BOOK

In writing this book I settled on a few ground rules.

No Jargon. In this book you won't find worn-out words such as *disruption*, *pivot*, *value-add*, *win-win*, *leverage*, and *monetization*; nor core (or non-core), bandwidth, ideation, hacking (of any kind), blitz scaling, market engineering, or futureproofing. You'll be spared reading about burning platforms, takeaways, journeys, deep dives, decision rights, syncs, inflection points, pain points, moon shots, white space, blue skies, red oceans, and adjacencies; and you'll never see phrases like "thinking outside the box," "finding product market fit," and "seeing around corners." Nor will you have to look up SWOT, TAM (or SAM), MVP, KPIs, OKRs, ROI (or ROMI), EBIDTA (or EBIT), TSR, SMART (or RACI or RATSI), or ESG and CSR. And above all, you'll never see the loaded word "strategic" except in a quote or paraphrase.

There is nothing always wrong with using words, phrases, abbreviations, and acronyms like these, but they do tend to obfuscate more than elucidate, especially when over-used.

Now, I know that jargon is in the eye of the beholder. So, if I use words you consider to be jargon, please let me know at *act2advice@gmail.com*.

No Overpromising. This is not a book you can buy and read in an airport lounge that promises you have only "X steps to strategic success." There are no controlled experiments that can prove what those X steps are! Strategy is more art than science. Science can be learned in a systematic and logical way, whereas expertise in an art has to be acquired by example, experience, and practice. Nevertheless, acquiring the art of strategy can be accelerated by learning a few general principles. These include: what strategy is and is not; why great execution depends on having a great strategy; what makes a strategy great; and how to *keep* it great. The promise of this book is that readers will learn such principles and how to apply them to the many questions about strategy they will confront in their careers.

No Overpromising, part 2. This book is not called The Sole Truth About Strategy, The Last Strategy Book You'll Ever Need, The Final Word on Strategy, or Everything You'll Ever Want to Know About Strategy. That's because it's not. It's necessarily a result of my particular experience, the many business leaders and board directors with whom I've worked, and the learning I've gained from practitioners, experts, and even charlatans. In writing it, I made a promise to tackle only those questions that arise most often in my work…and to which I think I truly have something to add.

FEEDBACK ON THIS BOOK

I welcome your thoughts on whatever you choose to read, whether that's a particular page, chapter, part, or the whole book. I've not seen everything under the sun. I don't have the one and only truth. And I'm sure you can help me improve what there is to say about strategy and how to rescue it from the muddle, misuse, and, well, all the B.S. it suffers in the real world.

And if you have a question on strategy that's not addressed in this book, I welcome hearing about it. I'm sure I've missed some important ones. And next time, I'll include them.

Finally, this book *Real Strategy* will be followed by two others, *Real Innovation* and *Real Organization*. Both will tackle the most important questions for their respective topics. If you have any such questions that I should include, please do let me know. I will be grateful for your suggestions. Again, you can find me at *act2advice@gmail.com*.

---

1   Reader beware: chatbots will produce different responses for the same prompt because they are based on probabilistic algorithms rather than deterministic ones.

This book in three minutes

Great execution means consistently producing superior business results. That's not guaranteed with a great strategy, but it's impossible without one.

Every great strategy stands on the shoulders of a big idea—a novel solution to an unsolved problem or unmet need or unsatisfied want. The bigger the idea, the more potent a strategy can be. No strategy and no amount of great execution can make up for the lack of a big idea that is still a "big" idea.

Ask ten leaders of a company what "strategy" means, and you'll get ten very different answers. That's okay as long as their strategy answers three questions: *Who* should be the target customer for our products and services? *Why* should our target customers choose us over their perceived alternatives? *What* capabilities should we become the best at, in order to be better than anyone else at meeting our promise to our target customers?

The answers to these three questions—*Who? Why? What?*—tell leaders, their organization, and their owners and investors how they will build a growing, profitable, and loyal customer base. The more those answers are sharply differentiating and powered by a big idea, the more likely great execution will follow.

But what about leaders at the helm of multibusiness companies? They must answer a different set of questions: What should be our company's unique way of contributing to the future earnings power of our various businesses? What capabilities should we be the best at, in order to make us better than anyone else at our way of contributing to our businesses? What businesses should we own because they fit best with our unique way of contributing to our businesses?

Mutually-reinforcing and internally consistent answers to these three questions form a coherent multibusiness strategy and increase the odds that the whole will be worth more than the parts.

Strategy is neither a business model nor a business plan. A business *model* is how leaders turn their strategy into economic value, how their organizations operate to turn their strategy into reality, and how their leaders fund their strategy to give them life. A business *plan* spells out what leaders will actually do, the resources the organization will deploy to help them do it, and the performance it will need to achieve so as to implement their strategy *and* their business model.

A strategy, a business model, and a plan form a powerful trio of tools to help leaders get the most out of their organization and their big idea. But they should never be conflated. Strategy is always the victim when it's conflated with a business model or plan.

The strategies that leaders have for their company can inform or be informed by their vision, mission, purpose, and goals. Yet leaders should never confuse these with strategy, for strategy will always suffer if they do.

The questions that headline most of the chapters in this book touch on the multitude of confusions, received wisdoms, and misconceptions that can destroy the power of strategy to facilitate great execution. The answers found in this book will help leaders preserve and fortify that power.

A note on Covid-19

While I was writing much of this book, Covid-19 upended the world. In a few short weeks, in early 2020, whole industries were brought to their knees. Companies large and small were knocked off their carefully considered strategies, business models, and plans. Leaders fell into chronic crisis mode to keep their businesses alive. Their people were tossed into a world of crushing uncertainty and sacrifice. It seems hard to believe now, but at the time, having customers and revenue seemed a distant, nostalgic memory when much of the economy shut down in response to the pandemic.

Yet, except for a single chapter on the retailing industry (see chapter 62), readers will find no reference to this attack on our way of life. How is that possible? Well, after careful thought, I concluded that the important questions of strategy addressed in this book have not changed. And the answers to those questions remain the same.

Of course, the *context* for strategy changed dramatically during the Covid pandemic. It did this very much as it did during the financial crisis of 2008; the 9/11 terrorist attacks; the civil rights, oil, and inflation crises of the 1960s and '70s; two world wars before that; and so on.

Yet the substance and principles of strategy proposed in this book hold steady for any particular context. And, in fact, they provide leaders the tools to steer their ship with a firm grip and steady hand through whatever tailwinds, headwinds, crosswinds, and currents they will face in the future.

....

PART I

What Is Strategy?

One day, a colleague and I were taking
a break from our work on a strategy assignment
for a client.

Suddenly, he blurted out "What is strategy, anyway?"
I don't remember my answer. It was decades ago. But I'll never forget the
feeling that my answer could have been better.

1

How is strategy typically defined?

So many answers to a simple question

Some people collect baseball cards. Others, vintage cars. I collect answers to a simple question: *What is strategy?* Here are the top ten most common:

1. The sum of choices a company makes and executes over time.
2. The act of making choices under uncertainty, constraints, and competition.
3. Where you play and how you win (or: What business to be in and how to compete in it).
4. How you create and capture value.
5. The search for a favorable competitive position in an industry (optional addition: Based on your view of where that industry is headed).
6. What you want to become and how you will become that (or: Where you want to go and how you will get there).
7. Analyzing, envisioning, and framing (or shaping) your future.
8. Setting a goal and planning actions to achieve it.
9. An integrated set of actions designed to create a sustainable advantage over competitors.
10. A set of actions to overcome the biggest hurdle(s) in achieving a particular objective.

These definitions come from business leaders, corporate strategists, strategy consultants, and business school professors. And each one has serious drawbacks.

The first five are too broad. Every day, everyone in a company—from frontline workers to board directors—makes decisions and takes actions that could be included in any one of those definitions. For example, in a retail business, a regional manager might decide where to locate the next store in her region while letting each of her store managers decide what they stock in their stores to appeal to the preferences of their local communities. Their decisions are choices, and at their level, those choices affect where their company plays and how it competes, how the company creates and captures value, and how it wins (or loses) a favorable competitive position. If that's included in strategy, then everything is included! But by including everything, it means nothing. It amounts to defining strategy as "everything we decide and do." Not very helpful.

The next five (6–10) have another problem. They conflate strategy with plans, vision, mission, purpose, and goals. For sure, these are important tools for leading any enterprise. But they serve very different functions. In chapters 4 and 5, we'll dive into this. For now, I'll assert that leaders end up with very little strategy when they conflate it with things like plans, visions, missions, and goals.

There's another type of response to the question of *What is strategy?* This defines the term based on its objective or intent. Here are the most common:
- *To achieve leading market share.*
- *To establish a profitable and sustainable position in an industry.*
- *To create sustainable competitive advantage.*
- *To capture market territory.*
- *To maximize the share of potential opportunity areas.*
- *To build market leadership.*
- *To maximize shareholder value.*
- *To maximize customer satisfaction.*
- *To optimize stakeholder value.*
- *To maximize social value (or shared value).*
- *To serve a social purpose.*

Each has been promoted and popularized by various business stars, famous academics, leading consultancies, and even powerful money managers.

For example, in the 1970s, Bruce Henderson, founder of Boston Consulting Group, argued that maximizing "relative market share" should be the intention of strategy because of what he called the "Experience Curve" effect. He got the idea from T.P. Wright an aeronautical engineer, who in the 1930s studied airplane factories. Wright found that the more often an airplane model was manufactured, the quicker and cheaper the next plane became. The second plane would be 15 per cent cheaper to produce than the first; the fourth would be 15 per cent lower than the second; and the eighth 15 per cent cheaper again. Wright called this phenomenon "the learning curve." Henderson's conclusion was that the higher your relative market share, the further up the learning curve you would be and the lower your unit costs would be, compared to competitors'. Hence, he reasoned, "maximizing relative market share" is the best way to beat your competitors.

In the 1980s, Michael Porter broadened this to "competitive advantage," which, according to him, could be obtained in one of three ways: through lower costs, differentiation, or focus (see chapter 44).

Around the same time, Jack Welch—General Electric's long-standing CEO—was building his empire at GE and declared that being number 1 or 2 in every business should be the central intent of the company's strategy (see chapter 6).

Yet Welch's time was also one of empire-busting by corporate takeover artists who argued that management was working in its own interest rather than for shareholders. In their seminal paper, "Theory of the Firm: Managerial Behavior, Agency Cost and Ownership Structure," Michael C. Jensen and William H. Meckling sowed the seeds for a movement that took off in the 1980s and '90s to make "maximizing shareholder value" central to strategy (see chapter 35 and appendix 1).

Then, early this century, the inevitable backlash began when none other than Welch announced in 2009 that "shareholder value is the dumbest idea ever" and gave new impetus to the so-called stakeholder school of strategy. Ten years later this was supposedly endorsed by the Business Roundtable, an elite club for CEOs of America's largest companies (see appendix 1). Variants of the stakeholder model include a call for strategy to "maximize customer satisfaction" (for example, see "The Age of Customer Capitalism," by Roger L. Martin, in the *Harvard Business Review*) and calls for CEOs and their boards to make "social purpose" the north star for their strategies (see chapter 33).

Yet all these ways of defining "strategy" in terms of its intent or objective have the same problem: they drag us into an endless philosophical debate about what companies are generally for. They pull us away from the practical use of strategy as a leadership tool. And, from a practical perspective, these ways of defining strategy fail to define what's in and what's out. Every decision and every action taken—by the frontline, by folks in the boardroom, and by everyone in between—affects the company's market share, competitive advantage, and value to shareholders, customers, other stakeholders, and society overall. So where does strategy begin and end? Nowhere and everywhere! Again, not very helpful.

I often ask leadership teams with whom I work to write down whether they agree or disagree with each of the statements in the two lists above. You can guess the typical result. They're all over the map! Few teams agree on what strategy is. It's under-specified, frequently conflated with other leadership tools, unhelpfully equated to the governing objective or general purpose of business, or sometimes even all these things. Perhaps the question—*What is strategy?*—is the wrong one. The better one is: *What questions should a strategy answer?*

2

How should strategy be defined?

However you wish, but at the very least know your *Who? Why?* and *What?*

A successful business has a thriving base of customers who are willing to buy, use, and recommend its products and services. In competitive, transparent markets with level playing fields, that requires leaders to know *Who* they want their customers to be, *Why* those customers should choose them, and *What* makes their business better than any other at marketing, selling, and meeting their promise to those customers. These are the *Who? Why?* and *What?* questions that every strategy must answer:

1. *Who* should be our target customer?
2. *Why* should our target customer choose us?
3. *What* capabilities should we prioritize and nurture to make us the best at marketing, selling, and making good on our *Why?*

No matter how leaders define "strategy," they should at least be able to articulate *with one voice* their choice for each of these three questions. The sharper and more distinctive their choices are, the better their execution will be. It's that simple.

But this doesn't make strategy easy. I often ask a group of executives to write down their *Who? Why?* and *What?* They typically find the exercise challenging.

To begin with, leaders often struggle to be specific about their *Who*. This is frequently because they feel it limits their business. But sometimes they can't even agree on who their customers *are*. For example, "is our customer the reader or the advertiser?" is the subject of endless discussions among the leaders of a world-leading newspaper. For most health care businesses, an evergreen question is whether the customer is the patient, the payor, the physician, the hospital, an employer, a pharmaceutical company, or someone else. Then there's Uber. In its SEC filing to go public, it declared that its customer is the driver, not the passenger, even though the rider is receiving the service and paying for it. (Does this mean that its push into autonomous driving was an attempt to get rid of its customers?)

Likewise, many executive teams labor to describe their choice for *Why*. This happens when they conflate what customers buy with what they pay for and thus default to describing features rather than benefits. It also happens when leaders confuse solving an unmet need and "job to be done" with the benefits gained from meeting a need and getting a job done. And it also happens when leaders underestimate the intangible benefits (such as social validation, security, peace of mind, and status) and costs (like risk, hassle, and internal disruption) that their products and services entail.

Finally, leaders can be stymied by the *What* question—the handful of capabilities they should prioritize for continuous investment and deliberate nurturing. Here are some examples (with thanks to *Strategy That Works*, by Paul Leinwand and Cesare Mainardi):

- Frito-Lay's direct-to-store delivery system, which makes it better than anyone else's at rapid-fire, real-world, trial-and-error testing of snack promotions and innovations in the field;
- Honeywell Systems' expertise in working with the distributors and contractors who deal with the buyers of HVAC systems, which Honeywell is using to fend off companies like Nest that are offering digital building devices;
- Netflix's head start in using the behavioral data of viewers to understand what they do and want, which could make or break the streamer's future in the increasingly crowded streaming business;
- Starbucks' innovative methods for recruiting and motivating dedicated

employees, giving the company a leg up in the notoriously difficult task of staffing quick-service retail businesses.

Leading capabilities like these typically span multiple internal boundaries and are hard to pin down. That is especially so if leaders are fuzzy about their *Who?* and *Why?*

Who? Why? and *What?* aren't as easy to answer as they might seem. Moreover, their answers have to fit within a context that's always changing. That's because some customer populations grow while others hit a wall or even shrink. Customers' needs and wants are always evolving. New technologies generate new possibilities and close down others. Innovation opens up new opportunities or creates new threats. Regulation tilts the playing field, for better or for worse. Political movements and moments create headwinds or tailwinds.

Changes like these can wilt a winning strategy. To avoid this, leaders need to regularly revisit their strategy, and sometimes even start over. That requires a certain degree of diligence that is easier said than done when leaders feel overwhelmed by other matters—from capital crunches to budget battles, people problems, customer crises, partner predicaments, supplier snafus, intellectual property issues, operational obstacles, competitor challenges, legal liabilities, and even survival scrapes.

This can create a vicious cycle: Putting out fires understandably stands ahead of spending quality time on strategy; lack of quality time on strategy allows it to stagnate and lose its punch; a stale and punch-less strategy means playing catch-up and leads to more and hotter fires breaking out; and this makes spending time on strategy even more difficult to justify. Trying to break into that vicious cycle and reverse its direction is no fun.

All this may explain why strategy has been so muddled over the years. Perhaps it's easier to default to "big picture" statements with the warm feeling of motherhood and sweet aroma of apple pie. Who can argue with a "strategy" *to be the leading company in this or that,* or *to be number 1 or 2 everywhere we compete,* or *to create the world's best this or largest that?*

Maybe it's more exciting to adopt a big, hairy audacious goal *to put a computer on every desk,* or *to make health care more affordable for all,* or *to organize the world's information,* or *to elevate the world's consciousness.*

Perhaps it's smarter to focus on what Wall Street or "corporate" wants to hear, like where growth will come from, how margins will fare, and what kind of returns investors can expect. Or to talk about what employees are *really* interested in when they ask to hear more about the company's "strategy," like its vision, mission, goals, and priorities.

The good news is, there's nothing wrong with any of this. Embracing a bigger picture and having broad, ambitious goals can truly be motivating. Giving information to Wall Street, corporate, and employees is no bad thing. But all of these tend to be mostly silent on leaders' answers to *Who? Why?* and *What?*

Leaders can't escape the reality that businesses are successful only when they are attracting the right customers with meaningful and unique benefits, and with the capabilities to market, sell, and produce those benefits better and at a lower cost than anyone else. Vision, mission, purpose, and goals can be powerful multipliers of strategy if they meaningfully enhance why customers choose offerings *or* materially boost the ability to attract and build the know-how, skills, tools, technology, and assets that are essential to leading capabilities. But they can't substitute for the all-important choices leaders must make for their *Who? Why?* and *What?*

To further explain this, consider Ford Motor Company. In 1913 it was an also-ran. By 1921 it had captured over two-thirds of the market. Henry Ford's goal was big, hairy, and audacious: "to make the automobile affordable to the masses." Was having that goal the key to his company's success? Or was it great execution?

The answer to both questions is "Yes." But it was Henry Ford's strategy that made both his goal and superior execution possible. He was the first to focus on the "the little guy" for his *Who?* rather than the wealthy. His *Why?* offered all the benefits of owning a reliable car, but at a fraction of the prevailing market price ("as long as it was a Model T and came in the color black"). And no one else could match Ford's *Why?* because of his *What?*—a breakthrough production capability that combined a moving assembly line and standardization of parts with a unique selling capability based on franchising the first nationwide network of car dealerships.

Today, however, every car company has those two capabilities. And Ford is once again an also-ran. Its original ambition has evolved—now it's to be a "mobility company," whatever *that* means—and it still has excellent operators. But you can't distinguish Ford's *Who? Why?* and *What?* from those of any other car company. No amount of vision, mission, purpose, ambition, or operational excellence can make up for that.

All this goes to say that leaders lose a powerful tool to bring out the best of their companies when their strategies are simplistic, too complex, just a goal, or merely a philosophical statement on the purpose of their business or of business in general. They can avoid that by having and maintaining distinctive choices for their *Who? Why?* and *What?* and by keeping those choices at the heart of their strategy, no matter what "strategy" means at their company.

Finally, when leaders know their *Who? Why?* and *What?* they can answer all the questions implied in the most common definitions of strategy such as those listed in chapter 1. These include, for example, "What business are we in?" "Where do we play?" "How will we compete, create advantage, earn market leadership, and win?" "How do we create value for customers, staff, shareholders, and society at large?" And "How do we serve the social purpose of our business?"

Unfortunately, it doesn't work in reverse: answering these questions doesn't always lead to clear choices for *Who? Why?* and *What?*

3

What about multibusiness companies?

A different set of questions

In chapter 2 we explain why the strategy that leaders have for their business must spell out *Who? Why?* and *What?* But what about the leaders of a company with multiple businesses, such as The Walt Disney Company or Berkshire Hathaway? Is strategy for these companies just an aggregation of the strategies for their individual businesses? No, not at all.

"Strategy" for a multibusiness company[1] should answer a different set of questions:

- What should be our company's unique way of contributing to the future earnings power of our individual businesses?
- What capabilities should our company prioritize and nurture to make us better than anyone else at our way of contributing to the future earnings power of our businesses?
- What businesses should we own because they fit best with our way of contributing to their future earnings power?

The answer to each question depends a lot on the answers to the other two. Thus, leaders have to iterate between all three to find answers that reinforce each other and reflect the practical realities their company faces.

A great example of multibusiness strategy is the one that the long-time CEO

Bob Iger had for Disney. He called it the "corporate franchise strategy." To him, corporate franchises are a character, such as *Mickey Mouse*, or a group of characters, like *Toy Story*. They can be home grown (*Frozen*) or acquired (*Star Wars*). But all of them can be commercialized in multiple ways through Disney's various businesses, including resort parks, theater, consumer products, TV, streaming, and more. Every business is expected to actively contribute to and benefit from all of Disney's corporate franchises.

Over the years, it's clear that Disney has built and honed an extraordinary ability to create new characters, strengthen the characters it buys, and commercialize its characters multiple times over. None of Disney's businesses could do what they do—as well as they do it—on their own, or with any other company.

Iger's strategy for Disney made clear how the company contributes to its businesses, what capabilities enable that, and what businesses fit best with that. With one glaring exception,[2] Iger's strategy is a poster child for a company that has a coherent multibusiness strategy.

Another poster child is Berkshire Hathaway. Its founder and long-time CEO, Warren Buffett, built a company with three world-beating capabilities: sourcing enormous amounts of low-cost capital (called "insurance float," which is the delay between collecting premiums and using them to pay out claims in its insurance businesses), deploying capital profitably (both through stock purchases and capital allocation to the businesses it wholly owns), and attracting high-quality companies run by superb leaders who could retire but don't because they never tire of the challenge to maximize the long-term value of their businesses.

No company—diversified or not—can match the strength of these three capabilities. And every business in Berkshire's empire, from the insurance businesses to the heavy industry, transportation, energy, consumer, and retail businesses, contributes to all three capabilities…*and* benefits from them.

Like Iger's strategy, Buffett's strategy makes crystal clear what his company's special capabilities are, how those capabilities contribute to each business, and what businesses belong (and don't belong) in its portfolio.

Unfortunately, Iger and Buffett are exceptions. Most leaders of multibusiness companies obsess over what should be in their portfolios. Yet they don't give much thought to how their companies should contribute to the long-term earnings power of their businesses, nor to the capabilities their companies should have to realize that contribution. Instead, they default to a form of financial engineering (see chapter 6), where they prioritize what they *think* the stock market and investors value: businesses with particular growth rates, profit margins, risk profiles, or price-to-earnings ratios. They end up chasing businesses that everyone else covets and dropping businesses that have lost their luster.

The result is a set of businesses that don't gain much from being part of the company except for a lot of extra overhead, bureaucratic processes, and "strategic direction" from the ivory tower. The leaders have no good answer to "What makes the whole more than the sum of its parts?" Their enterprises are really just investment portfolios masquerading as operating companies; and they themselves are effectively more like amateur stock pickers choosing winners and losers than they are operating executives creating operational value that their businesses could not otherwise replicate somewhere else or on their own.

This is why Richard Rumelt reports in his book *Good Strategy, Bad Strategy* that "an average multibusiness corporation has little if any systematic effect on the businesses it owns and manages." And it's why the "conglomerate discount"—where a company's observed value is less than the estimated values of its businesses—is so common (see chapter 15).

Multibusiness companies can trundle along just fine as long as their individual businesses are performing. Yet it's only a matter of time before one or two of their businesses stumble and the stock price falters. If leaders lack substantive answers to those questions listed above, they are on the back foot when the inevitable happens and the board, Wall Street analysts, or activist investors start to agitate for the company "to realize its hidden value" and split apart (see chapter 45). This happened to Viacom, Kraft Foods, Tyco (twice), ITT (twice), and even to the venerable corporations HP, Philips, AT&T, Siemens, and GE. In the future, don't be surprised if it even happens to Novartis, that pharmaceutical behemoth cum health-care conglomerate, and Unilever, the purposeful, but growth- and margin-challenged consumer packaged goods (CPG) company. Or to Salesforce, the buyer of Slack and Tableau.

Yes, leaders can demand more growth or profits from their businesses, require each of them to be number 1 or 2 in their market, and acquire, divest, restructure, and refinance to their hearts' content. But sooner or later, leaders must fashion a multibusiness strategy that yields a robust economic and commercial purpose for their individual businesses to be under the same corporate roof. That demands compelling answers to those three questions above. Otherwise, the company has no sustainable *raison d'être,* no matter how admirable its corporate purpose might be.

All the above is straightforward enough. But there are three complications. The first is **strategy for business units within a multibusiness company**. Each business unit must have its own strategy and, as explained in chapter 2, that strategy must answer three essential questions:

1. *Who* should be our target customer?
2. *Why* should our target customer choose us?
3. *What* capabilities should we prioritize and nurture to make us the best at marketing, selling, and making good on our *Why?*

However, because business units operate within the context of a multibusiness company, their strategies must also address two other questions:

4. How should we contribute to our company's multibusiness strategy?
5. How should we benefit from our company's multibusiness strategy?

Of course, this demands that business unit leaders internalize (and even provide input to) their company's multibusiness strategy. Ensuring this is an essential role of CEOs (see chapter 55).

A second complication arises **when companies have organizational layers between their CEOs and their business units**. Executives in these layers are charged with leading multibusiness entities such as "groups," "sectors," or "divisions." Does this mean they should have their own multibusiness strategy, separate from the company's multibusiness strategy? Absolutely not. That is a recipe for creating companies *within a* company that gain no value from operating under the same corporate roof. Instead, executives in these layers should be charged with ensuring that every business unit is contributing to and benefiting from the company's one multibusiness strategy. This, too, demands that they understand and commit to that strategy. This is also addressed more fully in chapter 55.

The third complication is **when leaders think of their business unit as a collection of products, customer segments, or geographies** for which they need a "portfolio strategy" to allocate resources across the various parts of their business. At a minimum, this is conflating strategy with planning (see chapter 4). But it might also indicate that their business unit is not really a single business, after all. Instead, their different product lines, customer segments, or geographies are businesses that demand their own distinctive strategy choices for *Who? Why?* and *What?* (see chapter 2). In this case, the leaders are actually in charge of a multibusiness entity that represents another organizational layer between the company as a whole and its various businesses.

---

1   Note, "corporate," "enterprise," and "portfolio" strategy are imperfect synonyms for "multibusiness" strategy. "Corporate" and "enterprise" strategy can apply to a single-business entity. "Portfolio" strategy can encourage corporate leaders to make decisions on what businesses to divest, acquire, and keep based on financial engineering (see chapter 6) rather than the more fundamental choices described in this chapter. "Portfolio" strategy can also mean choosing how to allocate resources to and across their businesses. This is planning, not strategy (see chapter 4).

2   In 2015 I wrote a piece for Forbes.com with the title "ESPN: The Exception to Disney's Strategy" (see appendix 2). ESPN is the sports-oriented cable TV channel owned by CapCities/ABC, which was acquired by Disney in 1995. If you think of Disney as a media company, you can see the connection. But ESPN neither contributes much to Bob Iger's "corporate franchise" strategy nor materially benefits from it. That must change, otherwise ESPN and the rest of Disney will have to part ways. Neither scenario will happen anytime soon, because ESPN is such a big part of Disney's profits and because Iger himself grew up in ABC. But at some point, something has to give. Disney's streaming service, Disney+, could offer a partial or temporary solution: the company is bundling Disney+ and ESPN+ (along with Hulu, its partly owned general entertainment streaming channel). This could enhance the offering and customer base for both. Skeptics might say Disney does not need to own ESPN to do this. But that assumes that the market for bundling separately owned streaming services is deep and efficient enough to establish "fair" pricing of the spoils to be shared between them (see chapter 49). Time will tell. In the meantime, *Financial Times* reported in December 2020 that Iger "told friends that once-mighty channels such as ABC/ESPN were 'over,' and Disney's future was streaming and theme parks." *FT* added that the company's interest in Hulu, which also doesn't fit Iger's strategy very well, has diminished while Disney+ has become an emerging success, signing up more than 100 million subscribers in its first two years. The fact is, ABC, ESPN, and Hulu do not fit well with Iger's corporate franchise strategy.

Note to readers

From here on out, the word *strategy* will be used as shorthand for the three choices framed in chapters 2 or 3. The exception is when "strategy" is in quotes: this flags that something is different from what's described in those two chapters.

PART II

....

What Is Not Strategy?

It's not always enough to say what
something is. Sometimes you
have to say what it's not.

4

How is strategy different from a business model and plan?

A powerful trio that's weakened when it's muddled

Sometime in the 1990s the term "business model" became ubiquitous. This was during the dot-com boom. Hundreds of newly minted internet companies ("dot-coms") were attracting huge valuations despite having no clear way of generating revenues. "What's your business model?" became synonymous with "What's your path to revenues?"

Over time "business model" morphed into something broader: how we make money (our economic model); how we organize our leaders, team, activities, and work (our operating model); and how we fund our company and returns to owners (our capital model). The term has become so popular that many leaders now use "strategy" and "business model" interchangeably.

Clearly, strategies and business models are close cousins, as they are so interdependent. For example:

- The price point that leaders choose for their economic model affects the calculus of benefits versus costs in the *Why?* of their strategy.
- The *Why?* for a medical device company might include "we get paid only when a patient's outcome is improved," thus injecting a

contingency-based fee into its economic model.

- The leaders of a clothing company may wish to distinguish its *Why?* by who makes its products, and where, thus affecting its supply chain operating model.
- A durable goods company may offer a customer financing option to enhance its *Why?* thus affecting its capital model.
- The choice that leaders make for their *Who?* affects how the marketing and sales aspects of their operating model work.
- How a multibusiness company contributes to its businesses influences what's centralized versus decentralized in its operating model.
- The capabilities that leaders choose to prioritize—their *What?*—will determine how R&D, Production, Sales, Finance, and other functions should work together in the company's operating model.

Yet interdependencies do *not* make a strategy and a business model the same thing. Each answers very different questions (see table below). And when leaders conflate the two, business model questions inevitably dominate the agenda. This forces strategy questions into the back seat, and that's when it begins to fall off the rails.

Something similar can happen between strategy and another leadership tool—the "business (or 'strategic') plan." The 1970s marked a high point of excitement for "strategic planning." Like so many other business practices, General Electric validated it as a management process that every company should institutionalize. Even with ferocious criticism from high-profile leaders such as Jack Welch (the former CEO of GE!) and business academics such as Henry Mintzberg (Cleghorn Professor of Management Studies at McGill University), strategic planning has survived as an annual ritual that's followed by most companies. And somewhere along the way, "plan" became synonymous with "strategy." But they are not the same thing.

The heart of a plan is the action, resource, and performance commitments that leaders make to implement and improve their strategy (*and* their business model). The plan's action commitments spell out what the leaders and organization will do over a particular time frame. Resource commitments call out the investments, expenses, and staffing that will be deployed in that same time frame. And performance commitments represent the results that leaders promise to produce over that time frame, as well.

To be sure, strategy without a plan is just a set of choices that will never see the light of day. Yet a plan without a strategy is akin to rowing furiously in a boat without a rudder, where its direction is determined more by water and weather conditions than by the rower.

Clearly, leaders need *both* a strategy *and* a plan. But they have to draw a clear line between them in order to know when one or the other is missing. If they allow that line to blur, the questions a plan must answer (see table below) will inevitably—and understandably—come to dominate the essential questions of strategy. Leaders will end up taking a lot of action, deploying a load of resources, and promising the moon for the performance they'll achieve. But this will be more in reaction to market tides and winds than in support of a clear strategy.

Here's a table that summarizes the difference between a strategy, a business model, and a plan based on the questions each must answer:

Business Strategy (Chapter 2)	Multibusiness Strategy (Chapter 3)	Business Model	Business Plan
Who should be our target customer? *Why* should our target customer choose us? *What* capabilities should we prioritize and nurture to make us the best at marketing, selling, and living our *Why*?	What should be our unique way of contributing to the future earnings power of our various businesses? What capabilities should we prioritize and nurture to make us the best at our way of contributing to the future earnings power of our businesses? What businesses should we be in because they fit best with our way of contributing to their future earnings power?	What should our **economic model** be—that is, how we create value with our strategy through our revenue, cost, and profit model? What should our **operating model** be—that is, how we work with each other, customers, suppliers, and partners to turn our strategy into reality? What should our **capital model** be—that is, how we fund our strategy and investor returns?	What are we going to do to implement and improve our strategy and business model? What should our **action commitments** be? What resources are needed to meet our action commitments? What should our **resource commitments** be? What will we achieve through our action commitments? What should our **performance commitments** be?

Together these determine how leaders compete, create value, and guide decisions, actions, resources, and performance throughout their organizations. Each is a powerful leadership tool in its own right. But strategy almost always loses out when these are conflated, confused, or muddled. Business model and planning questions often overwhelm leaders' thinking, time, and communications. Then leaders' strategy choices become stale and their company loses its edge. Ultimately, the business model stops working as well as it used to. Growth stalls. Plans become increasingly desperate. Financial engineering rises to the top of the agenda (see chapter 6) and Mergers and Acquisitions (M&A) become a savior (see chapter 41). But none of that is enough to make up for a strategy that is past its sell-by date. It's just a matter of time before new leaders are asked to take over so current leaders can "spend more time with their families."

Postscript: The term "business model" was given a huge popularity boost in 2005 when Alexander Osterwalder and Yves Pigneur published their "business model canvas." It looks like this:

Business Model Canvas				
Key Partners	Key Activities	Value Proposition	Customer Relations	Customer Segments
	Key Resources		Channels	
Cost Structure			Revenue Streams	

If you agree with the distinctions made in this chapter, then you might agree that Osterwalder's and Pigneur's business model canvas has three issues. First, it contains parts of a strategy, a business model, and a business plan, and thus, it conflates all three.

Next, it's missing critical parts of a strategy, a business model, and a business plan.

- It includes two of the three essential elements of strategy—value proposition (*Why?*) and customer segments (*Who?*)—but it ignores the third: leading capabilities (*What?*).
- It excludes many of the operating and capital elements of a complete business model (see table above).

- It covers two of the three parts of a business plan—"key activities" and "key resources"—but leaves out the third: "key performance commitments."

Given this, and its label, the third issue is that the business model canvas is both too broad and too narrow. It's too broad because it incorporates parts of a strategy and a business plan; and it's too narrow because it drops critical pieces of a business model.

In my work with leaders, I use an alternative that I call a "Leadership Canvas." It looks like this:

Leadership Canvas		
Business Plan Our action, resource, and performance commitments to implement our strategy and business model		**Vision, Mission, Purpose, and Goal** How we make everything we do meaningful and compelling to all our stakeholders
Strategy How we will build a growing, profitable customer base: our *Who? Why? What?*	**Business Model** How we bring our strategy to life through our economic, operating, and capital model	
Big Idea The problem we solve, the novelty of our solution, and how we will protect it—the foundation for everything else		

This organizes the most important leadership tools that leaders have into a coherent whole. It's designed to make clear that:
- strategies, business models, and business plans are worth nothing unless they stand on the shoulders of a big idea (see chapters 9 and 16).
- together, a strategy and business model spell out how to turn a big idea into commercial reality and value, and they inform and mutually reinforce each other (hence they stand side-by-side in the canvas).
- a business plan lays out how leaders will implement their strategy and business model (hence, it sits on top of strategy and business model in the canvas).
- a vision, mission, purpose, and goal both inform and are made possible by one's big idea, strategy, business model, and business plan (see chapter 5).

The leadership canvas helps leaders to put their strategy into its proper context and to keep it from getting run over by all the other leadership tools they have at their disposal.

5

Should vision, mission, purpose, and goals be part of strategy?

Complementary tools that lose their punch when conflated

When Lou Gerstner took over the reins of a troubled IBM in 1993, he famously declared, "The last thing IBM needs right now is a vision." This was widely interpreted as a statement that strategy was a luxury that IBM could not afford, so it would take a backseat, at least while Gerstner was busy turning around the company. But he promptly proceeded to change IBM's priority customer (from information technology executives to CEOs), its lead offering (from mainframe computing to corporate IT solutions), and, most important, its leading capabilities (from selling to the IT department to partnering with the C-suite). In other words, he focused on the essential questions of strategy (see chapters 2 and 3) to make his elephant dance again.

Gerstner knew that IBM was suffering from a lack of clear and coherent strategy choices that adequately addressed the existential challenge to its mainframe business. And he rightly saw that fixing this was priority number one. Envisioning the company's future could wait. Without a winning strategy, there would be no need for that.

Yet when Gerstner downplayed vision, why did so many business leaders think he was rejecting strategy? Because they were conflating the two. This happens a lot. When discussing strategy, executives often invoke some version of a vision (for instance, "to be the leading biotech company"), a mission ("to find and commercialize innovative drug therapies"), a purpose ("to improve patients' lives"), or a goal ("to bring three innovative molecules to market in the next five years"). But none of these things says much about the essential elements of a company's strategy (see table below).

Leaders lose a powerful tool for driving execution in their company when they allow vision, mission, purpose, and goals to masquerade as a "strategy." As a result, they and their organization can't tell what's "on strategy" and what's not. Everything becomes important. Indiscriminate growth creeps into the company's plans. Sooner or later, with no strategy as a guide, the business drifts.

Take Procter and Gamble. It had a mission "to touch and improve the lives of more consumers, in more parts of the world, more completely." Yet the company stalled after the Great Recession in 2008 because its strategy got lost while the vast, complex enterprise struggled to operate effectively in a more volatile and challenging business environment. It regained some momentum after offloading a bunch of brands, focusing on its biggest geographic markets, and enhancing its customer promises such as diapers free of bleach and fragrances, and razors designed for men with beards and sensitive skin. In other words, it has gained renewed traction by *less* completely touching the lives of *fewer* consumers in *fewer* parts of the world.

All this is not to denigrate the power of having a vision, mission, purpose, or goals. For sure, these are important tools for leading companies, too. Leaders can use them to rally the troops and help their people find meaning in their work. Each can help leaders bring their strategy to life; each gives leaders a means to excite, inspire, focus, mobilize, and challenge their stakeholders; each can be part of "the glue" that binds an organization together and "the grease" to ensure that things get done; and each can help an organization to perform at its very best.

Gerstner knew this, too. After stabilizing the company and establishing IBM's strategy, he did, in fact, create a vision: "To lead big companies into the brave new networked world, IBM will devise their technology strategies, build and run their systems, and ultimately become the architect and repository for corporate computing, tying together not just companies but entire industries."

But even then, he recognized the need to connect that vision to IBM's strategy (and also its business model and plan). In 2004, when reflecting on his company's turnaround, he remarked, "Vision is easy. It's just so easy to point to the bleachers and say, 'I'm going to hit one over there.' What's hard is saying, 'OK, but how do I *do* that? What are the specific programs, what are the commitments, what are the resources, what are the processes in play that we need to go implement the vision, to turn it into a working model that people follow every day in the enterprise?' That's hard work."

When employees ask about their company's strategy, they are usually asking to learn more about what the company is seeking to achieve, its longer-term ambition, the bigger picture of why the world needs it. That's okay—even necessary—and that is what vision, mission, purpose, and goals are good for. They help leaders establish and maintain the perspective, commitment, inspiration, and excitement required by their organization to perform at its very best.

Still, customers mostly don't care about a company's vision, mission, purpose, or goals.[1] They care much more about the benefits of being a customer, the company's ability to follow-through on those benefits, and whether they justify the costs of being a customer. That is what strategy is for.

Here's a table summarizing the differences between strategy and vision, mission, purpose, and goals, based on the questions each must answer:

Business Strategy (Chapter 2)	Multibusiness Strategy (Chapter 3)	Vision, Mission, Purpose, and Goals
Who should be our target customer? *Why* should our target customer choose us? *What* capabilities should we prioritize and nurture to make us the best at marketing, selling, and living our *Why*?	What should be our unique way of contributing to the future earnings power of our various businesses? What capabilities should we prioritize and nurture to make us better than any other at our way of contributing to the future earnings power of our businesses? What businesses should we be in because they fit best with our way of contributing to their future earnings power?	Vision: where (or what) will we be in the future? Mission: what do we do? Purpose: why do we exist beyond the purpose of making money? (Or, why does the world need us?) Goals: what are our ambitions? (Or, what do we seek to achieve?)

These are highly complementary tools that serve very different functions. They can inform each other. They must reinforce each other. But they cannot replace each other.

---

1   This point needs some nuance. Some leaders feel that customers choose products and services based on a judgment they make about the companies offering them: Is their vision a responsible one? Is their mission good for society? Is there purpose meaningful to me? Do they have the right goals? This suggests that vision, mission, purpose, or goals can play a meaningful role in one of the central questions of strategy: Why should our target customer choose us? There is actually no problem with this. To the contrary, if leaders can enhance their strategy (in this case, their *Why?*) with their vision, mission, purpose, or goals, more power to them (see chapters 2, 13, and 33).

6

Does financial engineering belong in strategy?

A powerful tool that's dangerous when it takes over

The practice of financial engineering is pervasive throughout the corporate world. Here are some real-world examples:

- Cutting costs to meet a target for-profit margin.
- Issuing bonds to create a more tax-efficient balance sheet.
- Replacing low-margin businesses with high-margin ones to lift a company's average margin.
- Raising a company's growth profile by replacing low-growth businesses with high-growth ones.
- Investing in businesses to diversify a company's portfolio and reduce its earnings volatility.
- Using the debt capacity of one business to fund another.
- Repurchasing shares to increase earnings per share.
- Delaying capital expenditures to fund a share repurchase program.
- Splitting shares to make them more affordable for investors.
- Discounting products to accelerate their purchase and boost current-quarter revenue.
- Buying companies that have low price-to-earnings ratios (PEs) with high-PE stock.

At too many companies, these are all considered "strategy." Consider General Electric Company. Before it imploded in the second half of the 2010s, the modern-day GE was built by Jack Welch, its CEO for 20 years. His tenure started in 1981. One of his favorite mantras was "fix it, close it, or sell it." He wanted every business to be a market leader. He expanded into growing businesses because they were growing and he shed weaker ones because they weren't. He obsessed over targets and hitting them.

This "strategy" led Welch to turn GE Capital, the company's financial arm, from a modest business financing the purchase of GE's traditional consumer durables such as appliances and industrial products like jet engines into a giant conglomerate of commercial banking, investment banking, insurance, and other financial services.

GE's powerhouse industrial side earned it a triple-A credit rating that—for a time—allowed GE Capital to borrow money at a lower rate than prevailing bank deposit rates. GE Capital exploited that apparent advantage to finance fast-food franchises, suburban McMansions, plane leasing, power plants, office buildings, and even credit card receivables.

Returning the favor, GE Capital provided a ready supply of party tricks to engineer GE's financials. For example, GE could have GE Capital peddle half a parking lot or part interest in a power plant on the final day of a quarter, book the gain as earnings, and then purchase it back after the quarter closed. Or buy the receivables of one of the industrial businesses to help it generate short-term cash flow. Or finance its customers' purchases with debt at below-market rates to prop up demand.

In 2001, when Welch was succeeded by Jeffrey Immelt, GE's portfolio was superficially similar to Berkshire Hathaway's today: a highly diversified set of industrial and consumer businesses[1] with an enormous financial arm.[2] But unlike Berkshire (see chapters 3 and 8), no one at GE could answer in any compelling way the first two of three questions that a multibusiness strategy must answer:

- What should be our unique way of contributing to the future earnings power of our various businesses?
- What capabilities should we prioritize and nurture to make us better than anyone else at our way of contributing to the future earnings power of our businesses?

- Which businesses should we own because they fit best with our way of contributing to their future earnings power?

As a result, GE's answer to the third question was driven by financial engineering—not by clear and compelling answers to the first two questions.

Welch built GE's group of businesses based both on their financial attributes—their growth outlook, market position, margin profile, and so on—and on the financial maneuvering—smoothing earnings, massaging cash flow, exploiting a high credit rating—that they facilitated. It seemed to work. But Welch's tenure coincided with two big trends: one of the greatest bull markets for stock and bonds of all time; and the booming growth of financial services in the U.S. economy.

To put this in perspective, in March 1981, the month before Welch took the reins at GE, the average stock traded at a multiple of nine times its underlying earnings, while the yield on 30-year Treasury bonds stood at 15%. In the month Welch retired, September 2001, the yield had collapsed to just over 5% and the average stock multiple exceeded 35 times (after peaking at 44 two years earlier). Moreover, the corporate tax rate fell from 46% to 35% during Welch's tenure.

Thus, you could, for example, buy a company in 1981 with pre-tax earnings of $100M for just under $500M; and if all you did was grow with the general economy, that $100M would be worth $4,300 million in 2001, more than eight times the original investment for doing nothing special. It was a beautiful time to be a serial acquirer and to build a financial services conglomerate. Welch's timing was superb.

Unfortunately, in 2001, when Immelt inherited Welch's role as CEO of GE, he also inherited Welch's tendency to conflate financial engineering with strategy. After laudably navigating through the aftermath of 9/11, Immelt resumed GE's financial-engineering ways. For example, he:
- Spun off GE's oil-&-gas unit into a publicly traded merger with Baker Hughes to "unlock hidden value."
- Jettisoned assets like the plastics division and insurance lines to sustain GE's dividend promise and fund share repurchases to boost earnings per share.

- Made GE's largest acquisition ever (Alstom SA) to replace the earnings lost by downsizing GE Capital.
- Discounted long-term service contracts to allow for billing customers sooner and thus accelerate their (now-lower) profits.
- Hammered out sales and profit targets in an annual inquisition called the Growth Playbook.
- Doubled across-the-board targets for cutting costs; and tied executive pay to short-term profit hurdles.

None of these led to—or were the result of—compelling answers to those three strategy questions listed above.

Sure enough, fractures began to appear in the empire Welch built and Immelt inherited. In May 2007, I posted an opinion for *Harvard Business Review* with the title "Should GE Be Scrapped for Parts?" (See appendix 2.) My thesis: After years of financial engineering, GE lacked a coherent multibusiness strategy. I wrote: "Until Immelt cracks this…, his stock price will continue to lag and there will continue to be challenges to whether GE belongs together. I would not give up hope that GE can prove itself…. However, I would guess that some businesses no longer belong in GE's portfolio, and I would consider the alternative of creating two or three GEs…." That alternative was never considered until it was forced on the company some ten years later—after the stock price had cratered to nearly a tenth of its zenith. And lo and behold, creating three GEs is exactly what Larry Culp, the first-ever outsider CEO, has done.

Thomas Gryta and Ted Mann said it best in their 2018 article for the *Wall Street Journal:* "When needed most, the heirs to [Thomas] Edison's ingenuity had run out of ideas." Indeed, financial engineering can't replace a big idea and a great strategy to commercialize it (see chapter 9).

Gryta/Mann went on to write, "In the cruelest of codas, the last CEO of America's last great industrial conglomerate would be an outsider." Fortunately, the outsider is Larry Culp, who built Danaher Corp. into a powerhouse industrial conglomerate with a coherent multibusiness strategy (see chapter 3). As Gryta/Mann reported, Welch hoped Culp would go on to "build a new GE." Perhaps then Thomas Edison himself can stop turning over in his grave.

GE is just one example. There are many more. Leaders conflate financial engineering with strategy all the time. And they are often aided and abetted by the press. For example, in February 2020, *Financial Times* reported, "Cost-cutting is a big plank of the new boss's strategy [at Julius Baer]." In another instance, *The Wall Street Journal* opined, "Paying out cash is a crowd-pleasing strategy for companies." And here's a headline from an article in *Fortune*: "Does Apple's stock buyback strategy make sense in this market?" This kind of conflation in the public eye encourages leaders to let their financial goals and targets become the tail that wags their strategy dog (see chapter 31).

To be clear, financial engineering is a powerful tool when used well. There's good financial engineering, and bad. The good kind ferrets out inefficiency in a company's P&L or on its balance sheet, thus enhancing execution and liberating resources to fund a strategy's implementation, innovation, or both. The bad kind replaces strategy as the driving force of a company's direction, decisions, and actions. When that happens, the ultimate outcome looks a lot like a Ponzi scheme that's run its course.

Postscript: While I was writing this book, Jack Welch died. Plaudits poured in for a man selected by *Fortune* magazine in 1999 as Manager of the Century. He was rightly lauded for jolting American Inc. out of the moribund 1970s, for replacing a highly bureaucratic regime with a lean meritocracy and culture of accountability, for the time and investment he put into developing people into competent business leaders, and for the attention he paid to raising GE's quality control processes in response to the rise of Asian manufacturing.

He was also celebrated for raising the value of GE from $14 billion to $400 billion over his 20-year span. And that put his obituary writers into a quandary: GE's peak value turned out to be a mirage that became evident almost immediately after Welch retired. They tried to explain this away by suggesting that conglomerate-building was now "out of favor" and that the 2008 financial crisis made his expansion into financial services untenable. That does a real disservice to the practice, art, and substance of multibusiness strategy.

Consider this: GE's stock-to-earnings multiple was about equal to the general market in 1981 and more than 25% *less* than the market in 2001. In reality, building conglomerates and expanding into new businesses lacking a compelling multibusiness strategy has never been in favor. The "house that Jack built" could not withstand the heavy storms that periodically lash every company, because it lacked the solid foundation of a sound strategy. In his post-career book, *Hot Seat: What I Learned Leading a Great American Company,* Immelt confirmed it: "I'd become CEO of a company where perception didn't match reality."

---

1   In 2001, GE owned jet engines, power turbines, locomotives, MRI machines, plastics, light-bulbs, appliances, oil-field supplies, credit cards, auto financing, real estate, mortgage insurance, wealth management, a TV broadcaster, and more.

2   In GE's case, mostly commercial and investment banking; in Berkshire's, mostly insurance.

7

Should strategy include "strategic priorities"?

Don't confuse what's always essential with what's currently important.

Use of the word *strategy* was originally reserved for the military (see chapter 43). But as the *Mad Men* era was reaching its zenith, business leaders started to adopt it with a vengeance. The uptick seemed to begin with "portfolio strategy" during the go-go years of the 1960s and '70s, and it took off with "competitive strategy" in the 1980s. Then just about everything became a strategy. Today, the word *strategy* has attracted more modifiers than ever. You must have diversification, global, growth, and M&A strategies. And customer, product, and channel strategies. Plus, cost, manufacturing, supply chain, distribution, and sourcing strategies. Don't forget your technology and digital strategies. Or your people, communications, and investor relations strategies. The list seems infinite. *What's going on?*

The term *strategy* has degenerated into an all-purpose one of elevation. If it's important, it must be "strategy." If we append "strategy" to it, it will demand the top echelon's attention. *Strategy* has been co-opted as a way to lend status, import, and credibility to nearly anything that requires choices. Some might say, "We need a 'channel strategy' to choose the routes to market and distributors we will use." Or "We need an 'IT strategy' to choose the combination of infrastructure, applications, and vendors that will power technology at our company." And even "I need a breakfast strategy to choose whether I'm having eggs or pancakes today." But equating strategy to any and all choices makes it so broad that it becomes meaningless and loses its power as a leadership tool (see chapter 1).

Moreover, strategy is now a central feature of business fashion. Remember when "quality strategy" was *de rigueur* in the 1980s? Or when "reengineering strategy" was all the rage in the early '90s? Or how "dot-com strategy" ruled the late '90s? And how about "China strategy" and "blue ocean strategy" in the early 2000s? A few years ago, everyone was asking "What's your Google strategy?" and "Your IoT strategy?" Today it's "What's your digital strategy?" or "AI strategy?" or "Metaverse strategy?" or "Web 3.0 strategy?" In a few years, it'll be something else. It's enough to make a grown strategist cry. Companies struggle to implement just one strategy really well. How can they possibly implement one for every new, big development that comes along?

The answer is *they can't*. What they *can* do, however, is use the next big thing to challenge and stretch the strategy they already have. Take the digital technology wave sweeping across the business landscape. Today, business leaders are drowning in the hyperbole surrounding its game-changing potential—and creating some of their own. Such as (now former) GE proclaiming itself the world's first "digital industrial company" and Citigroup claiming to be the only "digital-first" bank.

But instead of rushing headlong into fabricating a "digital strategy," leaders should stop, take a deep breath, and think deeply about how digital technology—smartphones, 5G, social media, AI, Internet-of-Things, blockchain, metaverse, web 3.0, the lot—could change and enhance their answers to the essential questions of strategy (see chapters 2 and 3).

Here's what that looks like:

How could digital change the businesses we should be in? For example, Amazon's biggest profit generator is Amazon Web Services, which turned its back-office computing capabilities into a fast-growing, highly profitable new business serving enterprises' computing power and data storage needs. Another example is IKEA. It is reportedly considering a move to enter the e-commerce business by providing an online platform for all furniture retailers. On the other hand, the rise of Zipcar and other such tech-enabled services doesn't necessarily mean that big auto manufacturers belong in the ride-sharing business.

How could digital improve the way we contribute to the future earnings power of our businesses? For example, if (now former) GE wanted to foster a distinctive enterprise capability to develop skilled general managers for its industrial businesses, how could they leverage the EdTechs for that capability? Or could an eBay-like platform bring the discipline of competitive markets to a company's corporate services capability? Or could a company adapt the various online investment platforms used by angel investors to make prioritizing and funding a company's capital projects a faster and smarter enterprise-wide capability?

Could digital change our *Who?* Is digital technology eroding our target market as it did for newspapers and travel agents, or is it opening up new potential targets? For example, big data has prompted one company to change its primary customer from CFOs to CMOs. In addition to using digital technology for a financial service to CFOs, it can use it for services to CMOs that enhance their customer acquisition and loyalty efforts.

Could digital add to our *Why?* For example, how would we use digital technologies to enhance our service like McDonald's use of AI to automate its drive-throughs? Or as many hospital, device, and drug companies are seeking to do, could we promise an outcome in exchange for a share of the result that digital technology allows only *us* to produce? Or how could we use digital technology to enhance our physical products, as LEGO did with an augmented reality app that blends physical and digital play to stay relevant and cool with kids?

How can digital fortify our *What?* This is not adding digital capabilities but rather adding digital to capabilities. For example, USAA has digitized its claims processing capability by using AI to calculate the cost of damage based on photos sent in by claimants. Other insurance companies are sharpening their fraud management capabilities by gathering data through sensors embedded in buildings and even sending drones to disaster areas. Drug companies are using data mining and AI to enhance their R&D capabilities. And social media data and analytics could help a bank further differentiate its credit management capability.

Leaders can avoid jumping from one strategy to another by applying these same questions to whatever is top of mind for their company. For example, if

M&A is a high priority that demands choices, leaders shouldn't push for an "M&A strategy." Instead, they should address the following questions:

- How could M&A change the businesses we should be in or improve the way we contribute to our businesses (see chapter 3)?
- How could M&A change or extend the *Who? Why?* or *What?* for our business (see chapter 2)?

This is how leaders can handle all their top priorities—whether, for example, they be geographic expansion, AI, partnering, supply chain, or the next big thing that's surely just over the horizon. And this is how they can use the latest business trends, macroeconomic movements, and broad-based innovations as an impetus to reinvigorate the relevance and resilience of the strategy they already have.

PART III

What Is a Great Strategy?

Great strategies are no guarantee of great execution—but they sure help.

8

Why must strategies be sharply differentiating?

Oranges in a world of apples

In my work with business leaders, a favorite exercise is "Name That Company" based on seeing only its strategy. I start with these two companies:

Strategy	Company A	Company D
Who (target customer)	Leisure and business travelers on a budget who want to get from point A to point B in the fastest and most convenient, direct, and flexible way	"Every citizen of the world"
Why (value proposition)	Lowest, most transparent fares with friendliest, most reliable service	"Highest-quality air travel to widest selection of destinations"
What (leading capabilities) Fleet management Route management Customer service	Single make and model of airplane Point-to-point Happy, cheerful, lighthearted, fun-loving, and flexible staff who feel ownership for their company	Multiple makes and dozens of models Hub-and-spoke Professional, courteous, responsive staff with rigorous training

Most leaders waste little time in naming company A (Southwest Airlines). They struggle mightily to identify company D (American Airlines), though they know it's one of the larger global airlines.

Continuing the exercise, I ask them to do the same for these two companies:

Strategy for Company B	Strategy for Company E
Use insurance float to generate "free" capital, invest only in what we know, buy businesses that can productively use a lot of capital, and be a welcoming, hands-off home for great operators who love what they do.	*"Preferentially invest in a portfolio of technology-integrated, market-driven performance businesses that create value for our shareholders and growth for our customers. Manage a portfolio of asset-integrated building-block businesses to generate value for our downstream portfolio."*

Most leaders don't need long to name company B (Berkshire Hathaway). Yet they are mystified by the strategy for company E, even after I tell them it's from The Dow Chemical Company (before its merger with DuPont and subsequent split into multiple entities).

Finally, I show them two more strategies:

Strategy for Company C	Strategy for Company F
Create, buy, and grow family-friendly characters and action figures—our "corporate franchises"—that strengthen and gain strength from each of our businesses to the delight and wonderment of children and their families.	*"Improve efficiency, pivot towards high-growth areas such as wealth management and Asia-Pacific, and reduce capital allocated to our investment bank."*

Leaders quickly recognize the first as The Walt Disney Company. As for the other, they know it's a financial services company, but they can't tell which one (it's the former Credit Suisse).

After going through this little exercise, I ask two questions. First, "Why were you able to name companies A, B, and C, but not the other three?" They know where I'm headed! They readily understand that the strategy for D could be for *any* airline; strategy E could be for just about *any* multibusiness company; and strategy F could be for virtually *any* company in the global financial services industry.

In stark contrast, strategies A (Southwest), B (Berkshire), and C (Disney) are highly specific to these three companies and sharply differentiate them from any other. Their strategies make them oranges in a world of apples. And that's why they are easy to spot.

The second question, though, is the "money" question: "Which are the better-executing companies?" Again, they see what I'm after. They don't hesitate to name Southwest, Berkshire, and Disney. This is when I make the central point of the exercise. *Superb execution—consistently producing great results—depends on many factors. Having a great strategy is one of them. And great strategies are sharply differentiating.*

A *sharp* strategy facilitates three essential disciplines of executing well: clarity, prioritization, and opportunism. The sharper a strategy, the greater clarity everyone has on what is "on strategy"—what initiatives, projects, investments, acquisitions, innovations, market developments, ideas, customers, partners, key hires, and more—and what is just a distraction.

Furthermore, leaders are better able to separate the wheat from the chaff in prioritizing the barrage of internal requests and inbound approaches they face on a daily basis. And they can better recognize, find, and create opportunities that both fit with the strategy and amplify it—and moreover, they avoid wasting time, money, credibility, and reputation on opportunities that don't.

Yet if a company's strategy is just so much *blah-blah-blah* (see the strategy for companies D, E, and F, above), leaders lose a powerful tool for managing these three important ingredients of great execution: clarity, prioritization, and opportunism.

The other quality of a great strategy is *differentiating.* This creates an essential condition for executing well: avoiding as much as possible the destructive effects of head-on, zero-sum competition for customers, people, acquisitions, partners, and more. For example:

- Having a distinctively defined, ideal customer increases the efficiency and efficacy of marketing, selling, and innovating a company's products and services. That's a big part of why Amazon's cloud-computing business—Amazon Web Services—found success: by initially targeting independent developers and early-stage companies, and by steering away from big, complex corporate buyers until later when its success was already assured (see chapter 12).
- Offering a compelling, superior range of benefits supports higher prices at a given volume (or vice versa), thus mitigating an intractable trade-off between growth and profitability that makes execution all the

more difficult. That's how leaders of Pabst Blue Ribbon rescued it from near death: by offering a distinctly non-corporate, non-pretentious, unglamorous, hipster proposition to countercultural beer drinkers such as bike messengers and snowboarders (see chapters 12 and 13).

- Prioritizing and nurturing a handful of distinctive capabilities makes a company much better at creating value for its customers and gives a multibusiness company a comparative advantage in both contributing to its businesses' success and acquiring new ones. This is why Southwest, Berkshire, and Disney have a huge advantage in competing for customers, people, acquisitions, partners, and more.

Peter Drucker, the famous management thinker, has been credited with saying that "strategy is a commodity; execution is an art." We will never know exactly what he meant by that, but one thing is for sure: a strategy can't be great if it's a "commodity"—that is, if it's indistinguishable from any other company's strategy. More important, execution is better with strategies that are sharply differentiating. When a company's leaders are struggling to execute, they should look at their strategy and ask themselves, "How sharply differentiating is our strategy?" That's always revealing.

9

Why must strategies stand on the shoulders of a big idea?

Novel solutions prevent zero-sum competition

Crown Holdings (formerly Crown Cork & Seal) was once the most profitable and innovative company in metal containers. This industry is dominated by large companies serving national customers with enormous orders that make long, low-cost production runs possible. In the early 1960s, Crown's CEO, John F. Connelly, had the big idea of retooling Crown to be a leader in filling special orders for smaller customers. Crown became a "short-run" specialist and stopped going head-to-head with larger competitors for national customers.

Connelly crafted a coherent strategy to bring his idea to economic life. He tailored his pitch to what his ideal customer valued the most: rapid-response rush orders, high levels of technical assistance, holding inventory for customers, and carrying excess production capacity. All of this went against the grain of accepted wisdom in an industry in which success depended on minimizing costs. He bet on being able to charge higher prices by serving smaller customers with far less bargaining power.

As Richard Rumelt writes in *Good Strategy, Bad Strategy*, Crown was generating more profit than any other company in its industry, even without having the most revenue. But sadly, the big idea lasted only as long as the CEO's tenure, which ended in 1990. Connelly's successor shifted to a "strategy" of growth through acquisition. Seven years later, after completing 20 acquisitions, Crown was the world's largest container manufacturer. But it had lost sight of the big idea that made it so successful in the first place. And it had not found a new one. By 2006, it was one of the industry's least-profitable players.

Crown exemplifies what occurs when a company's strategy drifts away from the big idea that powered it. Something similar happens when the big idea behind a strategy is no longer "big." Chapter 2 tells the story of how Henry Ford—with a unique strategy—took his company from also-ran status in 1910 to market leader by 1921. But a decade after that, General Motors was the world's largest and most profitable car company. How did that happen?

In April of 1921, Pierre du Pont, president of GM, asked Alfred P. Sloan, his vice-president of operations, to develop a strategy for GM's ten vehicle brands. At the time, these brands collectively shared 12% of the market. Sloan came up with the big idea of "branded price points." Below a certain price point, GM would compete on quality and, above a certain price point, on price. Each vehicle brand was assigned a unique price range and commensurate quality standard, with Chevrolet taking the lowest price range, Cadillac taking the highest, and other brands such as Buick and Oldsmobile falling in between. When Sloan became president in 1923, he used his big idea to swamp Ford within a decade.

Ford and GM became great companies on the back of big ideas—Ford with its moving assembly line, and GM with its branded price points. But almost every car company has copied these ideas. Consider Toyota with its Lexus brand and Volkswagen with the Audi brand. Today, they are more faithful to Sloan's big idea than GM is!

Though Ford and GM remain enormous players, they long ago ceded their industry leadership because their big ideas lost steam and they were unable to replace or reinvigorate them. And when that happens, companies and their strategies are prone to wander.

Today, Ford and GM are diversifying into transportation services and becoming "mobility" companies, such as with GM's $500 million investment in Lyft, the car-hailing service, and its multibillion-dollar investment in Cruise, the autonomous vehicle business.

Both companies have "strategies" that amount to make some money here, to spend it there, and, by all means, to keep up with whatever is "hot" at the moment (EVs, anyone?). There's no "there" there—no big idea that's unique to their companies and provides a novel solution to a big unsolved problem, an unmet need, or an unrequited want.

Ford and GM can't do enough restructuring, reorganization, acquisitions, venture investment, product innovation, or financial engineering (see chapter 6) to compensate for lacking strategies that are powered by their own truly novel, scalable ideas.

I often ask leaders to compare the two lists below and consider two questions: Which companies are powered by a big idea that's still a big idea, and which are the better-executing companies?

List 1	List 2
Starbucks	Gap, Inc.
Google	Yahoo!
Netflix	Viacom
Microsoft	HP, Inc.

It's obvious to them that List 1 wins on both counts. In fact, as of this writing, the (unweighted) average price-to-earnings multiple for List 1 is more than six times the average for List 2 (using Yahoo's multiple just before it was acquired by Verizon). Evidently, the stock market thinks List 1 wins on both counts, too. This proves nothing, but most leaders I work with agree there's no coincidence here.

Having a big idea keeps a company's strategy out of a zero-sum game where it wins only if others lose (see chapters 43 and 44). For example, Howard Schultz's big idea for Starbucks—to bring the Italian espresso bar experience to the U.S.—created a new market with plenty of room for everyone to grow, not just Starbucks. That idea will eventually run its course, but until then, Starbucks doesn't have to steal growth from others in order to execute well. Compare that to Gap, Inc., which became a wild success on the back of two big ideas: first, offering the widest and deepest selection of Levi's jeans to fill the gap (hence, its name) in sizes and fit found in most stores; and then being the go-to place for fashionable "basics," such as T-shirts, underwear, socks, and sweatshirts. These were obviously great ideas, but they expired many years ago and they haven't been succeeded by a next big idea. Thus, today, Gap, Inc.'s execution has to be perfect just to avoid any further stagnation. Same for Viacom and Yahoo! (the latter acquired by Verizon in 2017 and sold just a few years later).

In addition to avoiding zero-sum competition, strategies powered by a big idea have another advantage: they have a lot of stretch in them. This means they have many opportunities to broaden a company's target market, add to its offerings, and commercialize its best capabilities in new ways (see chapter 18).

For example, take Google, the search business. Its success took off when its founders had the big idea of ranking web pages based not only on internal references to the search term, but also on links from other sites, created by humans using the content. (Both of them offspring of academics, the founders got this idea from how academic publications are ranked: based on the number of times they are cited in other papers.) Since then, Google has stretched its business to include YouTube, Chrome, Gmail, Google Maps, Waze, and Google House. All these sites are enormously successful in their own right as well as big contributors to the success of the search business itself.[1]

Things are different for the once-soaring Gap, Yahoo!, Viacom, and HP, Inc. Their leaders have all tried many, many "growth options" since their big ideas atrophied, and none have really moved the needle. Maybe this is due to poor execution, but these companies have great operators. The better explanation is they have strategies that can't stretch because they don't stand on the shoulders of a big idea that still a big idea (see chapter 20). These companies need big-idea innovators, not just terrific operators.

---

1   In 2015, Google changed its name to Alphabet, Inc., and Google became a subsidiary. Since then, Alphabet has poured tons of money into new ventures hoping to find its next "moon shot." In 2021, Facebook seemed to mimic Google/Alphabet when it renamed itself to Meta Platform and unleashed a torrent of investment in developing applications for the so-called metaverse. Unfortunately, in both cases, this amounts to investment looking for big ideas, not the other way around. It reverses the very sequence that led to the outsized success of both companies: first, the founders had a big idea; then they found the investment to commercialize it. This doesn't mean they won't eventually find a big idea or two with all the money, talent, and attention they are putting into their moon shots, though it's rare that investment-driven innovation is more effective than idea-driven innovation.

❿

Why must strategies belong to leaders, not companies?

Because strategies are like children

Who's the founder of Starbucks? When I ask leaders that question, they usually say Howard Schultz, its long-time, multiterm chief executive. And they're wrong. Starbucks was founded by three classmates from the University of San Francisco (Baldwin, Siegl, and Bowker). Their original store in Seattle sold high-quality coffee beans out of burlap sacks, and also sold roasting equipment. Schultz was one of their employees.

One day, the founders sent Schultz to Italy to scout out the latest equipment for roasting and grinding coffee. While there he landed on what he thought was a terrific idea: create an Italian-style espresso bar experience that would spark demand for Starbucks' high-quality coffee. Upon his return, he took his idea to the founders. They promptly turned him down. Schultz periodically resurfaced his idea but got shot down again and again. So, he quit and started his own business. Then the founders decided to sell, and Schultz bought the company. He created his "third place" strategy (between office and home) based on his big idea, and the rest is history. As he later reflected, "I could have...just dropped the idea. But I refused to let it die. [It] felt too right, and my instincts about it ran too deep to let it go."

The moral of Starbucks saga is that *great strategies belong to leaders, not companies.*

Great strategies separate companies from the pack (see chapter 8) and stand on the shoulders of a big idea that no one else has (see chapter 9). But this puts them on a collision course with the powerful immune systems that all markets and organizations seem to possess that causes them to resist anything going against the status quo and accepted wisdom. Or, as Niccolò Machiavelli wrote in *The Prince*, "there is nothing more difficult…than to take the lead in the introduction of a new order of things. Because the innovator has for enemies all those who have done well under the old conditions, and lukewarm defenders in those who may do well under the new. This…arises partly from…the [inherent] incredulity of men, who do not readily believe in new things until they have had a long experience of them."

Thus, great strategies—and the big ideas they depend on—take leaders who believe enough in them to be willing to fight the status quo for however long it takes. For example, J. P. Morgan stayed committed to turning Edison's lightbulb invention into the standard for residential lighting, even after Edison nearly burned down Morgan's home library containing priceless manuscripts and artifacts from all over the world. Only Sam Walton, founder of Walmart, believed that you could profitably serve small towns with a full-line discount store. Henry Ford was alone in seeking to democratize the automobile among the dozens of auto company leaders in the early 1900s (see chapter 2). Lou Gerstner had to resist loud, persistent calls to break up IBM in order to implement his new strategy for the company (chapter 5). Alfred P. Sloan faced fierce internal resistance to the pricing and style boundaries that his branded-price-points strategy placed on GM's divisions (chapter 9). Larry Page and Sergey Brin started Google (chapter 9) because no one would buy their idea even for a million dollars. When Reed Hastings sparked an 80% drop in Netflix's stock price by committing the company to replacing DVDs with streaming, he didn't blink. The founders of PayPal were ignored—even ridiculed—by what they called the "bankocracy," and faced down multiple near-death situations before emerging with a commercially successful innovation that seems so obvious today. And Schultz had to buy Starbucks from its original founders to realize his "third place" strategy, because they repeatedly rejected his big idea.

All this tells us that strategies are like children: you never love someone else's as much as you love your own. Or, as President Lyndon Johnson once said to another Schultz, his Secretary of State George P. Shultz, "If you have a good idea, and it's your idea, it's not going to go very far. But if it becomes my idea, it just might go somewhere. Do I make myself clear?"

The two men's experience belies the condition that we are all born with: the not-invented-here syndrome—deeply ingrained tendencies to love ideas and strategies that we conceive and raise to maturity, and to be skeptical of those we don't. This explains how the founders of Starbucks turned down one of the greatest ideas of all time; how the leaders of eBay—where PayPal flourished— actively refused to acknowledge its game-changing idea of email-based payments until it became a multibillion-dollar one; and why Netflix was rejected multiple times when it offered to sell itself to Blockbuster for a scant $50 million.

It also explains why history is littered with once-extraordinary companies that became mediocre when their leaders drifted away from the ideas and strategies that made those companies great. The history of The Walt Disney Company vividly demonstrates this.

In 1957, Walt Disney had the now-famous idea that family-friendly characters brought to life through films could power a broad constellation of entertainment businesses. Disney animated his idea with a hand-written diagram still held in the archives at his namesake company. It has the topic of "Theatrical Films" listed in the middle of a giant network of other businesses, including books, comics, merchandise licensing, music, TV, and a Disneyland resort park. The founder drew connections between every node of the network and annotated them to describe how each business supported and gained support from every other. Disney's idea was as creative as the characters he invented and films he made. And with it, he built a beloved company of world renown.

By 1984, a mere 15 years and four CEOs after Walt Disney died, the company was attacked by corporate raiders. The once-proud enterprise had become a serial underperformer. To counter that, its new leaders made moves like releasing films targeted at adults, acquiring a real estate development company, and even trying to buy the then-third-largest greeting card business. Meanwhile, the company's animated-film revenues had fallen to just 4% of its top line—the very antithesis of Walt Disney's big idea and strategy. Fortunately, instead of succumbing to raiders, the board hired Michael Eisner.

The first things Eisner did was to reignite investment in family films and to create new characters, such as *The Little Mermaid, The Beauty and the Beast*, and *The Lion King*. And he invested heavily in adding new businesses to Disney's system of interlocking businesses. This included retail stores, Broadway shows, cruise ships, and Saturday morning cartoons—all featuring its characters brought to life through those films. By 1994, Disney's film revenues had risen to 19% of its overall revenues. Character licensing had grown by no less than eight times. Theme park attendance and margins soared.

In 2005, Eisner's successor, Bob Iger, brought his own twist. Under his "corporate franchises" strategy (see chapter 3), a new *Cars Land* attraction—inspired by the movie *Cars*—was added to the company's California Adventure Park. The long-standing, but tired, Norway attraction at Epcot Center was rebuilt as "Frozen Ever After," based on the smash musical animation *Frozen*. The "Iron Man Experience"—Disney's first attraction based on a Marvel character—premiered at Hong Kong Disneyland. And a large *Pirates of the Caribbean* feature—based on the movie franchise that was originally inspired by a ride at the very first Disneyland—is now found at Shanghai Disneyland. Today, Disney-created or -acquired films such as *Cars* and *Star Wars* not only inspire new rides, but rides like "Pirates of the Caribbean," "Jungle Book," and "Tower of Terror" spark fresh new films.

Iger replaced himself with another Bob—Bob Chapek—who had caught Iger's eye after seeing what Chapek did when Iger put him in charge of Disney Consumer Products. Chapek reorganized the division around the company's corporate franchises like *Mickey Mouse*, the Disney princesses, and *Star Wars*, rather than around product categories such as housewares or action figures. The old structure led the category heads to chase each new movie or TV show to hit their numbers. Chapek's new setup gave his team an incentive to keep an eye on each franchise's overall health.

Iger saw an executive who had embraced the corporate franchises strategy and made it his own. In explaining his choice of Chapek to be his successor, Iger said, "It's less important that Bob knows the specifics of one business, and more important that he appreciates how all of these businesses fit into one company." Iger clearly wanted those 15 years of the Disney brand wandering in the wilderness to be an aberration that never happens again.[1]

Eisner and Iger found a way to make Walt Disney's innovative strategy their own—and they proved that it still had legs. The four CEOs before them had abandoned Walt's strategy and in doing so proved that companies don't *have* strategies, only their leaders have them—for better or for worse.

All of this goes to say that leaders have to create—and then make—the choices that form the backbone of their strategy. In-house and third-party experts can help, but leaders can't delegate the hard work of strategy to anyone else and simply be the chief "reviewer and approver" of someone else's inspiration and perspiration. Too many leaders spend too much of their time running from meeting to meeting, being the ceremonial chief, and putting out fires. It's all too easy for "strategy" to become one more item on a long list of things to get done during the day. That doesn't work. Great strategies—and the big ideas that power them—require leaders to step back from time to time, and to think hard about where they'll find inspiration and how they'll create the mental space for it.

---

1   Chapek did not last long, however. He allowed himself to be undermined by Iger (who for years has struggled to retire) after mishandling the politics associated with the idea that companies should engage in social activism. But despite some harsh behavior, you have to hand it to Iger: he feels deeply about Walt Disney's original big idea, and he cares a lot that it lives through leaders' strategy for the company.

11

Why do popular strategies always fade?

Wide adoption of favored prescriptions sows the seeds of their own destruction.

For over 60 years, the business of giving strategy advice has been to promote universal prescriptions that apply to any business. For example, in the 1960s and 1970s, the hot concepts were the experience curve, the growth-share matrix, and SWOT (strengths, weaknesses, opportunities, and threats). The 1980s gave us five forces, value chain strategy, scenario planning, and total quality management. In the 1990s, business process engineering, customer loyalty, time-based competition, core competencies, and growth horizons all gained traction. Those ideas were followed by co-opetition, BHAGs ("big, hairy, audacious goals"), growth adjacencies, and blue oceans in the 2000s. These hugely popular concepts, and many others, have largely faded after enjoying a few years of attention and acclaim. Few have had a lasting impact on the art, practice, and substance of strategy—though they've left behind a veritable mountain of jargon that persists in the lexicon of modern-day management.

Nevertheless, the business of strategy will continue to churn out the next big thing, because new concepts provide leaders a modicum of comfort in an uncertain, complex world. But creating a great strategy—and keeping it great—demands that leaders understand the limitations of such concepts and resist the allure generated by their popularity, while at the same time taking advantage of their potential to spark new thinking.

Three limitations ultimately sink popular strategies. The first is the effect of separating the true owners of a company's strategy (the prescription promoters) from those implementing it (the company's leaders). No doubt, the promoters work hard to win management's acceptance of their concept. But when the inevitable bumps in the road loom, the strategy concept is ditched, often with leaders saying, for example, "the McKinsey growth horizons strategy doesn't work"[1] and its promoters blaming poor implementation.

A second limitation is that, by nature, popular strategy concepts are not unique to any one company. That's problematic because when they become widely adopted, no one gains advantage from them. The "me-too" pursuit of strategy concepts stymies their supposed benefits.

For example, in 1972, the leaders of DuPont's titanium dioxide business adopted the experience curve concept for their strategy. Following the concept's prescription (see chapter 1), it invested more than $400 million in new capacity to maximize market share. The problem was that everyone *else* had already taken the same strategy prescription. By 1979, industry capacity utilization collapsed from 88% to 64% and DuPont's margins had fallen to half of what they were before.

Generalized strategy prescriptions don't answer the questions every strategy must answer in ways that are specific and differentiating for any one company (see chapter 8). Peter Drucker, the leading management guru of the last century, once remarked, "Strategy is a commodity; execution is an art." The first part of that is certainly true for strategy prescriptions that become widely popular.

Consider total quality management (TQM), a recipe for reducing cost by minimizing error. TQM is mostly silent on *what* kind of businesses should be in a company's portfolio, and why. It says nothing about *who* a company's customers should be and *why* they're glad the company exists. It's also a dangerously narrow perspective on the *Why?* and *What?* that together make for a winning strategy (see chapter 2).

Instead of asking "Should we adopt TQM?" leaders should ask "How can TQM improve the strategy we already have?" (see chapter 7). Diversified companies, such as Danaher, Berkshire Hathaway, and Disney, would have distinctly different answers to the latter question, because they have sharply different strategies for contributing to their businesses' success. Furthermore, because these companies have such distinctive strategies (their strategies are hardly commodities!), they can be disciplined about whether and how they use TQM. This enables them to get the most out of new strategy concepts without becoming hostage to them or distracted by them.

A third important limitation of popular strategy concepts is their tendency to conflate ambitious goals with big ideas (see chapter 31). For example, time-based competition and riding the experience curve are, respectively, edicts to operate faster than everyone else and to minimize cost by maximizing market share. But "maximize speed" and "maximize market share"—or, for that matter, "maximize net promoter score," "expand growth horizons," and "occupy white space"—are really just generic goals that any company might adopt. None is a big idea—meaning a novel solution to a specific problem, an unmet need, or an unfulfilled want—that's unique to a particular company (see chapter 9).

The wide adoption of popular, goal-driven strategies promoted by third parties essentially guarantees that they will fade over time. But why do they become so popular in the first place? Because they resonate with a widely shared problem in the corporate community. TQM came to life during the Japanese quality invasion in the 1980s; business process reengineering hit it big in the wake of the 1990–92 recession; and growth horizons and blue oceans arose in the early 2000s during a time of high growth for tech companies but growth stagnation for everyone else. More recently, we saw the rise of a new generation of popular strategies, such as lean startup, disruptive innovation, digitization, transient advantage, and "agile strategy."

The obvious solution might be to resist the ebb and flow of strategy fashion altogether. But each new strategy prescription offers a potential opportunity to challenge and improve the strategy leaders already have for their company (see chapter 7).

Leaders should always be seeking ways to open their eyes to new possibilities for their strategy. The latest big things in strategy are one such way, *if* they stimulate leaders' thinking without substituting for it, and *if* leaders use them to enhance their strategy rather than replacing it. However, those are two big *if*s, especially when leaders don't currently have a strategy to which they are truly committed. That's when they are most vulnerable to being captured by the latest fad in business strategy. And it's when the conditions are ripest for wasting executive time and organizational energy.

---

1   This is not to pick on McKinsey. Many times, I've heard executives use the name of some other consulting firm, including my own, to label their strategy. Whenever that happens, you can be sure the strategy will die on the vine. See chapter 10.

PART IV

....

How Do Leaders Create a Great Strategy?

There is no surefire, scientific way. And luck plays a big part.

But leaders can tilt the odds in their favor.

（12）

How should leaders choose their *Who?*

By defining the bull's-eye that differentiates their business

Customers can be defined by one or more characteristics, including the following:

- where they are (for example, in certain areas of the world or particular parts of town).
- how they buy (perhaps through specific channels, advisors, or the procurement department).
- who they are (their particular demographics, psychographics, occupational role, industry, and so on).
- when they buy (such as for particular occasions or at certain times of the year).
- what they buy (are they price purchasers? service hounds? brand buyers? style seekers? quality prioritizers? risk averters?).
- what they prefer (for where, when, or how they buy).
- for whom they buy (themselves, family, friends, their company, or their customers).

There is no one way for leaders to define their ideal customer. The possibilities are endless. That's why choosing one may not be as easy as it seems…

and why some leaders don't bother. Instead, they let customers self-select and if customers don't materialize, the leaders modify the offering until it attracts enough customers. In Silicon Valley–speak, this is called "finding your product market fit." In other words, "Our ideal customer is whoever buys our stuff."

Sooner or later, though, this come-one-come-all approach will require sharper thinking about *Who*? For example, consider Starbucks. Howard Schultz built it by offering high-quality, espresso-based drinks in a comfortable setting that could serve as a "third place" between office and home, and he invited anyone and everyone to join in. This effectively let consumers decide for themselves whether they were his bull's-eye customer.

Then, in the early 2000s, Starbucks accelerated store openings and added a broader food menu, inadvertently making it look, feel, and smell increasingly like a fast-food joint. When McDonald's and Dunkin' Donuts added high-quality, but affordable, coffee drinks to their fast-food format, Starbucks was exposed for its high prices and comparatively mediocre food offerings, causing the company's growth to stall.

That's when Schultz had to think harder about his *Who?* Is it the coffee enthusiast who wants to enjoy it in a social setting, or the fast-foodie who wants good coffee with her value meal? Schulz chose the enthusiast. He temporarily eliminated Starbucks' menu options such as breakfast sandwiches until the company figured out how to ensure their aroma didn't overpower the smell of coffee. He also redesigned Starbucks' stores to feel unique and sophisticated. Schultz's choice was a bold one, made in the immediate aftermath of the 2008 financial crisis, when consumers had become ultra-price-sensitive. But it worked.

For a similar reason—chasing margin growth—Walmart created a problem for itself in the late 2000s with what it called a "win-place-show" policy. This entailed stocking merchandise so that only the three leading brands in each product line would get shelf space. Because these were the brands most in demand, Walmart's leaders thought they could get away with charging higher prices and thus increase its margins, which were under pressure. But the policy put the company into more direct competition with Target Corporation, whose "cheap-chic" discount format is aimed at price-conscious yet affluent consumers—a somewhat higher-income demographic that prides itself on finding good deals. Perhaps not coincidentally, the Walmart executive who instituted the policy had previously worked at Target! But the new policy was a bust, and a few years later he left Walmart. Well-defined thinking on customer targeting would have helped him distinguish between smart strategy and plain 'ole financial engineering (see chapter 6).

All this goes to say that leaders miss an opportunity to sharpen their strategy—and consequently their execution—if they don't "think different" when defining their bull's-eye customer. For example, consider these target customer strategies:

- Andy Jassy, founder of Amazon Web Services (AWS), initially prioritized developers and startups for his new cloud-computing business, instead of big corporate-tech departments.
- Long-time Crown Cork Seal CEO John Connelly went after smaller, regional customers rather than the national, high-volume customers that all his competitors were chasing.
- Former NBA superstar Magic Johnson chose residents of minority neighborhoods in Los Angeles for building his empire of Starbucks coffee shops and TGI Fridays restaurants.
- Herb Kelleher, founder of Southwest Airlines, zeroed in on car, bus, and train travelers on a budget who just wanted to get from A to B in the cheapest, easiest manner without having to stop anywhere on the way.
- Henry Ford finally succeeded, after two failures, in building a world-beating car company by targeting the mass market when everyone else thought cars were only for the wealthy.
- The Casella brothers, makers of Yellowtail wine, recruited beer drinkers who are open to wine but put off by the rigamarole of fancy labels and "tasting notes."
- USAA targets only military personnel and their families.
- Leaders of Pabst Blue Ribbon doubled down on non-establishment types (surfers, skateboarders, delivery bikers, and the like) to revitalize this beer brand.
- Levi Strauss built its brand by making its blue jeans the garb of choice for cowboys, rebels, and movie stars.

These examples illustrate an aspect of smart strategy that's easy to overlook. It consists of choosing a *Who?* to achieve one or more of three objectives: minimize head-to-head competition, expand a market, or attract prospects who want to emulate those already buying or buying into the company's offerings. In the list above, there are examples for each of these three objectives.

Starting with AWS, today it accounts for the bulk of Amazon's profits and is the company's fastest-growing revenue stream. This was hardly a sure thing when Andy Jassy was asked to start the business. As he told *Financial Times*, "If one of the old-guard technology companies had built something like this and had been first to market, it would have been much harder for us to come in later." By 2010 every large IT company—from IBM to Oracle to Google to Microsoft—had caught on. But Jassy had a seven-year head start, in large part because he chose a *Who?* that allowed him to stay under the radar. And he offered computing power and data storage services on a pay-as-you-go basis, because his priority customers could simply not afford an expensive monthly subscription, which was then the standard model.

Likewise, while Crown Cork's John Connelly let his competitors duke it out for national customers, he built the industry's most profitable metal containers business by customizing his offering for smaller regional customers with the promise of rapid-response rush orders, high levels of technical assistance, holding inventory for customers, and carrying excess production capacity (see chapter 9). And Magic Johnson tailored his offering for people he thought were being ignored by the popular chains. In a speaker series at Stanford University's Graduate School of Business, he said, "I had to take the scones out of my Starbucks and put [in] sweet potato pie, pound cake, sock-it-to-me cake, peach cobbler. [And] I was the first Fridays in the nation to ever serve Dom Pérignon, Cristal, and all the high-end liquors…. That's what my [target] customer base wanted."

Southwest, Ford, and Yellowtail give us examples of the second objective for choosing a distinctive *Who?* And that is, to expand a market, then to benefit disproportionately from doing so. Before Southwest, airlines only served those who could afford the relatively high cost of air travel. Southwest's Kelleher flipped that by targeting a different kind of traveler, organizing his company's *Why?* and *What?* to attract and serve them, and consequently becoming the most successful airline ever. Henry Ford targeted those who could not afford a car and proceeded to invent a way to make and sell reliable cars at a fraction of prevailing industry costs. When he founded his company in 1902, only 5% of the U.S. population owned a car. Some 19 years later, 25% owned one, and Ford's market share was over 60%. And then there are the Casella brothers of Yellowtail. They created a new group of wine drinkers by drawing in beer drinkers with a high-quality wine sold like beer: with simple labels and straightforward taste profiles.

A third objective of choosing a bull's-eye *Who?* is drawing in others who want to emulate that customer. For example, veterans go to USAA because other vets do. Leaders of Pabst Blue Ribbon revitalized the brand by targeting non-establishment types and thus made it attractive to mainstream twenty-somethings who wanted to signal their non-establishment credentials. Decades earlier, Levi Strauss did something similar. Originally having marketed their blue jeans to farmers, mechanics, and miners, Levi's leaders created mass-market appeal by associating the duds with glamorous actors playing cowboys and hoodlums, and later with hippies. Today, even enterprises with business customers in sectors like professional services and software implementation use this approach by targeting "flagship" entities or leading lights that others want to emulate.

All this goes to say that great strategies typically include a sharply distinctive definition of the *Who?* Leaders should start with multiple alternatives for their *Who?* Each should be designed to achieve one or more result of minimizing head-to-head competition, expanding the market, or creating buyers that others will want to emulate. And then, leaders should choose the alternative for which the company's products or services are likeliest to have the most compelling package of benefits that determine customer preference.

13

How should leaders frame their *Why?*

By asking what people pay for, not what they buy

When we have a free choice of whether to buy a product or service, our choice is governed—explicitly or instinctively—by a calculus of perceived benefits and costs. The calculus is both absolute and relative:

"Is the balance of benefits and costs attractive?"

"Is that balance more attractive than my alternatives?"

A compelling *Why?* makes it easy for the answer to be an enthusiastic "Yes!" to both questions. And to choose their *Why?* leaders must answer three questions of their own.

First: **What alternatives does our bull's-eye customer have?** The most obvious of these is whether other providers offer similar products or services. Yet leaders often behave as if this is the customer's *only* choice. That can lead them into a "we say…they say…" dynamic of claims and counterclaims about whose offering has the lowest cost or best quality or richest functionality or superior experience or even the highest ROI. And it encourages customers to make apples-to-apples comparisons that lead to competitive stalemates or destructive corporate behaviors (see chapters 43 and 44).

The best *Why?* minimizes head-to-head competition by enabling customers to do something they couldn't do before. For example, as we saw in chapter 8,

Southwest Airlines established a viable alternative to driving, taking the bus, or traveling by train as a convenient, affordable, and faster means of getting from point to point with no stops in between. Likewise, instead of drinking cheap, bland coffee at home or the office, Starbucks invented a "third place" where people could enjoy high-quality coffee in a communal setting. And Peloton—the stationary bike company—became a multibillion-dollar company by creating an alternative to joining a gym for its fitness classes.

In each case, the *Why?* offers a better alternative than what their customers had before: traveling by dingy bus; drinking mediocre java from an over-used kitchen coffee pot; and schlepping down to the gym for a spinning class. That helped the companies escape head-to-head competition until they had established a brand, scale, or network advantage to protect their big idea (see chapter 16).

Nevertheless, success always invites imitators. Leaders rarely find themselves without direct competitors forever. Thus, in choosing their *Why?* most leaders must answer a second question: **What are the benefits we offer that will compel our ideal customer to choose us over someone else?**

When I put this question to leaders, I often hear statements like "We have the best products." or "We are the biggest supplier of XYZ." or "We have the most experience in ABC." or "We meet an unmet need." or "We help you get a 'job to be done.' "

My response to such statements is always the same: "Put yourselves in the customer's shoes and ask, 'So, what? Why does that make you better than my alternatives?' " The point is that customers may buy products and services, but they pay for benefits. Being the best, biggest, or most—and meeting a need or getting a job done—is only relevant if customers can readily see what they gain relative to their alternatives. Sometimes that's obvious, but when it's not, leaders need to spell it out. And what *that* involves depends on whether the offering is tangible, like a physical product that customers can inspect, hear, smell, or touch and feel; or an intangible one, such as online dating or professional services that customers can only really know from experience.

For tangible offerings, a powerful way to distinguish a *Why?* is with *intangible* benefits. For example, in the early 2000s, the leaders of Always, the feminine hygiene product line, and of Dove, the personal care product line, adopted causes for women: "like a girl" for Always and "real women beauty" for Dove. This encourages people to buy Always and Dove products because it makes them feel like they are supporting a worthy social purpose (see chapter 33). That's a real benefit, even though it's an intangible one.

The leaders of Pabst Blue Ribbon pursued a different approach: they made mainstream beer drinkers feel cool about choosing "PBR" by promoting it as the choice of people generally considered to be cool, like surfers and skateboarders (see chapter 12). Similarly, many companies use "flagship" customers, like an iconic company, CEO, or celebrity—or they boast flashy locations such as Fifth Avenue in Manhattan or Silicon Valley—to make their target customers feel validated or special. Feeling "cool," validated, and special are real benefits that can be a big difference-maker to the choices that customers make.

Leaders can also use exclusivity, scarcity, sponsorships, trust, and transparency (for example, of fees, ingredients, and suppliers), or knowledge dissemination, or many other approaches to fortify their *Why?* For example, to enhance their reasons for drivers to work exclusively for Lyft, the ride-hailing company gives bonuses in many markets to people who complete a certain number of trips in a row without rejecting or canceling any or going offline during peak hours. And while rides are in progress, Lyft provides drivers new requests for pickups very close to their current passengers' drop-off locations, thus reducing idle time. Approaches like these are especially important when customers see very little difference between competing offerings.

For intangible products and services, a *Why?* can be fortified by conveying *tangible* benefits. This is especially important if the customer has little firsthand experience with competing offerings. Tangible benefits could include promising a particular result. If the target customers are enterprises, that could be faster growth, lower costs, or reduced risk. In consumer businesses it could be a better match from an online dating service or improved health markers from a fitness tracker.

Here's a multi-pronged *Why?* for a business that offers a mental health solution to companies and their employees:

"Spring Health is the only employee mental health solution proven to produce both clinical and financial ROI (JAMA 2022) through a dramatically improved user experience from a traditional EAP. Unlike any other solution, Spring Health uses clinically validated technology called Precision Mental Healthcare to pinpoint and

deliver exactly what will work for each person—whether that's meditation, coaching, therapy, medication, and beyond. With Spring Health, an employee can sign up and directly schedule a next-day appointment with a mental health provider— in just eleven minutes, right on our platform.

"Spring Health delivers the following benefits to employers:

- *Reduces provider wait times from the national average of 21 days to 1.1 days.*
- *Increases EAP engagement among employees from less than 5% to greater than 28%.*
- *Returns $2,150 in net health care cost savings per patient to the employer, with the potential to reduce an employer's total health care spend by 1% with just 6% of employee conversion into care with Spring Health.*
- *Enables employers to offer a competitive employee mental health benefit that serves PepsiCo, Microsoft, Pfizer, Allstate, Goldman Sachs, and other leading employers."*

This is a good example of making an intangible offering—mental health support—more tangible with a performance-based *Why?*

Other tangible benefits could include granting use or ownership of an asset or capability like proprietary data sets, algorithms, or analytical models. Or joining a community of fellow travelers, such as CEOs or marketing executives or millennials or moms or alumni. There are innumerable ways to turbocharge the *Why?* of intangible offerings that have tangible benefits.

The bottom line is that leaders must choose a healthy mix of tangible and intangible benefits to put front and center in their *Why?* In doing so, a good practice is to apply the "So, what for me?" test. For example, if leaders want to promote size or quality as a benefit, they should articulate *why* that matters to the customer. Customers don't care about size or quality unless they can readily see the benefits they gain from such things.

This brings us to the third question that will help leaders choose their *Why?* **What are the costs of our offering versus our target customer's perceived alternatives, and how do we justify or mitigate those costs?** Beyond obvious considerations such as price, installation, and any ongoing costs of ownership (like maintenance, tech support, or insurance), leaders often overlook the intangible costs that can make a big difference. The most important of these is risk—the exposure customers feel in switching to someone else's product or service; or doing something in-house that was previously done externally; or using a third party to do something that used to be done internally; or having to adopt new operating procedures, create new organizational roles, change habits, learn new skills, or look or even feel different.

Doing something genuinely new and different creates energy and excitement for a customer, but also can breed fear, uncertainty, anxiety, and other such emotions. Will there be side effects? What will others think of me? Do I have to get permission? Am I risking my career or reputation? Will my workload increase? Will it be a hassle to get the budget and authority I need? Do I have to fire a long-time vendor and perhaps let go of a close professional or even personal relationship?

Worries like these might seem trivial, compared to the enormous benefits all leaders think their products and services bring to the table. But they can often be the tail that wags the choice-making dog. Even if they are not voiced by the customer, and often they are not, leaders should be alert to them and either preempt them (implicitly or explicitly) or be ready to solve them when they arise.

In sum, choosing a *Why?* entails using the art of appealing to what customers pay for. They buy products and services, but they pay for an attractive mix of tangible and intangible benefits, which can be economic, professional, altruistic, emotional, or rational. A compelling *Why?* convinces customers that such benefits are more than worth the costs they'll bear—financial and otherwise—to gain them.

All this applies to businesses that serve other businesses (B2B), not just those that sell to consumers (B2C). In a B2B company, we like to think that the customer is a company that makes purely rational decisions based on economics. But companies *don't* make decisions; the people within them do; and neuroscience tells us that emotions drive decisions. Thus, even in B2B businesses, a winning *Why?* appeals to both the rational and the emotional brain with a compelling combination of tangibles and intangibles.

14

How should leaders select their *What?*

By starting with their *Why?* and with where their company already excels

In the early days of Frito-Lay, the salty snacks company, its leaders chose to build a capability known as direct-to-store delivery (DSD). This was a very different path from the more-common one of relying on third-party distributors.

Frito-Lay's DSD capability is a mix of know-how, procedures, tools, technology, and assets from across multiple functions such as sales, marketing, R&D, manufacturing, logistics, and IT. It's fortified by the latest technology in wireless devices and communications; by battle-tested procedures that make crystal clear who does what in any field experiment; and by deep, specialized training of its ground force of drivers and merchandisers. DSD is always high on Frito-Lay's priority list for continuing investment in things like machine learning and driver-assist technology.

DSD gives Frito-Lay abilities to shorten the time between plant and store; to minimize the physical handling that causes its products to fracture and settle into an unappealing lump at the bottom of the bag; and to quickly and cost-effectively test new ideas for product, packaging, and merchandising in a few stores before making bigger bets.

Moreover, as Paul Leinwand and Cesare Mainardi describe in *Strategy That Works*, Frito-Lay has two other capabilities that exploit and fortify its DSD capability. One is consumer engagement to rapidly scale up demand for successful field experiments, while the other is an innovation capability that sucks in store-level response data from its field experiments and transmits it directly to the R&D operation. According to Leinwand and Mainardi, these three capabilities make Frito-Lay better than any other company at meeting its promise to customers, which depends on having a range of classic and contemporary products that are consistently fresh, reliable, and "on trend."

Like Frito-Lay, every company with sustained success has a handful of capabilities that make it the best at marketing, selling, and making good on its customer proposition. For example, Southwest's proposition is impossible to match without its three leading capabilities: simplified fleet management, point-to-point route management, and a consistent, institutionalized ability to foster happy, cheerful, and flexible staff (see chapter 8). And Amazon Web Services (AWS) couldn't win with its pay-as-you-go pitch unless it had a formidable capability in growing and managing an immense network of distributed, secure computer capacity; its parent company's famous e-commerce capability; and a less-talked-about ability to transmit enormous amounts of data over the internet.

To be clear, none of these companies—Frito-Lay, Southwest, and AWS—is the best at everything. No company is. All viable companies have hundreds of capabilities to keep them going—from functional to technological and managerial capabilities; from global to local ones; and from mundane to wildly sophisticated capabilities. But no company can be better than *every* company at *all* of these.

Moreover, like DSD at Frito-Lay, truly special capabilities typically cut across internal boundaries. No one is singularly in charge of them, and most everyone has a role in both exploiting and nurturing them. That means that only a company's leaders can be the keepers of its leading capabilities, and only they can choose what those capabilities should be. But, like the other essential choices of strategy (see chapters 12 and 13), this is easier said than done.

When I ask leaders to jot down their company's leading capabilities, the result is always the same: lengthy laundry lists, typically organized by function or department, with few, if any, common entries among them. This is partly due to we humans' tendencies to give highest priority to the familiar—salespeople tend to rate selling capabilities most highly—and to be all-inclusive for fear that something important will be ignored if it's not on the list. But these are symptoms of the bigger problem: not starting in the right place—the *Why?* of their strategy.

Different *Why's* demand different choices for leading capabilities. As an example, consider a pharmaceutical company that has amassed a portfolio of innovative drugs for treating the same disease. Its leaders have three alternatives for their offering: one based on providing breakthrough solutions for different manifestations of the disease by using their drugs; another rooted in having the foremost clinical expertise and treatment support to help doctors improve outcomes; and a third that stands on being the expert in all the various experiences that different patients have with the disease. Each alternative is a different way of capitalizing on the company's unique range of novel therapeutic drugs to treat the disease in its many forms.

Here's a table that summarizes the capabilities leaders prioritized for each offering:

Most important capabilities for Alternative 1: Innovative Solutions Provider	Most important capabilities for Alternative 2: Clinical/Outcomes Expert	Most important capabilities for Alternative 3: Patient Experience Expert
• Providing customized solutions to different segments of doctors • Designing and providing recurring services that simplify management of different forms of the disease • Selling solutions (versus just products) • Measuring/reporting the economic benefits of solutions for each doctor segment	• Generating/disseminating medical evidence on which drugs to use in which situations • Influencing clinical protocols • Providing a support service call • Arming MDs to have crucial conversations about treatment	• Building/maintaining a master brand that patients trust for all things related to the disease • Providing a consistent customer experience across the entire drug portfolio • Codifying/disseminating learning across the disease spectrum to inform patient experience design and implementation • Executing rapid-cycle piloting and prototyping of ideas for innovating the patient experience

All the capabilities in this table are important for most pharma companies to have. But the list above names a dozen capabilities. This company can't possibly be the best at all of them. No company can. Fortunately, though, this one doesn't have to be the best at all 12 capabilities. It need only be the best at four, and what those four should be depends on which alternative leaders choose for their *Why?*

Note that the choice can work in the other direction, too. This is where the choice of offering depends, in part, on what the company is already able to do better than any other. For example, if it already has strong capabilities in designing, selling, and implementing solutions, alternative 1 might be the best choice. But alternative 2 could be the way to go if the company is already better than most at supporting doctors' clinical and patient-support needs. Still, alternative 3 might be the winner if the company has a well-honed ability to develop and implement novel approaches to patient experience.

In their article for *Harvard Business Review*, "The Discipline of Market Leaders," the authors Michael Treacy and Fred Wiersema argue that leaders must choose between three "value disciplines": Operational Excellence, Customer Intimacy, or Product Leadership. Each is a complex capability—or rather a complex set of interdependent capabilities. The authors argue that no company can be the best at all three simultaneously. If that is the case, leaders have to choose. And there are two ways to choose: by which is closest to the *Why?* that they have already articulated for their strategy; or by which fits best with the strengths and weaknesses the company already has.

All of this goes to say that leaders should ask themselves three questions when considering their leading capabilities:

- What is our *Why?* (see chapter 13)?
- What must we be the best at in order to be better than anyone else at marketing, selling, and living our *Why?*
- And how much of a stretch does that require of our current capabilities?

Answers to these three questions provide the best way for leaders to zero in on their *What?*—the small number of capabilities they will choose to nurture and prioritize for investment.

15

How should leaders examine their multibusiness strategy?

Use the A-B test to avoid self-delusion.

For a time in the 1990s, General Electric, a sprawling conglomerate of industrial and financial might, was the toast of the town for its consistently stellar earnings growth. It was easy to conclude that GE was a supremely successful company. But we now know that its success was the product of serial financial engineering and could not last (see chapter 6).

GE's leaders would have known this if they had defined their success differently and honestly applied that definition to their own company. That's how, ten years before GE fell into disarray, I anticipated its decline in a piece I wrote for *Harvard Business Review* in 2007 (see appendix 2).

The success of multibusiness leaders should be defined by (A) the performance of their businesses compared to (B) what that performance would be if those businesses were on their own. If A is consistently greater than B, then the company's businesses are clearly benefiting from being under its corporate roof. Unfortunately, though, there is no way to construct a real-life A-B test, and thus we are left with using proxies, most of which are no good.

One no-good proxy is to compare a company's stock market value to what Wall Street analysts call its "sum of parts" value. Computing that value entails three steps: assuming a value-to-sales or value-to-earnings ratio for each business as if it were independent; multiplying those ratios by the sales or earnings of the company's businesses to calculate an assumed value for each of them; and then summing up those assumed values. If that sum is more than a company's actual market value, one is supposed to conclude that B is greater than A and therefore that the company should be broken up.

But this proxy suffers from several drawbacks. For one, it assumes that current sales and earnings would be the same for each business, whether it had been trading independently heretofore or not. Plus, most analysts infer the valuation ratio for any business by looking at ratios for publicly traded businesses that operate in its industry—that's possible sometimes, but often it's not. And perhaps most troublesome, it replaces the judgment of leaders and directors with that of some analyst who stands on a visibly shaky foundation of assumptions. All this makes this proxy very easy to dump when leaders don't like the answer.

Another suspect proxy for the A-B test is to ask the leaders of each business questions like "Would your business be better off if it were an independent company?" and "Does belonging to this company confer material benefits to the performance of your business?" If the two responses are consistently "No" and "Yes," respectively, and if those responses fairly reflect reality, corporate leaders can happily conclude that they are passing the A-B test with gusto. But I knew many business leaders who *wanted* to be good corporate citizens and would always answer "No" and "Yes," regardless of what they really thought. And on the flip side, I remember one leader of a business who was bound to say the opposite because he wanted nothing more than to be the CEO of his own independent company. Short of giving everyone a truth serum, the likelihood of false positives—and negatives—is too high for this to be a reliable proxy. (Corporate leaders would, however, learn a lot from—and about—the leaders of their businesses if they openly discussed the matter from time to time and were skilled at reading between the lines of what they hear.)

So, we are left with a third proxy for applying the A-B test. This asks corporate leaders to examine their company on half a dozen factors that make the most difference to how A compares to B.

The first of these factors concerns the use of **centralized services** such as managing receivables, payables, payroll, IT, HR, and legal—and even core business processes like R&D, manufacturing, sourcing, and sales—on behalf of the company's individual businesses. Centralization of such services does not come free, as it can slow responsiveness, increase bad bureaucracy, uncouple costs from the revenues they support, and dilute accountability for top- and bottom-line results. These are real costs even if they aren't physically visible. Corporate leaders who don't keep a watchful eye on such costs are likely to let them grow unchecked until they swamp any benefits of scale economies or specialization that centralization theoretically produces.

Another important factor is **capital allocation.** All else being equal, A will top B if leaders consistently allocate capital to their businesses better than the capital markets would do if those businesses were on their own. And corporate leaders *do* have some big advantages here: Unlike capital markets, they have access to proprietary inside knowledge that helps to allocate capital well; and they can influence how effectively capital is deployed once it has been allocated. But leaders can also squander those advantages by, for example, making their capital allocation process an exercise in rationing rather than investing, where if one business gets more capital, another must get less. This politicizes capital allocation and inevitably leads to some businesses getting less capital than they should and others getting more. That's not the way capital markets work! Adam Smith's "invisible hand" is a Spock-like creature devoid of emotion and political interest. It only wants capital to find the highest and best use, and millions of people have a vested interest in making sure that happens. So, the bar is set high for allocating capital in a multibusiness company. And that bar is impossible to hurdle if it's not guided by a great multibusiness strategy (see chapter 3).

Developing and deploying people is a third make-or-break factor. In theory, having a rich mix of businesses under one corporate roof confers the ability to offer a variety of flexible and enriching career paths that will be more attractive and developmental than what those businesses could offer if they were independent entities. That's a big recruiting and retention advantage. And even more so if corporate leaders actively match their company's strongest people to its most important priorities, whether these are specific to businesses, span multiple businesses, or transcend them. But the advantage is spoiled if they let "corporate headquarters" be the dead hand that allows inbreeding, cultural silos, and hoarding of talent within the businesses to prevail, especially if it's aided and abetted by an enormous, costly HR department operating lavishly in the "corporate center."

Governance processes: All companies require deadlines, policies, regulatory compliance, operational controls, targets, plans, and more to operate well. Companies that pass the A-B test go beyond that. Their leaders work hard to shield their individual businesses from the worst of short-term behavior—be it from customers, employees, or especially shareholders—while also holding everyone's feet to the fire when it comes to producing results and investing wisely. The leaders challenge and help shape the strategies that underpin the plans of each business, rather than sit back and wait until those plans are submitted for "corporate" to review and approve. And they actively work *with* the businesses to determine how they will meet their targets, instead of handing them down from on high and then crossing their arms while waiting for the results to come in. Operating this way requires a certain kind of attitude from corporate center leaders and their staff, where the question is not what the businesses can do for them, but what they can do for their businesses (see chapter 3).

The penultimate factor may be the most important: nurturing and exploiting **leading capabilities**. Chapter 14 takes a deeper look into what these are and how to choose them. In a multibusiness company, leading capabilities bring difference-making benefits to every business in its portfolio. Examples: Apple's superlative user-design flair that gives it an edge in personal computers, smartphones, wearable devices, and the like; and Disney's aptitude for creating family-friendly, child-engaging characters that fuel all its many entertainment businesses (see chapter 3).

Moreover, leading capabilities are fortified—not merely exploited—by every business in its portfolio. For example, LEGO's proficiency in making its plastic, brightly colored building blocks come alive is reinforced multiple times over through its resort parks, movies, TV game show, education business, and original toy division (see chapter 47).

Much of what makes A greater than B is made possible by having capabilities that make a company distinctive. Judicious corporate services, wise capital allocation, smart people-development, and enlightened governance processes can't make up for the lack of having a handful of such capabilities.

Finally, passing the A-B test depends a lot on a sixth factor: a company's

portfolio coherence. That is, do its various businesses draw on the same hand-ful of difference-making capabilities and, as important, contribute to them? Without this kind of portfolio coherence, a multibusiness company will likely fail on the five factors discussed above.

For instance, consider "universal banks"—those with both commercial and investment banking businesses. The best-performing banks tend to specialize in one or the other, but not both. Wells Fargo is good at commercial banking, especially retail, but it long avoided investment banking until, unfortunately, it bought Wachovia during the 2008 financial crisis. Goldman Sachs is the best of investment banks and does very little commercial banking. (We'll see how its more recent push into consumer financial services goes.[1])

Few, if any, universal banks pass the A-B test on the five factors listed above, because the needs and nature of commercial and investment banking are so different (see chapter 27). Yet Disney, Berkshire Hathaway, and Danaher score big on those factors because their leaders have created coherent business port-folios, even though all three are highly diverse conglomerates (see chapter 3).

Returning to GE, when I wrote that piece for *HBR*, it was clear that GE was falling short on all six factors! And that started with Jack Welch. As CEO, he said that he had only two jobs: allocating capital and evaluating people. He later added a third, that of transferring ideas between parts of the company. These jobs sound good on the surface; but they aren't worth a lot without a big idea and compelling strategy for a multibusiness company; and they alone are nowhere near enough to pass the A-B test. If, instead, Welch had defined his job by all six of the factors discussed above and had measured himself against the A-B test, perhaps GE would be in a very different place today.

---

1   This parenthetical was written before Goldman subsequently abandoned its consumer ambition, thus illustrating how leaders can use the A-B test to distinguish between good and bad multibusiness strate-gies. For more on why and how Goldman went wrong with its consumer "strategy," see chapter 31.

16

How should leaders evaluate their big idea?

Three questions provide the answer.

The world is full of stellar companies that are struggling to grow because their leaders lack a big idea or one that's still "big enough." There are four main scenarios for how this happens. The most tragic of these is drifting away from the big idea that made a company great. This happened to Crown Holdings (formerly Crown Cork & Seal), when long-time CEO John Connelly retired in 1990, after which his successors abandoned his "short-run specialists" idea to go on an acquisition spree (see chapter 9). It also happened to eBay when the company diluted its big idea of providing a marketplace for trading used merchandise by adding an Amazon-like platform for small retailers, buying the ticket reseller StubHub, and building a classified listings business (see chapter 19). It even happened to The Walt Disney Company when its founder died in 1966 and when for 15 years a succession of CEOs chipped away at his idea of building a constellation of businesses powered by its animated films studio (see chapter 10).

The second scenario is a company's outgrowing its big idea. This means the company has reached the limits of how much that idea can power further growth. For example, Microsoft hit the ceiling of its founders' original break-through—interoperability of operating software for personal computers—in the early 2000s. Walmart did the same a few years later, when Sam Walton's innovation of building mega discount stores for rural and suburban communities ran out of steam. More recently, the about-face commitment that Facebook made to the so-called metaverse not only led to a corporate name change—Meta Platforms Inc.—but it likely signals that Apple's privacy changes, TikTok's emergence, and the intensifying concerns with social media's impact on mental health and political discourse has put a growth ceiling over its original idea.

It's not so much that these companies' big ideas are no longer big. It's more that Microsoft, Walmart, and Meta outgrew them and, in the case of Microsoft and Walmart, they weren't replaced with even bigger ones until recently, as described in chapters 20 and 62. (As for Meta, its ballyhooed pivot to the metaverse seems like more of a sinkhole for its prodigious cash flow than a big idea—at least so far.)

A third scenario is when a company's big idea is copied and surpassed by other companies. This happened to Ford Motor Company and General Motors when Toyota borrowed Ford's assembly-line breakthrough, copied GM's branded-price-points idea, and added its own innovation—the Toyota Production System. More recently, Netflix, the entertainment streaming pioneer, could be experiencing this third scenario as other media companies—like Disney, HBO, Apple, and Amazon—pile into the business with their own particular advantages.

The fourth scenario is having a big idea dwarfed by the innovations of newcomers. Nokia's leaders experienced this scenario in the late 2000s when Apple's iPhone made roadkill out of Nokia's innovation to make pocket phones a global fashion accessory; and Blackberry's leaders experienced something similar when the company's innovative mobile email idea was overrun by Apple's even bigger smartphone phenomenon. Today, we see this scenario playing out in retail with Amazon overwhelming the department store and "category killer" formats that used to be big ideas in that industry (see chapter 62).

In a world where everyone is hungry for growth, full of ingenuity and aspiration, and willing to emulate any successful innovation, these four scenarios are happening everywhere all the time.

Four scenarios for why stellar companies end up struggling to grow	
Scenario A	A company's leaders drift away from the big idea that made it great
Scenario B	A company outgrows the big idea that led to its success
Scenario C	A company's big idea is copied and surpassed
Scenario D	A company's big idea is dwarfed by the innovation of others

That's why there are so many great companies struggling to grow—because there's just no amount of portfolio tinkering, financial engineering, operational improvements, or organizational change that can make up for being stuck in one of these four scenarios.

The most effective solution is preventive care—for leaders to be diligent in knowing what their big idea is and whether it's vulnerable to any of the four scenarios before it's too late. Such diligence demands that leaders periodically revisit three simple questions for their business.

First: **Is the problem (or need or want) we solve still relevant and material?** For example, Walt Disney's problem was "How do we realize the full entertainment and commercial value of the characters we create in our animated films studio?" Bill Gates's was "Different makes of PCs cannot talk to each other." Sam Walton: "How can you profitably serve small towns with a full-line discount store?" Henry Ford: "Cars are too expensive to make and sell for the mass market." And Amazon's Jeff Bezos: "How can you make finding and paying for any book, anywhere, a seamless, friction-free online experience?"

Leaders need to articulate the problem their company solves and be honest about how big and apt it remains.

Next: **Is our solution still unique and, if not, is it protected in some other way?** Few solutions remain unique forever, thanks to the flattery of imitation. Sooner or later, it needs to be protected by an advantage. The most common types of this are a network advantage (the more people or entities using your solution, the better it becomes), a scale advantage (which yields a unit cost no one else can match), or a brand advantage (which makes your offering "cooler," healthier, safer, more trustworthy, or in some other way better than other offerings in the eyes of your target customers).

For example, with its Amazon Web Services (AWS) business, Amazon all but invented the cloud-computing industry. The original idea was as a unique solution for the needs of software startups and individual developers (see chapter 12). Before becoming Amazon's CEO, Andy Jassy transformed AWS from a sideline renting out spare server capacity into a vast new industry. It now generates almost two-thirds of Amazon's profits, while contributing less than 15% of its sales. Meanwhile, seeking to reverse years of stagnation, IBM is hoping to out-do Amazon by making a big play in "hybrid cloud" where companies can use multiple clouds in addition to their own on-premises servers. It will be interesting to see whether AWS's big idea is sufficiently protected to withstand this latest assault. (If the lukewarm response of IBM's shareholders was anything to go by, the answer is most likely "Yes.")

Finally: **Is our big idea still big enough?** A "big idea" is a novel, protected solution (question 2 above) to a materially important problem, need, or want (question 1). But companies can be so successful with their big idea that they outgrow it. Both Microsoft and Walmart ran into this scenario. Their founders' original ideas remain protected solutions to the problems they were trying to solve, though their success in bringing those ideas to market was such that they outgrew their own innovations. Hence, as great as they were, these two companies struggled to find high-quality growth until new leaders found newer, bigger ideas.

Netflix and Starbucks may be facing a similar situation. Online, subscription-based entertainment and expresso-based drinks in a communal "third place" setting were big ideas that, respectively, turned Netflix and Starbucks into global juggernauts. But they could face stagnant growth unless they find new, even bigger ideas. To their credit, leaders of both companies are considering a range of ideas, such as weekly releases, gaming, and advertising in the case of Netflix, and in-store automation and doubling down on store growth in China in the case of Starbucks. But it's far from certain that any of these ideas have the novelty, scale, and profitability potential to power either company's growth for another few decades.

Companies for which the true answer is "Yes" to all three of these questions have the strongest possible foundation for growth (see chapter 20). If growth is not forthcoming for them, it won't be for lack of a big idea. Rather, it'll be due to a failure of strategy, implementation, or execution (see chapter 29).

For companies where the true answer is "No" to *any one* of the three questions, growth will be a continuing struggle. That's because they've slipped into one of the four scenarios, much like the companies in the following table did:

	Is the problem we solve (still) relevant and material?	Is our solution (still) unique and/or protected?*	Is our big idea (still) big enough?	What scenario are we in (see earlier table)?
Disney, 1966-84[1]	Yes	Yes	Yes, but...[2]	A
Crown Cork after 1990[3]	Yes	Yes	We'll never know[4]	A (or B)
Microsoft 2013	Yes	Yes	No	B
Walmart 2015	Yes	Yes	No	B
Ford	Yes	No	No	C
GM	Yes	No	No	C
Nokia	No	No	n/a	D
Blackberry	No	No	n/a	D

* e.g., by its novelty or by a network, scale, or brand advantage
1   Walt Disney died in 1966 and Michael Eisner was hired as CEO in 1984.
2   In the period 1966–84, Disney drifted away from the big idea that made the company great (see chapter 10).
3   1990 is the year when John Connelly, the originator of Crown's big idea, retired as CEO.
4   Connelly's successors moved away from his big idea (see chapter 9).

Once a company finds itself in any of the scenarios, it is extremely difficult to escape them. The only way out is for leaders to rediscover or replace the big idea that made their company great in the first place. Still, big ideas don't grow on trees, and most leaders lack a reliable method for generating a new one (see chapter 21).

Even worse, as the going gets tough, a lot of leaders obsess over execution (especially) and strategy (sometimes) when the situation they face is one of these scenarios. To avoid this, leaders should periodically return to the problem their business solves, explore how protected their solution is, and assess whether that solution is big enough to fuel further growth.

17

How should leaders draw on history to inform their strategies?

Beware competing in a certain way because it's currently popular.

Since the late 1800s, we've seen at least eight distinct movements in how companies compete. The first was **efficiency.** This was the original purpose of forming corporations—to facilitate the least amount of wasted time, materials, and labor. "Taylorism"—the attempt to turn management into a science of efficiency—marked the high point of this movement. Many companies still compete this way, and successors to Taylorism still crop up now and then, including business process reengineering and lean production techniques.

The second movement was **scale,** a close cousin of efficiency. This is where companies use size to drive down their unit costs. It was given a big boost during the 1970s, when the Experience Curve was lifted from the manufacturing floor and adopted as a strategy tool in the corporate boardroom. Scale drove consolidation and globalization of industries throughout the mid-1900s and it still does today, such as in steel, airlines, life sciences, and telecommunications.

Scale and efficiency are ways of competing by reducing costs to facilitate lower pricing without sacrificing a healthy margin. In the early 1980s, a new way of competing broke on to the world stage: the **quality** movement, the third in our list. W. Edwards Deming introduced this as a way of life for Japanese companies. Many attributed Japan's economic ascension after World War II to Deming's quality movement. "Made in the USA" gave way to "Made in Japan" as a badge of superiority. "Quality is free" became a mantra. And processes like Six Sigma quality control became standard practice after GE publicly adopted it in 1995.

Today, quality, scale, and efficiency stand side-by-side as ways of competing. For every Dollar Store, Kohl's, and Kia that competes mostly on price, there's a Whole Foods, a Nordstrom, and a BMW that competes mostly on quality. Some companies brought together Six Sigma and lean production into "Lean Six Sigma" as a way of competing with both lower costs and higher quality.

In the 1990s, the fourth on our list emerged: **speed.** This was memorialized in a book called *Time-Based Competition.* The idea was that the world was accelerating, so businesses had to speed up to keep up. The only sustainable advantage was thought to be faster than everyone else. Faster innovation. Faster manufacturing. Faster service. Faster delivery. Faster adaptation. Faster everything!

Also in the 1990s, a fifth way of competing became prominent: **loyalty-based management.** As described in *The Loyalty Effect,* the premise is that customer, employee, and investor loyalty is the *sine qua non* for creating value, so retaining it should be the central focus of strategy.

A different—sixth—movement gained popularity in the late 1990s and early 2000s. It's awkwardly called **premiumization,** or **trade-up.** Gillette was an early pioneer and exemplified this for decades with a succession of razors containing two, then three, and now five individual blades. The spirits company Diageo is another pioneer: for years it had only two labels of Johnnie Walker whiskeys, Red and Black. It now has labels spanning almost the entire color spectrum—Green, Gold, White, Platinum, Blue—with each one sold at a successively higher price point. Today, practically every brand in every spirits category—tequila, vodka, gin, bourbon, rye, etc.—is playing the same game of premiumization. And this way of competing now permeates all kinds of industries, from consumables (like coffee, ice cream, chocolate, cheese, nuts, and the aforementioned liquor) to consumer durables (smartphones, cars, home appliances), services (digital news, streaming, lodging, and retailing), and business equipment (copiers, printers, mowers).

The rise of Internet commerce led to a new, seventh movement: the **network effect**. This is the notion that a product or service becomes increasingly valuable as more people use it—that is, the more users a product has, the greater value it seems to have for new and existing users alike. Microsoft found this way of competing when it developed its operating system for the personal computer (see chapter 31). IBM, McKinsey, Google, Facebook, LinkedIn, Airbnb, and many others benefit from a "network effect." That effect is both a beneficiary and a multiplier of efficiency, scale, quality, speed, and loyalty.

The network movement has led to an eighth: the **ecosystem** (or **platform**) way of competing. This entails co-opting third parties to use a company's assets— technology, data, customer base, and the like—to build their own products, services, and businesses. Having an advantage comes from the number of companies tied to its ecosystem. Steve Jobs famously resisted opening up Apple's app store to everyone; he relented when his team convinced him that the iPhone would gain advantage by allowing anyone to build apps for it. Ryanair, the cut-rate Irish airline, has sought to create an ecosystem comprising hotels, restaurants, and other such businesses to serve its passengers, and thus make it their go-to airline.

While the network and ecosystem movements took off in the early 2000s, they are far from new. For example, newspapers have always heavily subsidized their "users" (readers) in order to provide more benefits to their "customers" (advertisers). The consolidation of phone companies and professional sports leagues in the last century was largely driven by creating fewer, bigger networks, each having many more customers, thus enhancing their service and experience. And in the late 1800s, lodging and resort businesses used the railroads as a platform (no pun intended) for building hotels near points of interest along their tracks, and that helped rail companies increase the attraction of their particular routes.

Moreover, the network and ecosystem movements have not supplanted the other ways of competing. There will always be phases of heightened, even fashionable, views on how to compete in certain situations. Efficiency takes center stage when there's a downturn, as does premiumization when customers are feeling their oats; scale and speed take priority when industry growth is slowing, or when competitive entry is exploding; quality and loyalty come to the fore when market growth is healthy or when there are systemic product or service failures; and the network and ecosystem movements shine when product and service differentiation becomes too difficult as a way of producing or sustaining a compelling customer proposition.

All the above raises a challenging question: What will be the *next* movement? There are many candidates, some of which may already be upon (or even behind) us:

- **Agility,** a variant of speed that comes from the world of software development. It has now become a broader business concept of gaining advantage by being faster to adapt than anyone else.
- **Subscription,** or offering products as a service. This way of competing is currently growing 100% a year. It now includes software, tractors, furniture, guitars, financial planning, and more.
- **Purpose,** directly linking a company's products and services to serving a social cause (see chapter 33).
- **Health & Wellness,** meaning differentiating everyday products and services (apparel, fast food, cosmetics, lodging, travel experiences, financial services, and so on) with "good for you" features and benefits.
- **ESG** (Environment, Sustainability, Governance), driving efficiency and loyalty by promoting one's doing-good-for-society credentials.
- **Metaverse,** creating new ways to market, sell, and deliver new or existing products and services in the next generation of how we engage through the internet.
- **Artificial Intelligence,** giving the means to drive greater efficiencies, exploit scale, and create higher-quality and more-customized products, services, and experiences.

These potential movements all go to show that if today there's a much bigger menu of ways to succeed than we had a century ago, the menu will be even bigger decades from now. This is how "leading a business" becomes more complex over time. To navigate through that increasing complexity, leaders must use their own specific strategies as a true north. Their way of competing needs to be particular both to their unique circumstances and to the essential choices only they can make for their strategy (see chapters 2 and 3).

PART V

How Do Leaders Keep a Strategy Great?

Strategies are like bicycles. They are either moving forward or falling over.

18

How should leaders stretch their strategy to keep it great?

Three ways to create new headroom for growth

A company's growth prospects are bounded by the *Who? Why?* and *What?* that leaders choose for their strategy (see chapter 2). Stretching these choices is one way to keep a strategy great.

Leaders can stretch their *Who?* in any number of ways to increase its universe of potential buyers. Here are four examples: Mercedes-Benz has grown by stretching its ideal customer from the wealthy who buy the most expensive cars to those who want superior quality for whatever car budget they have. McDonald's found new growth by adding breakfast eaters and coffee breakers to expand its population of fast-food customers. Belgian chocolate maker Godiva has plans for a global chain of 2,000 cafes designed to target millennials and other younger consumers who are less aware of its century-old confectionaries. And Mahindra Finance, the financial services arm of Mahindra Group, a multi-billion-dollar Indian conglomerate, decided to offer its vehicle financing service to India's rural people.

Leaders with great strategies are always debating how best to stretch their *Who?* This demands careful thought and on-the-ground trial, learning, and experience. To complicate things, many businesses don't have just one type of customer. For example, media companies such as newspapers, broadcasters, and social media sites have readers, viewers, or users on one side of their business and advertisers on the other. Market-matching companies such as talent agencies and online car-hailing services must target workers and passengers, respectively, as well as employers and drivers. Health care companies must choose which physicians, payors, and in some cases even patients to target for their offerings (see chapter 60). Consumer product companies must define their ideal customer at two levels: retailers and consumers. Companies that sell big-ticket products or services to other companies have to decide not only what type of enterprise to target, but which people within them to target. This complication, the myriad of ways to profile customers, and an ever-evolving environment are always opening up new opportunities to stretch a company's *Who?*

The second way to stretch a strategy is by enhancing a company's *Why?* in ways that secure and generate more demand for what it already sells. For example, consider Microsoft, Securitas AB, Google, and Amazon. In the early 1980s, Microsoft grew (and reinforced) demand for its core MS-DOS business by adding its suite of Office products (Word, Excel, Power Point, and more). Securitas increased demand for its physical guarding service by bundling it into a "security solutions" offering that includes electronic security and risk management. Google invested heavily in services such as Chrome, Google Maps, Waze, Gmail, and Google Home to stimulate more demand for its core search business, which still generates the vast majority of the top line for its parent company, Alphabet, Inc. And Amazon, the online retailer, added entertainment streaming to its Prime member service because people who stream content through Amazon shop more frequently there and spend more. Or as Jeff Bezos, Amazon's founder and CEO, remarked, "When we win a Golden Globe, it helps us sell more shoes."

More generally, many leaders are now stretching their strategies by adding a promised outcome to their offering, such as a higher success rate for a particular medical device or perhaps lower hospital readmissions from a provider of home health services. Others are turning their products into subscription services, such as Neeva, founded by the former head of Google's $115 billion advertising arm, which offers internet search for a monthly fee and promises no display ads to distract users. Amazon and Walmart sell subscriptions to their e-commerce service that feature subscriber-only benefits. Other companies are offering subscriptions to access passenger vehicles, construction equipment, and even private airplanes; yet others are adding coffee, home appliances, furniture, guitars, toothbrushes, and contact lenses to the growing list of subscription-based propositions. Venture capital firms are even turning to a subscription model whereby their investors (whom they call "limited partners") commit capital on an annual, rolling basis to a stream of quarterly investment funds.

The third possible path to stretching a strategy involves capabilities. Every successful business thrives by having a handful of these (see chapter 14). And some of these can become new revenue sources in their own right. For example, decades ago American Airlines turned its innovative reservation capability into a high-growth business, branded SABRE. Another example is Amazon. In the last decade, its revenue growth has accelerated tremendously by adding a seemingly infinite array of new categories to its original online retail business, though most of its profit growth has come from two other sources: offering e-commerce capabilities to other retailers, and selling its enormous cloud-computing capability, initially to developers and startups, and these days to major corporations. Today Amazon's cloud-computing business—AWS—accounts for almost two-thirds of its annual operating income, even though AWS generates less than 15% of Amazon's revenue! Moreover, Amazon is building an entirely new business—AWS for Health—that further commercializes its cloud-computing infrastructure by offering AWS-powered solutions to health care providers and self-insured employers.

Hennes & Mauritz (H&M), the second-largest fast-fashion retailer, and Walmart give us two more examples that are similar to each other. H&M is opening up its global supply chain capability to other clothing brands, including help on designing their own supplier networks to avoid disruptions caused by trade wars, pandemics, and other such things. Walmart is turning its local "last-mile" delivery capability into a new business, called Walmart GoLocal, that serves local and national retailers such as bakeries and auto parts stores. Going even further, Walmart is partnering with Adobe Commerce to integrate and sell its marketplace, fulfillment, and pick-up capabilities to other companies.

American, Amazon, H&M, and Walmart all stretched their strategies— and raised their growth ceilings—by commercializing their best capabilities in new ways. Moreover, they strengthened those capabilities by exposing them to the rigors of market competition.

Note that none of these three paths for stretching a strategy is independent of the other two. For example, by adding breakfast and coffee occasions to stretch its target-customer definition, McDonald's can utilize its assembly-line cooking capabilities during a part of the day when they would otherwise have sat idle. Mahindra Finance learned how to serve customers who were mostly poor, illiterate, and unbanked, and used this new capability to stretch into helping them finance their homes, working capital, and agriculture equipment, and even to obtain insurance for their tractors, health, and very lives. And by targeting millennials with its café concept, Godiva has created new ways to enjoy its products, thus enhancing their proposition to its traditional customer. The odds are good that when leaders generate ideas for stretching their strategy in one dimension, they will end up producing a rich set of ideas for the other two.

Leaders keep their strategy great by always looking for ways to stretch their *Who? Why?* and *What?* They are limited only by their imagination. They intuitively understand that a limber strategy is a healthy one. And a static strategy is an aging one.

Finally, a word of caution: There are good and there are bad ways to stretch a strategy. And some strategies stretch better than others. See the next two chapters—19 and 20—for more on that.

19

Why do some strategy stretches work better than others?

Three factors make the difference.

The world is littered with failed strategy extensions. The Coca-Cola Company tried making wine and films. Eastman Kodak ventured into pharmaceuticals. Drug companies leapt into consumer products. Philip Morris bought Miller Brewing. Anheuser-Busch jumped hard on the hard-seltzer bandwagon. Amazon tried an eBay-like marketplace. And eBay itself tried to be a marketplace for buying and selling tickets. Walmart dabbled in premium wines and tried to attract urban shoppers with a small-store format that can fit into tighter spaces. And the oil companies followed each other's unsuccessful forays into mineral extraction.

But this doesn't mean that flexing strategy never works. To the contrary, it can work spectacularly. For example, in the early 1990s, chief executive Lou Gerstner rescued IBM by adding both technology partnering to its customer pitch and corporate CEOs to its customer focus (see chapter 5). Apple created more demand for its Mac computers by stretching into highly competitive mp3, smartphone, and online music businesses. And Berkshire Hathaway has successfully stretched into industrial parts manufacturing, energy utilities, cargo transport, and many other seemingly unrelated businesses.

Why do some strategy extensions work and others not? Three factors make the difference. The first is whether they expand the base of customers for a company's current proposition. This alone explains many of the failed strategy stretches mentioned above. Premium wines are simply a poor fit with Walmart's traditional proposition of "everyday products at everyday low prices." Small urban stores do little to add new customers for the large format offering that makes Walmart attractive to rural and suburban shoppers. Beer, hard seltzer, and cigarettes might go well together at a party, but how does buying a beer business bring new customers to a cigarette business or selling hard seltzer add customers to a beer business? While many of us order soft drinks at the cinema, how does being a producer of movies draw in more consumers of Coke? Buying a marketplace (like StubHub) for reselling tickets did little to grow the buyers and sellers of second-hand goods in its original marketplace.

The second factor that affects the success of stretching a strategy is whether it enhances a company's customer proposition. IKEA provides an excellent example. It sells home furnishings at a low price. And now it's selling televisions. Is this the typical adjacencies thinking?[1] "Hey, if our customers are buying furniture, they might also be in the market for TVs.… Why not capture that business while they're already in our stores?" Well, no. IKEA aims to solve a furniture challenge that many customers complain about: how to fit the TV—and all the components, gadgets, and tangles of wires that come with it—more seamlessly into the living room. IKEA has integrated the television into a furniture solution. It's not trying to enter a new business (retailing electronics); rather, it's enhancing the customer proposition of its current business (functional home furnishings).

The third factor is whether a strategy extension exploits enough of a company's strongest capabilities. Extracting minerals from the ground may seem very similar to the business of pulling oil out of the earth, but it requires very different capabilities. Hewlett-Packard is another example: It started out in high-tech measurement machines that require hardware engineering capabilities. When the PC revolution occurred, HP realized that desktop printers were a natural extension of those capabilities—and printers became one of its best businesses. But another big stretch—enterprise computer services—was unsuccessful, because HP's capabilities were ill-matched to their requirements. Desktop printers were a solid extension of HP's best capabilities; offering enterprise computer services was not.

Berkshire Hathaway provides a further example. Its CEO, Warren Buffett, built a company adept at sourcing mountains of zero-cost capital ("insurance float") and well-managed businesses with oceans of opportunities to invest that capital (see chapter 3). The insurance side of the company generates the capital, while the other part (rails, utilities, retailing, stocks, and so forth) makes productive use of it, all guided by the investment expertise of Buffett and two lieutenants, Tom Weschler and Todd Combs.

Berkshire is the ultimate conglomerate, and yet every business in its massive portfolio consists of a new way to commercialize its extraordinary capabilities. To be sure, the company's capabilities are rare. But other diverse companies have their own unique capabilities that they use to stretch their strategies successfully. This includes Danaher and its famous Danaher Business System, Disney and its ability to create and commercialize family-friendly characters (see chapter 3), and United Technologies with its ACE (Achieving Competitive Excellence) system.

The best strategy stretches do all three of bringing new customers to a company's current proposition, fortifying that proposition, and then exploiting the distinctive capabilities it already has. This is why Apple's move into mp3 players is one of the all-time-best strategy extensions. In the late 1990s, Steve Jobs was thinking hard about how to make the Macintosh computer more central to consumers' digital lives. The internet was becoming mainstream, and Jobs wanted to make it easier for consumers to connect their photos, videos, and music with their Mac computers. Thus was born the iPod, which leveraged the company's leading capability to bring together technologies that already exist into a beautiful, ergonomic, user-enjoyable package. Not only was the iPod a wild success, but it also dramatically enhanced the perceived benefits of owning *other* Apple products. The Macintosh business benefited enormously because the iPod increased the computer's utility and made it even more hip to buy.[2]

The worst strategy stretches are usually born of the wrong motivations, such as to compensate for slowing growth, exploit a hot market, keep up with others, or engineer a particular growth, margin, or risk profile (see chapter 6). Such come-ons are why the car rental business once seemed attractive to airlines ("We are a travel services company") and also auto manufacturers ("We offer mobility").

And they led steel companies into buying construction aggregates ("We're a building materials company"), drove oil companies into mineral mining ("We extract stuff from the ground"), and seduced pharmaceutical companies into over-the-counter products ("We do consumer health"). With the wrong motives, these strategy changes were all doomed. Most had to be reversed. Their promise of growth proved illusory. *None* of them made their original businesses any stronger. Worst of all, they gobbled up precious executive time and attention.

The correct motivation for flexing a strategy, then, is to *expand a company's boundaries in ways that also strengthen the businesses it already has*. Done the right way, the only limitation is leaders' creativity, imagination, and will.

---

1   "Strategy stretches" (see chapter 18) aren't the same as "adjacencies"—selling new stuff to current customers; or selling current stuff to new customers; or selling current products and services in new markets; or selling new products and services in current markets. Yet the success of both is governed by the same three factors explained here.

2   We'll see how Apple's latest stretch into the streaming market unfolds. In March 2019 it announced original-content partnerships with Hollywood A-listers such as Oprah Winfrey and Steven Spielberg, and also tie-ups with third-party content creators like HBO, CBS, and the *Wall Street Journal*. Producing original content, aggregating third-party content, and building a subscription streaming service around both is an enormous stretch of Apple's capabilities; and it pits Apple against the likes of Disney, Netflix, and Amazon, which already either have these capabilities or have a big head start in building them. But Apple has a capability for building quality, style, and ease of use into hardware and software. And people are getting confused and frustrated by the proliferation of online content and channels. They could be attracted to a service from a company they trust that simplifies and enhances their reading and viewing lives, as Apple is already doing with the news and sports subsections of its TV app. That could enhance the perceived benefits of owning an iPhone, iPad, iMac, and Apple TV box, and could draw in new customers for those offerings as well.

20

Why do some strategies stretch better than others?

Big ideas make the difference.

Around 1980, Bill Gates and his cofounder, Paul Allen, landed on a big idea: software interoperability across all makes of PCs (see chapter 31). Based on that idea, they changed their original business of selling software programs for microcomputers to licensing the MS-DOS operating system to the personal computing industry. The company's valuation skyrocketed from 10 times its earnings in the mid-'70s to 45 times its earnings in 1995. Clearly, the market agreed that Microsoft's big idea was gigantic.

Gates and Allen rode their idea hard, stretching the company's strategy by, for example, increasing the number of developers writing apps for Windows to a peak of 6 million, adding the Microsoft Office product suite (Word, Excel, Power Point, and other apps), creating its own version of email (Microsoft Outlook), and aggressively pursuing international expansion. Every stretch worked because it grew and entrenched demand for MS-DOS, thus reinforcing and feeding off the company's one big idea. By the mid-1990s, Microsoft had achieved almost complete global dominance of the PC software industry.

Yet by 2013, Microsoft's price-to-earnings multiple had fallen to a mere 12, well under a third of its multiple 18 years earlier. It wasn't for lack of effort. From the mid-1990s through 2013, Microsoft launched an incredible array of growth initiatives. It started a gaming division, called Xbox, and also an online news channel, now called MSNBC. It created Bing, its search business, to take on Google and Surface tablets to compete with Apple. It bought Skype, the messaging platform. And in his final days on the job, then-Chief Executive Steve Ballmer bought Nokia's mobile telephony devices business. Nevertheless, the company's price-earnings ratio had taken a nosedive. Why?

The market had rightly caught on that Microsoft had hit a growth ceiling with its big idea, and no amount of flexing its strategy would be enough to compensate for that. Moreover, internet apps, which worked across different operating systems, diminished the developer network advantage of Windows, lowering entry barriers and allowing Android, Chrome, and iOS operating systems to make inroads. Finally, many of Microsoft's strategy stretches neither reinforced its big idea nor gained much from it. It was having to run just to stay in place. That's why its multiple was more like other companies—such as Gap, Inc., Viacom, and Yahoo!—whose big ideas had long ago lost steam (see chapter 9).

The general lesson is that strategies stretch better when they are powered by the same big idea that fuels the company overall, *and* when they make that idea even bigger. But when a big idea has run out of runway, its leaders will struggle to extend their strategies in ways that generate durable, profitable growth. Sears stretching into financial services (see chapter 46); Novartis getting into eye care; GE buying NBC Universal; Walmart's move into a small-format urban store; and Verizon's acquiring the legacy AOL and Yahoo! web properties—all these failed, because they were less about exploiting and fortifying a big idea and more a reaction to the lack of one.

If the big idea that made a company great in the first place is no longer big enough to power its future, the only solution is to find another one. This is a bit like saying the only solution is to find another unicorn. But it's possible. And as it turns out, Microsoft is a prime example.

Shortly after becoming chief executive in 2014, Satya Nadella introduced the idea of Microsoft's becoming a cloud-based software services company through a new business called Azure. He effectively called for a startup-like pivot of a company that was already worth nearly $300 billion. And ever since, he and his team have been busy stretching Microsoft's strategy to both strengthen and build on that big idea. For example, Microsoft Office, still one of the company's biggest earners, is now offered through the cloud as a subscription business called

Office 365. Updates to the Windows operating system are now done through the cloud. What's more, Nadella declared Microsoft an "open software development" company and bought GitHub to crystallize a policy shift long considered heresy. He reversed the company's purchase of Nokia's mobile phone business and bought LinkedIn, the online professional networking application. He has refocused the company's primary customer back on enterprises, big and small. And in July 2019 he invested $1 billion in OpenAI to ensure that its work on developing "artificial general intelligence" happens on Azure.

The year before Nadella was tapped as CEO, Microsoft generated almost $80 billion of revenue. That number has almost quadrupled under Nadella. As impressive, the company's market value is approaching $3 trillion and, even at that gargantuan size, its stock price is worth over 30 times its current earnings. Clearly, the market has judged that Nadella found his unicorn! The flurry of activity he's unleashed to stretch his strategy is still going on today. But in its intensity, it's no different from the activity driven by his predecessor, the famously energetic Steve Ballmer. What's different is that Nadella came up with a new big idea—one that creates enormous opportunities for stretching his strategy for Microsoft.

You don't see this every day. But you *do* see it. For example, in 1925, almost 40 years after Sears was founded as a catalog business, its chairman at the time, General Robert E. Wood, had the big idea of creating a new kind of store serving a broad range of homemaking needs with high service and periodic deep-discount sales. In the 1980s, Intel's then-CEO, Andy Grove, realized that his company's big idea—Dynamic Random Access Memory (DRAM)—had been overtaken by the Japanese; he and his team found the inspiration, courage, and resolve to replace that idea with a new, bigger one: microprocessors for IBM-compatible PCs. A little less than a decade later, IBM pulled off a dramatic strategy switch when Lou Gerstner landed on the big idea of becoming an IT partner rather than just a mainframe provider (see chapter 5). In the mid-2000s, LEGO was revitalized when its then-CEO decided to diversify *for* its original business rather than *away* from it.[1] And today we are witnessing Walmart finally realizing that strategy stretches—such as international flag planting, urban expansion, and buying companies like jet.com and bonobos.com—are insufficient responses to the aging of its original idea. Instead, we are seeing the behemoth inch its way from a bricks-and-mortar business with 4,000-plus superstores to an e-retailer with 4,000-plus store outlets that double as fulfillment centers and a Disney-like portfolio strategy (see chapter 62).

Failed stretches are often due to bad strategy (see chapter 19). But sometimes they happen because they don't exploit the big idea that made a company in the first place. Or worse, because the company's big idea has run out its string. That's what happened to Sears (see chapter 46) and also to Eastman Kodak, Blockbuster, and Nokia. Leaders have to know what their company's big idea is and be ever-diligent in assessing whether it's still a big one (see chapter 16). If they find it's not, their focus has to be on finding a new one (see chapter 21). They can buy time with cost cutting, asset sales, tax optimization, acquisitions, and other tweaks, but that will merely mask their stagnation. The only durable solution is to find the company's *next big idea.*

---

1   In 2004, LEGO had lost money in three of the prior five years, despite efforts to make the company less dependent on its original business (those famously colored plastic bricks) that had lost its appeal to children born in the 1990s. The company's then-new CEO, Jorgen Vig Knudstorp, came up with the idea of diversifying *for* that business rather than *away* from it. For example, he created LEGO Land, LEGO Education, "The LEGO Movie," and the LEGO Digital Designer, all aimed at making LEGO cool again with its bull's-eye customer and generating new demand for its toy construction sets. His strategy stretches worked because they nourished—and were nourished by—the same big idea for revitalizing the company.

21

How should leaders innovate their strategy to keep it great?

By looking in other boxes to think "outside the box"

The retired Army General David Petraeus is known as a deep thinker on strategy and leadership. In an interview at the Stanford Graduate School of Business, he said there are four tasks that leaders must master: get the big ideas right; communicate them effectively; oversee their implementation; and determine how to refine them. Then repeat.

In other words, no strategy can afford to stand still. Even great strategies need innovation from time to time if they are to remain great. And that is a challenge for most leaders. Mustering the creativity and inspiration required for genuinely new thinking and ideas demands mental capacity and relaxed physical conditions that can be hard to find when every day is consumed by more urgent matters. But as Petraeus said, "You have to sit down…and do it…. [And] it needs to be undertaken as part of a formal, structured process." The problem is, most leaders have no such process—or if they do, it doesn't reflect how strategy innovation and our brains actually work.

Fortunately, there *is* such a method. And by practicing it, leaders can become highly skilled at innovating their strategy. The key is to reverse engineer how innovative strategies happen in the real world, and then to mirror that when a strategy needs innovation.

Let's begin with what the most creative people in their field already know.

Mark Twain remarked: "There is no such thing as a new idea. We simply take a lot of old ideas and…make new and curious combinations."

Henry Ford: "I invented nothing new. I simply assembled the discoveries of others."

Albert Einstein: "If I had an hour to solve a problem, I'd spend 55 minutes thinking about the problem and five minutes thinking about solutions."

These reflections capture in a nutshell how strategy innovations happen in real life and thus how to innovate a strategy when it's needed:

- Start with framing a specific challenge that best describes the innovation a strategy needs.
- Find the most relevant innovations of others.
- Reassemble them—or the apropos parts of them—into a novel solution to the challenge.
- Build (or rebuild) a strategy to bring that solution to commercial fruition.

Take two real-world examples. One comes from Reed Hastings, the founder of Netflix. He committed himself to making movie rentals a more enjoyable experience. His innovation combined the models of monthly gym memberships, centralized warehousing of boxed software inventory, and online ordering and payment. He invented none of these; but he was the first to combine and apply them to the movie rental business.

Warren Buffett, long-time CEO of Berkshire Hathaway, gives us another example. He turned a failing textiles company into a value-creating juggernaut by connecting two ideas. The first came from a legendary investor and Buffett's business school professor, Benjamin Graham, and from Buffett's long-time partner, Charlie Munger. Buffett calls it the "intrinsic value" approach to investing, where the price of a stock is compared to the "value" of its future earnings stream (this innovation goes back to England in the early 18th century when Archibald Hutcheson reverse-engineered the earnings that the South Seas Company would need to produce to justify its ever-increasing price during the famous bubble named for the company).

Buffett combined this idea with a second one that came from Lorimer Davidson, then an investment officer for Geico (and later its CEO). This was the insight that "insurance float"—the cash collected from premiums before it has to be used for paying out insurance claims—is a source of free capital that could massively boost Berkshire's returns if invested well (see first idea).

The inspiration for both Netflix and Berkshire Hathaway hardly came from received wisdom in their respective domains, or even their own particular expertise. That's no exception. Research shows that deep expertise in a particular area (industry, function, geography, and so forth) can be a severe constraint on conjuring new thinking and ideas in that area. For example, Marion Poetz, from the Copenhagen Business School, found that carpenters, roofers, and skaters were all better at generating ideas for improving the others' gear than their own. That explains why a geologist developed the plate-tectonic theory of earthquakes, not a seismologist; why the hypothesis for how dinosaurs became extinct came from an astronomer, not a paleontologist; and why the breakthrough Odon device for obstructed labor when giving birth came from an auto mechanic, not a doctor, nurse, or medical device expert.

These examples show that when leaders need to innovate their strategy, they have to get past their own domain expertise and escape the orthodoxy that can kill their creativity. And to do this, they must move away from the specifics of their particular situation. This means recognizing that whatever their challenge might be, they are not the first to face some form of it.

For example, if leaders have the opportunity to launch a new product and their challenge is doing so in a crowded field, they might look into how JetBlue differentiated itself in a highly commoditized sector (see chapter 43). Or if their opportunity is changing the way an industry works and their challenge is to avoid the buzz saw of established-industry inertia, they should investigate how

Intuitive Surgical changed the practice of surgery in the face of enormous resistance to Da Vinci, its robotic surgery machine. Or if leaders face the challenge of a growing, perceived stigma associated with their product—because, for example, its ingredients are being questioned, or it's associated with labor abuse, or it has lost its "coolness" factor, or it's gained a reputation for being dangerous—they might find a creative breakthrough by studying what McDonald's Australia did about its Big Mac, or how Nike addressed protests over its overseas production, or how LEGO became cool again with kids, and even how the Colombian city of Medellín resuscitated its tourist industry.

William Duggan, who teaches innovation at the Columbia Business School, says that, to think outside the box, you should look in *other* boxes. What leaders will find in those other boxes is the feedstock for reassembling the old into a new idea that's big enough to crack their challenge *and* whose antecedents have been proven successful.

So, when leaders need to innovate their strategy, here are the steps they can follow: First, frame as creatively and specifically as possible the challenge that demands innovation of their strategy. Henry Ford once remarked, "Ideas are everywhere. You just have to know what you want [them for]." When venture capitalists interrogate entrepreneurs about their startup, they typically start with "What's the problem your company solves?" Ford himself knew, and venture capitalists (VCs) in general understand, that innovation is a novel solution to a particular challenge. The more-creative and more-specific leaders can be when framing their challenge, the more likely that they will spark new thinking and ideas.

Then leaders should deconstruct and disassociate their challenge into domain-agnostic discovery questions. For example, if the challenge is to commercialize a novel and complex technology, product, service, or payment model that goes against the grain of an industry's norms, here are some discovery questions they might pose that could fit the bill:

- Who successfully commercialized a new category of products or services in any industry with pervasive inertia, and how did they do it?
- Who successfully moved an industry from one pay or contracting model to another, and how did they make that happen?
- Who successfully transitioned an industry from buying products to

buying an outcome, and what made it work for them?

- Who successfully changed the way an industry works by introducing a new technology, product, or service, and what changes did they make?
- Who successfully changed the standard of customer service, and how did they succeed?
- Who successfully made a complex product or service as easy as possible for customers to implement, use, buy, and the like, and how did they do it?

Next, leaders should ask each other to search their memory banks; talk to others (particularly those outside their particular domain); crowdsource; interrogate Google's Gemini and OpenAI's ChatGPT; and do whatever it takes to find innovation precedents guided by discovery questions such as those listed above.

Once leaders feel satisfied that they have looked in enough other boxes and found a rich-enough set of precedents that are relevant, applicable, and proven, they should challenge themselves to recombine the most-promising parts of those precedents into new ideas for solving the business problem that demands innovation of their strategy.

These steps are simple in concept, but beware: They are cognitively taxing and inevitably entail multiple dead-end searches for inspiration that mostly feel like a waste of time. That's why we all tend to default to incremental improvement based on what we already know, or to blue-sky brainstorming that has no grounding in what's worked before. And it's why so many strategies—no matter how great they might once have been—become stale over time and lose their innovative edge. The good news is that the more that leaders mirror and practice how strategy innovation actually happens, the more skilled they will become at innovating their strategy when and where they need it most.

22

How should leaders work together to keep their strategy great?

By periodically challenging their choices and testing their alignment

The power of a strategy to facilitate great execution depends on the strength of conviction that leaders have for the essential choices that constitute that strategy (see chapters 2 and 3). Lack of commitment inadvertently creates the license to "unpick" choices some leaders may not like; it invites leaders to abandon a strategy too easily when the going gets tough; and it inevitably sows doubt in the rest of the organization. This drains strategy of its ability to bring clarity and momentum to a company's priorities, imperatives, decisions, and actions. And that ultimately undermines an organization's effectiveness and execution (see chapters 26 and 28).

So, how do we ensure commitment to strategy within a leadership team? Human nature is such that people commit to something when they have been part of shaping it, rather than having it handed to them. Plus, when it comes to strategy, the work is never done, because the context for a strategy is always changing. A strategy is either keeping pace with its context or falling behind it and becoming irrelevant. Like bicycles, strategies fall over if they aren't moving forward. Leaders have to continuously advance their strategy—together—to maintain its strength as a leadership tool. And they need a process for doing that.

Such a process has two parts. Both are designed to help leaders commit to their strategy while also moving it forward.

The first part is for leaders to engage each other in a regular exercise that tests their alignment. The best format for this is a roundtable discussion. Before it takes place, leaders write down their own thoughts on the following:

- The choices their strategy comprises today (see chapters 2 and 3)
- How sharp and differentiating these choices are (see chapter 8)
- The big idea behind their strategy (see chapter 9) and how well protected it is (chapter 16)
- Where their strategy needs stretch in order to raise the company's growth ceiling (see chapter 18)
- Where their strategy needs innovation in order to keep its edge (see chapter 21)

Everyone should record their thoughts *before* the meeting takes place. This enables them to share their original thinking, rather than simply responding to what they hear from others in the roundtable discussion.

To kick off the roundtable, each participant should be given a maximum of three minutes to share what they have written down. Except for clarifying questions, everyone should hold their fire until each person at the table has had his or her three minutes. Then the discussion can flow freely. After that has run its course, it's time to take stock of where there's common ground and where there's misunderstanding or disagreement that needs to be ironed out.

When leaders do this at least annually, they achieve a lot. They fortify their collective and individual commitment to their strategy and what it needs to stay great; they arm themselves to speak more consistently about that strategy to the rest of the organization; and they are enabled to take actions more coherently on its behalf. But the impact will be short-lived unless it's repeated on a regular basis, especially given the executive and staff turnover that every company faces.

The second part of the process is to carve out regular time for leaders to work together on their strategy. This starts with agreeing on which business issues and opportunities demand a decision now—one that could have the most material implications for their strategy. Here are some real-world examples from three different companies:

- *Online ride-hailing services are making us obsolete while at the same time potentially creating a new growth avenue for us.*
- *Our government business is highly relevant to corporate clients, but we lack the capabilities to win in the enormous commercial sector.*
- *Our products are increasingly stigmatized because of the obesity epidemic.*

Then, for each of the prioritized issues/opportunities, everyone is expected to contribute to generating genuine alternative responses *and* to evaluating those alternatives. Based on their evaluation, they agree on which alternatives they should choose and how the company's strategy should change accordingly. (For more on this approach, see chapter 23.)

Working on these things together is what it means for leaders to actively co-create strategy. And it produces many benefits. It forces differences to the surface when leaders are making their strategy choices, thus making these choices less vulnerable to unpicking down the road. It creates trust and respect such that the leaders can challenge each other in ways that move the strategy ball forward. And it helps those leaders convey their confidence, commitment, and conviction when communicating their strategy to others, both inside and outside their company.

As important, it operationalizes the practical reality that strategy should not be a one-and-done thing. After all, technology, competitors, and customers are always moving forward—why shouldn't strategy be doing the same? Leaders' attitude should not be "We set strategy and then execute like hell!" It should be "We execute like hell and never stop pushing our strategy ahead!" That's because issues and opportunities will *always* be appearing over the horizon that demand change to some aspect of a strategy. (If not, that strategy is likely pitched at such a high level that it's not an actionable one, but rather a series of big, sweeping statements with no practical value.)

Finally, leaders' work together on strategy should be kept separate from their operational meetings. Strategy-making is a creative act (see chapter 21) that benefits from an unrushed agenda with external inspiration, new insight, and collaborative iteration. It does not mix well with the typical operating agenda that dominates most executive team meetings.

To be sure, the two-part process described above is demanding. But it *is* highly effective in facilitating the collaboration that leaders need to keep their strategies moving forward and also to reinforce their commitment to it. Without it, their strategy will lose its punch and the company's execution will suffer.

(23)

What approach should leaders use to keep their strategy great?

That depends on the need: alignment, growth, or innovation?

Over the last 60 or so years, many intellectual giants have invented dozens of clever approaches to strategy development and strategic planning (see chapter 24). But many of these suffer from conflating strategy and plans...or strategy and vision, mission, purpose, and goals (see chapters 4 and 5). Few of them mirror how great strategies materialize in the real world. And, thus, most of them fail to produce great strategies or prevent them from becoming mediocre. That explains much of why so many startups with great ideas never see their commercial potential fully realized, and why so many world-beaters become also-rans.

To be fair, in a dog-eat-dog world, the odds of creating a great strategy and keeping it great are lottery-like long. Especially when leaders are getting hammered by the unrelenting daily crush of urgent, important matters that can't be ignored or deferred. But fortunately, there are a few approaches leaders can use to tip the odds in their favor. Each attacks a different need, though each also entails a bit of the other two.

One is aimed at solving misalignment on strategy within a leadership team or between it and the board. I call this the "Strategy Alignment" approach.

Lack of alignment typically results from strategy drift over time that goes unnoticed. The three most common reasons for drift are incremental decision-making, turnover of leaders and directors, and over-delegation of strategy to staff or third parties. The Strategy Alignment approach tackles this by having leaders periodically work together on the following steps:

- Identify and prioritize those issues and opportunities that have potentially strategy-changing implications for the company and that need to be addressed *now*.
- Frame each issue/opportunity so that it calls for a rethink of the strategy in some important way.
- Generate alternative responses to each particular issue/opportunity, and define the criteria that will guide how they are evaluated.
- Assess whether the strategy alternatives have been evaluated well enough, and if so, which is best for the company.
- Determine how the current strategy should change in response to the chosen alternative(s), and weigh whether or how the company's plans or business model should evolve accordingly.

Each issue/opportunity should be a factual statement that cannot be ignored—for example: "The differentiation of our downstream offering is eroding, and it's not speaking to the new needs of customers."

No issue should be framed as a question that doesn't explain why it should be addressed *now*. Like, "How should we improve our downstream offering?" That question is always important, as are many others. But it says nothing about why the question is urgent and why your team should allocate precious time to it versus the many other demands on leadership's time.

As important, every issue/opportunity should be framed to suggest the need for multiple alternatives. There is never just one "right" solution to any material issue/opportunity—only a best one among a handful of valid alternatives. For example, consider these two ways to frame the same issue/opportunity:

"Our commercial engine is no longer geared to the realities of today's market."

"Should we acquire company X to fix our commercial engine?"

The second phrasing implies that there are only two alternatives: to acquire company X or not to acquire it. This is not a recipe for sparking more-creative, aspirational thinking about how to crack the issue/opportunity. Moreover, choosing between alternative solutions to an issue/opportunity should call for making tough trade-offs. Otherwise, it's not an issue/opportunity that demands a real choice; it's merely a "to-do" that needs action.

Finally, in the list of steps outlined above, no step should be taken unless there is genuine alignment on the previous one. And if board alignment is a priority, directors should be engaged in every step.

I have seen this "Strategy Alignment" approach in action hundreds of times. Because each step cannot proceed without genuine alignment on the previous one, it makes strategy development a truly collaborative effort that produces better choices *and* stronger commitment to them.

Another approach tackles a different need: growth. This entails finding ways to expand one or more of the three choices that define the boundaries of any strategy (see chapter 18).

I call this the "Strategy Stretch" approach. It tackles growth head-on and entails these steps:

- Generate as many ideas as possible for stretching the company's strategy (see chapter 18). The preparation for this step can be as light or heavy as leaders want; but in my experience, leaders need new insights—about customers, competitors, value chains, technologies, and more—to inspire the new, aspirational thinking that generating good ideas requires.
- Combine different ideas into coherent strategy alternatives. This is important because ideas for stretching one dimension of a strategy typically spur ideas for stretching other dimensions (see chapter 18).
- Assess whether the strategy alternatives have been evaluated well enough, and if so, which is best for the company.
- Determine how the current strategy should change in response to the alternative(s) chosen, and whether or how the company's plans or business model should adjust accordingly.

The time to use this approach is either when leaders have an embarrassment of scarcity—too few growth ideas and they need to make a concerted effort to generate more—or the opposite: when they have an embarrassment of riches, meaning too many growth ideas and thus they need to prioritize. This approach should also be used for finding new ways to invest in organic growth or acquisitions that reflect and reinforce a strategy rather than substitute for it (see chapter 41).

A third approach—the "Strategy Innovation" approach—is best for when leaders need a new, big idea to power their strategy (see chapters 16 and 20); or for when they face a business challenge where industry wisdom and their own domain expertise are insufficient to solve it. In either case, leaders should follow these steps:

- Frame the business challenge that needs innovation. The more novel the framing, the more likely it will inspire creative thinking.
- Search for examples of who—from any domain, business or otherwise—has cracked any part of the challenge with a novel solution. These are called "innovation precedents." The more of these that leaders can find, the more fodder they have for the next step.
- Creatively combine the most-promising innovation precedents into unique and novel ideas.
- Select the best ideas and change the current strategy as necessary to turn those ideas into commercial reality.

This approach replicates how strategy innovations happen in the real world (see chapter 21). It has many benefits: It helps leaders "think outside the box" by pushing them to "look in other boxes," beyond their own industry. It also reflects the reality that there's nothing new under the sun except creative combinations of what's worked before; that those with a big, hairy challenge are never the first to face it; and that finding out how others found innovative ways to tackle it is the best way to find the innovative solution they need for their own unique situation.

Here's a table summarizing when to use each approach:

Strategy Alignment	When there's insufficient alignment on strategy, or on the big issues and opportunities that could change it. The lack of alignment could be within the leadership team, *or* between the leadership team and the board, *or* between the leaders and their direct reports.
Strategy Stretch	When the current strategy has reached its limits and is no longer enough to spur further growth; *or* when there are too many growth ideas to pursue at once and thus, prioritization is needed.
Strategy Innovation	When the big idea powering a strategy is no longer enough *or* when leaders face a business challenge that demands new thinking and novel ideas beyond established orthodoxy in their industry and company.

None of these is guaranteed to produce a great strategy or to revitalize a stale one. But if leaders follow the approach that fits best with their present need (alignment, growth, or innovation), they will bolster their chances of cracking it.

(24)

Why does strategic planning fail to keep strategies great?

Fitting a square peg into a round hole

Over the years, I have kept a list of the many strategic planning approaches used by companies, both large and small. I haven't seen them all, but I have seen many. Here are the most common:

- **Goals and actions:** start with a big, hairy, audacious aspiration and figure out the steps to achieve it.
- **Objectives and options:** develop a range of "strategic" options to achieve a set of business outcomes, and then prioritize and sequence those options.
- **70/20/10:** divide the future into 70% near-term actions; 20% medium-term plays; and 10% "moon shots."
- **Growth horizons:** generate growth initiatives for three time frames: short, medium, and long term.
- **Growth-share matrix:** identify the Stars, Cash Cows, Question Marks, and Dogs, and then divvy up resources accordingly.
- **Market-back:** start with competitor and customer analysis, then infer action priorities from that.
- **Hypothesis-based:** develop hypotheses about the industry's future and

infer from them the best set of actions and investments.

- **Scenario planning:** develop a variety of scenarios for the future and pick the "strategic" path that fits best with them.
- SWOT: take stock of the company's strengths, weaknesses, opportunities, and threats, then stand up the initiatives that best address them.

Some of these were popularized by admired enterprises such as Google's parent, Alphabet Inc. (the 70/20/10 approach), the oil company Royal Dutch Shell (scenario planning), and the Stanford Research Institute (SWOT). Others were invented by top consulting firms—such as the Growth-Share Matrix (BCG) and Growth Horizons (McKinsey). But I struggle to cite one great strategy that came from any of these approaches. (Can *you?* If so, I'd love to hear from you.)

The problem with all these approaches is that they are methods to create a *plan*, not a strategy. They are designed to conjure up "strategic initiatives," slice the corporate resource pie, and hand out financial targets. They aren't designed to answer the questions that every strategy must answer (see chapters 2 and 3). They aren't set up either to sharpen and differentiate those answers (see chapter 8) or to regenerate the big idea that stands behind every great strategy (see chapter 9). They aren't geared to stretch a company's strategy in ways that raise its growth ceiling (see chapter 18) or to innovate a company's strategy so as to sharpen its edge (chapter 21). Nor are they intended to facilitate a collaborative effort for leaders to generate alternatives and make choices for the most important strategy issues and opportunities they face today (see chapter 22). All of this explains why these approaches fail to produce great strategies.

Customers generally don't care about a company's goals, actions, options, and SWOTs unless they get some benefit. They care even less about whether a company divides its focus according to a 70/20/10, a 10/20/70, or a 33.3/33.3/33.4 rule—*or* whether a company organizes its growth initiatives into three or ten horizons. And they aren't concerned with the trends and scenarios that might affect a company's future. In other words, most of the approaches listed above are too company-centric. Strategies should be customer-centric. They should come *first,* ahead of plans. They should be the horse that pulls the planning cart.

The approaches listed above may be help leaders sort out internal battles for scarce resources, plot skirmishes to win market share, deal with intense short-term performance pressures, and ensure they are investing for the longer term—all good things! But they leave a strategy void that leaders are tempted to fill with lofty statements about vision, mission, purpose, and goals (see chapter 5). And such things rarely say much about why customers should buy the company's products or services; how the company will grow a thriving base of customers who are willing to use, recommend, and pay for its offerings; or the capabilities that will make the company better than any other at marketing, selling, and following through on those offerings. That is what strategy is for, and most approaches to strategic planning simply don't serve that function.

In 1994, Henry Mintzberg, a business professor from McGill University, published his popular book *The Rise and Fall of Strategic Planning*. In it, he shows how the typical approaches to planning destroy commitment, narrow a company's field of vision, discourage change, and breed an atmosphere of politics. Such conditions are hardly conducive to creating great strategies and keeping them great!

Instead, leaders should leave plenty of time on strategy—outside of the planning process—to make their strategy sharply differentiating, to ensure that it stands on the shoulders of a big idea, to stretch it regularly, to keep it novel, and to make it an ever-evolving work of genuine collaboration that never really ends.

25

What role should annual planning play in keeping a strategy great?

Free them from each other to get the most out of both.

For many companies, the *de facto* objective of annual planning is to agree on how to divvy up corporate resources and assign performance targets for the coming year or more. In the face of intense competition for investment and pressure for profits, that has to be done. But what often get lost in that process are the essential strategy choices that determine the efficacy of their investments and sustainable growth of their profits. These choices are:

- What businesses should we be in, and how should we contribute to their earnings power?
- Who should be the ideal customers for each of our businesses, and why should they choose us?
- What capabilities should we prioritize and actively nurture to make us the best at how we help our individual businesses succeed, and which capabilities should each of our businesses prioritize to be the best at what they do in their respective markets?
- What's the big idea that underpins our company, and should we stretch or revitalize it?

These questions are rarely visited or challenged in the typical annual planning process. This can create a strategy void, and leaders will often fill the void with something lofty that's more like a vision, mission, purpose, or set of goals. For example, consider the following "strategies" as stated by five top airlines:

- *We are committed to providing every citizen of the world with the highest-quality air travel to the widest selection of destinations possible.*
- *We are dedicated to providing air transportation services of the highest quality and to maximizing returns for the benefit of our shareholders and employees.*
- *[We aim] to be recognized worldwide as the airline of choice.*
- *We exist to deliver the world's best in-flight experience.*
- *We fly our customers at convenient times to the best-located airports across the world.*

In my work, I'll often ask leaders three questions: Can you name the airline behind each "strategy"? Will these strategy statements help their respective organizations produce consistently better execution than their peers? Based on these statements, can you say anything about how these companies are trying to differentiate themselves, either by whom they serve, what they offer, or what makes them able to do what they do better than anyone else?

The answer I hear from leaders to all three question is always "No," and, of course, that's the point. These airlines surely have good processes for annual planning, but such processes are poorly suited for developing great strategies and keeping them great. Let's explore why.

Annual planning is an important tool for managing strategy implementation and execution (see chapter 29). But strategy *development* is a creative act. It requires new thinking, creativity and innovation (see chapter 21), and a lot of collaboration and iteration (see chapters 22 and 23). If annual planning and strategy development are mashed together into one exercise, formulating plans will dominate and developing strategy will be relegated to high-level packaging such as those airline examples above. This is a lost opportunity. There is no better tool than strategy to fortify a company's execution (see chapter 26). But to unlock its true power and reclaim it as a positive, driving force in their companies, leaders must free it from the annual calendar.

Annual planning typically happens at a certain time each year, with a kick-off and a wrap-up. This is fine for updating plans, but it is horrible for advancing strategies. It guarantees that big strategy issues and opportunities are either addressed superficially within the arbitrary confines of a fixed, time-bound exercise or tackled haphazardly throughout the year. It leaves very little room for looking in other boxes (see chapter 21) to inspire innovative solutions to strategy challenges. More likely, it produces status-quo-plus strategies than novel, ambitious strategy stretches (see chapter 18).

Instead, leaders need regular time to work together on strategy. And that time should have three purposes:

- To polish, hone, sharpen, challenge, iterate, and innovate their strategy choices (see chapters 2 and 3).
- To monitor, evaluate, and modify how their strategy choices are being implemented.
- To spot when their strategy choices—or their plan or business model (see chapter 4)—need a reset, and to act on that need.

Leaders should do this at least quarterly. Their agenda must be unrushed and sacrosanct. Operational matters ought to be reserved for leaders' regular staff meetings, and not be allowed to leak into their strategy process. Ideally, the venue for each strategy session is in person and away from the office where distractions and interruptions are less likely. Their strategy sessions should be facilitated (see chapter 51) so that each leader can be in the meeting rather than having to run it. And most important of all, at the end of every session, each leader should not only leave feeling engaged and heard but should also agree that the team produced meaningful conclusions and real decisions.

Strategies can have a short half-life and be overwhelmed quickly by ever-changing market conditions. All strategies are necessarily based on assumptions and expectations of an unknowable future, many of which inevitably turn out to be wrong. To keep their strategy moving ahead, leaders need a routine for advancing it that's not taken hostage by the annual planning process. Only then can leaders find the time and space to make their strategies great—and then keep them great.

PART VI

....

How Much Does Strategy Matter?

Why bother, when so many other
things make a difference?

26

Which is more important, strategy or execution?

"Give me six hours to chop down a tree and I will spend the first four sharpening my axe."

The question in this chapter's title could be the most important one in this book…and it couldn't be more wrong-headed. Perhaps nothing has weakened strategy as a leadership tool more than that which is implied in this age-old question. Let's explore why.

Most everyone would agree that you can't achieve good results without having good execution (in this book, they are equivalent—see chapter 29). And most would also agree that having a good strategy alone is no surefire formula for success. But too many leaders jump to the wrong conclusion that this makes execution more important than strategy. For example, here are some statements from executives, some made publicly and others said to me in private:

1. Great execution can turn mediocre strategies into winning performance.
2. I'd rather have superb execution with an average strategy than the other way around.
3. Fantastic execution is more likely to produce superior results than great strategy.
4. Business success is 1% strategy, 99% execution.
5. Execution is the difference between great and ho-hum performance.

6. You win with better execution.
7. Fixing execution is typically the key to fixing performance.
8. We don't need to change our strategy; we just need to execute better with the one we have.
9. Great execution is running your business really well.
10. Strategy is results.

That last one is a head-scratcher. The CEO of a Fortune 30 company said it to me with a straight face. I think he meant that strategy doesn't matter as long as you are producing results. Many leaders feel this way. That's because:

- They associate strategy with thinking and analysis (or "intellectualizing and philosophizing," as Ram Charan and Larry Bossidy write in their misguided book, *Execution*).
- They equate execution to doing (or to "The Discipline of Getting Things Done," as the subtitle of *Execution* tell us).
- And they attribute more value to doing than to thinking and analysis.

For such leaders, strategy is a lofty, self-evident statement such as "To maximize customer value" or "To become the market leader."

But strategy is not a bunch of high-level statements that no one can disagree with (see chapter 5). Rather, it's a small handful of choices that *only* leaders can make (see chapters 2 and 3). And for our purposes here, "execution" means producing results in the context of those choices (see chapters 26 and 29 for more on this). Thus: *It is impossible to sustain great execution without a great strategy.*

Consider Toyota and GM. For decades Toyota has produced better results than GM because it has executed better than GM. But it out-executes GM because it made better, sharper strategy choices about its target customers (*Who?*), promised benefits (*Why?*), and leading capabilities (*What?*). As a result, Toyota executes better than GM largely because it has a better strategy than GM. GM's decades-long struggle with unions, and Toyota's production system snafus in 2010 and 2011, both reinforce the point that good strategy alone isn't enough. But this shouldn't be confused with the point that a company's execution depends a great deal on the quality of its strategy.

The airline industry provides another example. Southwest Airlines has outperformed American Airlines for decades. Is this because Southwest has executed better than American? Absolutely. But it's no coincidence that Southwest also has a better strategy (see chapter 8). Its leaders chose a more sharply defined target market (the point-to-point traveler on a budget), a stronger package of benefits (price, convenience, passenger-friendly service), and a more-coherent set of capabilities to realize those benefits (maintaining a simpler fleet, running a point-to-point operation). Having a better strategy has enabled Southwest to consistently out-execute American.

Without a more-sharply-differentiating strategy, American will struggle to consistently overcome the lousy economics of its industry. It doesn't matter how much it improves on other execution factors—as important as they are—like labor relations, service quality, and operational excellence. Similarly, no matter how much GM improves its culture, engineering, dealer operations, or anything else, it won't be enough to produce superior results without a better strategy that stands on the shoulders of a big idea (see chapter 9).

To be sure, American and GM both face challenging conditions. But even when an industry's economics are generally attractive, standout strategies facilitate even better results than the industry as a whole. For example, most banks make buckets of money in their essential businesses of lending and cash management services, despite having strategies that are largely indistinguishable from one another. Their leaders all talk about targeting the same customers; having "intimacy" with those customers; and being the best at managing credit risk, fostering customer relationships, harnessing technology, blah, blah, blah. But some bank leaders really *do* choose distinctive strategies and are able to achieve even better performance without necessarily being better than other banks at the generic (but really important) stuff of underwriting, customer service, treasury management, and so on.

For example, from the early 1980s to the mid-1990s, chief executive Sir Brian Pitman, of Lloyds Bank, transformed his U.K. company from a billion-pound "also-ran" into a 55-billion-pound star by spurning investment banking to which it had nothing to offer; deemphasizing plain-vanilla commercial banking with elephantine companies; and reversing what he called "global flag planting." Instead, he invested to dominate consumer and small-business banking in the bank's domestic markets. That may not sound radical, but at the time

Pitman's strategy was ridiculed, causing him to face great resistance, even within his own organization. Yet it transformed Lloyds into a bank that consistently outexecuted its peers, even though its operators were no better. Other examples include USAA and Silicon Valley Bank, both of whose leaders chose strategies with very distinctive target customers: for USAA, military personnel and their families, and for SVB, technology entrepreneurs and VC firms (see chapter 12).[1]

Returning to that numbered list of executive quotes above: The first four statements convey a false choice—they're like saying it's more important for a race car to finish first than for it to have a great engine. Leaders won't have excellent execution without a great strategy, any more than race car drivers will win without a great engine.

The next five statements (5–9) are okay, though their implication is dangerous. Execution is indeed what separates the best from the rest. But the difference between great and ho-hum execution is almost always strategy. Again, *it is impossible to sustain great execution without a great strategy.* Fixing a company's execution almost always requires fixing some aspect of its strategy (see chapters 2 and 3); and the bottom line is that having a great strategy is essential to running a business really well.

As for the last statement in the list (no. 10), the CEO who said it was asked to move on to bigger and better things. Why? Poor results.

Peter Drucker, a leading light of management practice in the 20th century, once said, "Sooner or later strategy has to degrade into real work." Sadly, this encouraged too many leaders to think that they could get away with mediocre strategies and still execute well. Instead, leaders should think of execution as chopping down trees and strategy as their axe. And they should internalize the words of this chapter's subtitle, words attributed to Abraham Lincoln: "Give me six hours to chop down a tree and I will spend the first four sharpening my axe."

---

1   In the middle of my writing this book, SVB imploded. The bank had experienced a tsunami of deposits from early-stage companies that were flush with VC capital. SVB invested these "excess" deposits in government bonds that at the time were yielding very little. When the Fed started raising interest rates with unprecedented speed, the book-to-market value of those bonds tanked, and that crushed the bank's capital base. A failed attempt to raise fresh capital led to a panicky run on the bank's deposits, putting it into a death spiral. Many commentators criticized SVB's strategy for being overly concentrated

in a single sector: Silicon Valley technology. Others criticized it for failing to hedge the risk of rising interest rates, a standard practice in banking. Some even blamed the fiasco on the bank's customers—VC firms and tech companies—for pulling the rug out from under the bank that had served them so well. And some laid the problem directly at the feet of the company's investment bankers for botching the capital raise.

So, was SVB's demise the result of bad strategy or bad execution? If a great strategy comprises a distinctive target customer, value proposition, and capabilities (see chapter 2), then perhaps it was the former because SVB's strategy had failed to prioritize interest rate management as a leading capability. Or perhaps it was bad execution because there were organizational barriers—for example, a blind spot in the leadership team's skill set, or misplaced management incentives, or balkanized functional silos—that created the conditions for a sudden change in interest rates to put the company in peril no matter what its strategy was. I say the latter, but you are invited to decide for yourself.

27

Does culture really eat strategy for breakfast?

Making one a morning meal for the other does injustice to both.

"Culture eats strategy for breakfast" is a popular refrain in the world of business. It's frequently invoked by people who see "culture" as the beating heart of all great companies. Those same folks like to cite the likes of Southwest Airlines and Zappos, whose leaders point to their companies' cultures as the secret of their success. Or, as Arvind Krishna said in his first letter to employees when he became IBM's CEO, "Culture is everything. It's what drives capability in any organization."

The extended argument goes something like this: "Anyone can come up with a fancy strategy, but it's much harder to build a winning culture. Moreover, a brilliant strategy without a great culture is 'all hat and no cattle,' while a company with a winning culture can succeed even if its strategy is mediocre. Plus, it's much easier to change strategy than culture." That argument's inevitable conclusion is that strategy is mere ham and eggs for culture. But this misses a huge opportunity to enhance the power of both culture and strategy. Here's how:

Two of the most fundamental choices for strategy are:

- What businesses should our company be in (see chapter 3)?
- Why should our target customers choose us (see chapter 2)?

A company's specific cultural strengths (and weaknesses) are central to answering that first question. For example, high-margin, premium-product companies that serve wealthy customers do not belong in businesses where penny-pinching is a source of great pride and celebrated behavior. Southwest has chosen not to enter a NetJets-like business and, so far, that's been a sound decision.

Likewise, low-margin, high-volume, dog-eat-dog businesses won't gain much advantage from belonging to companies whose identity and self-worth are based on discovery and innovation that are rewarded with high margins. This is why few traditional pharmaceutical companies, if any, have succeeded in the generic drugs business. Their ethos is tied up in doing cutting-edge health science and discovering novel, patentable drug therapies. The cultural requirements for winning in generics are just too different.

In theory, different cultures can coexist under one corporate roof. But in practice, major cultural differences across different parts of a company create an enormous barrier to collaboration and to the easy flow of ideas, information, and people. This is why universal banks struggle to win in all three sectors: retail, commercial, and investment banking. Whatever synergies they might enjoy—for instance, from common customers and complementary capital needs—are offset by the cultural chasm between these businesses. For example, commercial bankers value *containing* risk and knowing the customer, while investment bankers value *taking* risk and selling the latest financial products or transaction.

Maintaining cultural coherence across a multibusiness company should be an essential consideration when answering that first strategy question listed above. Take General Electric: its late CEO, Jack Welch, conceded that his acquisition of Kidder Peabody was a failure because its culture did not fit GE's cultural strengths. This made it exceedingly difficult for Kidder to realize any of the benefits from being owned by GE, and hard for the rest of GE to gain from having Kidder as a corporate sibling. The cultural disconnect was likely forecastable and would have been a giant, frantically waving red flag for GE's strategy.

Culture also looms large in answering the second question above. In most businesses, customers consider more than tangible benefits and costs when choosing between alternative providers; they also consider the intangibles (see chapter 13). These often become the tiebreaker when tangible differences are difficult to discern. For example, most wealthy individuals choose financial advisors more for their personal chemistry or connections than for their particular range of mutual fund products. Virgin Airlines tries to attract passengers who like its offbeat, non-establishment service values. Culture experts are right to point to Southwest and Zappos, because these companies have instilled norms of behavior that are essential features of their winning propositions: from offering consistently cheerful service in Southwest's case to leading customer satisfaction at Zappos.

What these companies really demonstrate is how culture is an essential *input* that should be considered when creating a strategy—much like a company's other strengths and weaknesses. This is especially so when culture, particularly on the frontline, can affect customers' perception of a company's overall offering, the benefits it promises, and its ability to realize those benefits.

The bottom line is that strategy must be rooted in both the cultural strengths of a company and the cultural needs of its businesses. If culture is hard to change—which it *is!*—so is strategy (see chapter 39). Both take years to scale; both take time to change; and both need to evolve as fast as a company's fundamentals change.

This is one of the many reasons that established companies struggle with creative destruction in their markets. For example, credit card companies are transitioning from traditional to digital payments and commerce. This requires not merely a cultural change, but also a change in each company's most fundamental strategy choices: *Who? Why?* and *What?* (See chapter 2.)

All this is to say that making strategy a "morning meal" for culture does injustice to both. Limiting culture to the narrow role of "enabling" strategy prevents it from strengthening that strategy by being integral to it. It also weakens the power of strategy to turn your company's cultural strengths into a source of enduring advantage.

This brings us back to the refrain that opens this chapter. An alternative interpretation of its meaning is that a strategy and its implementation will fail when they are incompatible with a company's culture. That is indeed what will happen when the strategy neither exploits the culture's strengths nor accounts for its weaknesses. But that doesn't make culture more important than strategy.

The impact of culture on a company's success is only as good as its strategy is sound. Or as James Gorman, long-time CEO of Morgan Stanley, once said, "Having a clear strategy earns you the right to talk about culture." No culture, however strong, can overcome poor strategy choices.

28

How does strategy affect organizational effectiveness?

Ambiguity always fills the vacuum created by a fuzzy strategy.

An organization's effectiveness is reflected in its ability to realize the best possible results from a strategy. Theories abound on what determines organizational effectiveness. Here are some of the most common:

- Fostering engagement and empowerment
- Sharpening accountability and authority
- Enhancing autonomy and alignment
- Cultivating shared purpose, values, and goals
- Giving vision, pathways, and hope to your staff
- Increasing transparency and openness
- Reducing top-down planning and micromanagement
- Embracing change
- Breaking down silos
- Celebrating failures
- Democratizing strategy and innovation

It seems like the list goes on forever! Still, two determinants of organizational effectiveness stand above the rest: clarity and collaboration.

Clarity means that every individual knows what they are supposed to be doing, and why—from frontline employees to board directors and everyone in between. This also holds for every team, including product and customer account teams; executive and operating committees; boards and their subcommittees; special-project teams; and so on.

Collaboration means that each and every individual and team is engaging with those who can improve their work as well as helping those whose work they can improve.

Together, clarity and collaboration are the corporate ligaments that make teams more than the sum of their members, and organizations more than their parts. They enable an organization to have sharp lines of accountability *and* to coordinate across internal boundaries without the need for excessive, stifling process.

The combination of clarity and collaboration helps everyone see who is responsible for doing what and see where the company's strengths and weaknesses lie. Where there's crystal clarity and proactive collaboration, people feel highly engaged, empowered, accountable, autonomous, and even hopeful because they don't have to wait to be told what to do. And they aren't burdened by processes designed to fix the lack of coordination that occurs when clarity and collaboration go AWOL.

Moreover, research (for example, see *Smart Collaboration,* by Harvard professor Heidi K. Gardner) has shown that strong collaboration increases employee productivity, forges loyalty, reduces attrition, and fortifies recruiting.

All these benefits of clarity and collaboration make your organization more effective at adapting to market changes, while also achieving the performance that gives you the license and wherewithal to adapt, innovate, and eventually evolve.

On the flip side, lack of clarity and collaboration is soul-destroying. It makes people hesitant to decide and act; it breeds make-work for middle managers and those below them; it produces well-intended initiatives that inadvertently create headaches for others; and it leads to both over-delegation (abdication) and under-delegation (micromanagement). It also promotes groupthink; stunts creativity; keeps hidden where expertise, skills, and capabilities might lie; and it sub-optimizes the customer experience.

Moreover, poor clarity and collaboration produce bad meetings, bloated bureaucracies, and coordination snafus. Constant, unnecessary firefighting is a symptom of weak clarity and collaboration—as are turf protecting, tribal warfare, matrices that don't work, and both priority overload and blind spots. Without clarity and collaboration, companies gravitate to top-down command and demotivating control.

What does all this have to do with strategy? Imagine a business whose leaders are razor sharp on its strategy choices for *Who? Why?* and *What?* (see chapters 2 and 8). Now, imagine another in which everyone is fuzzy about those three things. If you know nothing else about these two businesses, which is more likely to have an organization in which everyone knows what they are supposed to be doing and with whom they need to be working in order to build and sustain a thriving base of committed customers?

Likewise, consider a multibusiness company whose leaders can speak with precision about how its various businesses gain real advantages from being under the company's particular corporate roof, and about the handful of capabilities the company has that make those advantages possible. Compare it to another that is nothing more than a collection of businesses that could just as well be on their own or part of some other company. Again, which company's organization is more likely to be acting and teaming in a way that makes its whole more than merely the sum of its parts?

The point is that everyday clarity and collaboration—and thus organizational effectiveness—are nearly impossible to achieve without a clear and well-understood strategy (see chapters 2 and 3). *Everything*—from strategic plans to business models, governance, delegation, accountability, who needs to play with whom, how to hire and pay and develop people, which new products to be innovating, and so on—becomes hazy when a company's strategy is foggy and drifts with the winds created by market turbulence.

Organizational ambiguity always fills the vacuum created by a murky strategy. And most people abhor ambiguity in what they should be doing, whom they should be helping, and who can help them. *Less* ambiguity is often what they are craving when they pester their leaders to say *more* about the company's priorities, plans, and goals. Yet without a strategy that is sharply differentiating (see chapter 8), those things are subject to the daily, unyielding pressures of dealing with customers, competitors, and costs.

Clarity of strategy is no guarantee of organizational effectiveness, but it can help enormously to prevent the waste, inefficiency, wheel-spinning, and entropy that undermines an organization's ability to perform at its very best.

PART VII

....

What Is the Right Scope of Strategy?

What's in? What's out?

29

Where does strategy end, implementation begin, and execution fit in?

And why should leaders care?

Do leaders "implement" or "execute" a strategy? Is there a difference between "implementation" and "execution"? If strategy involves making choices and if everyone in an organization has to make choices to do their job, does that make strategy everyone's job? If strategy demands thinking, creativity, and analysis, do these disciplines end when strategy stops? Where does strategy stop, implementation begin, and execution fit in?

For many leaders, thinking about such distinctions doesn't matter much. Still, the words that leaders use are important. For example, here's what Lim Chow Kiat, long-time chief executive of GIC, Singapore's sovereign wealth fund, had to say: "We are meticulous about word choice.... The right word engenders the right attitude and...behavior.... The wrong words can corrode, if not corrupt."

Charles Handy, the celebrated management guru, expressed a similar view in his *21 Letters on Life and Its Challenges*: "Words do matter. They change behavior. They shape our thinking because of the implicit messages they send; then our thoughts shape our actions. Always watch your language lest you send messages never intended."

Leaders should know what they mean by the terms "strategy," "implementation," and "execution." Ignoring, blurring, or making the wrong distinctions between them will inevitably weaken strategy as an essential tool to help leaders build and grow their companies.

Let's start with strategy. At a minimum, it's the answer to three questions (see chapter 2):

- *Who* should be our target customer?
- *Why* should our target customer choose us?
- *What* should be the capabilities that make us the best at marketing, selling, and living our *Why?*

For a multibusiness company, strategy is the answer to three different questions (see chapter 3):

- What should be our unique way of contributing to the future earnings power of our various businesses?
- What capabilities should we prioritize and nurture to make us better than any other company at our way of contributing to the future earnings power of our businesses?
- What businesses should we own because they fit best with our way of contributing to their future earnings power?

The answer to each of these questions is a choice that leaders are responsible for making. *Strategy is their job.* They should hear and learn from others (see chapters 51-54), but never delegate that job to anyone else.

Next, we turn to implementation. In *Merriam-Webster*, this is defined as "putting something into effect." For our purposes this means that if a strategy calls for, let's say, targeting a new type of customer, "implementing" that choice might require a change in the company's marketing and sales approach. For a multibusiness company, if leaders choose a new way of "adding value" to their various businesses (see chapter 3 for examples), "implementing" that strategy might entail establishing an alternative approach to interacting with those businesses—*or* having different staff or skills at the corporate center—*or* changing the company's processes for training, planning, resource allocation, budgeting, and so on.

In reality, a strategy is never fully implemented, because strategy is never done. That's because strategy choices are a bet on a future that is inherently unpredictable. Those choices are necessarily informed by assumptions about the future, including customers, technology, regulation, competitors, and more. As the future unfolds, those assumptions have to evolve, and so do the strategy choices they inform. That means there will often be a persistent gap between when those choices are made and when they go into effect. The ongoing effort to close that gap is "implementation." And while leaders must guide implementation, it's the job of everyone, from frontline staff to board directors.

What, then, is execution? Turning again to *Merriam-Webster*, "execution" is listed as a synonym for implementation. That explains why they are so often used interchangeably. But *Merriam* actually defines it as "performance." In other words, to execute is to perform—to produce results. In business that means generating sales, making profit, earning a return on investment, and so forth. As all decisions and actions taken by an organization will affect performance, execution belongs to everyone. The role of leaders is to coax the best possible execution (a.k.a. results) from their strategy through their organization's implementation of it.

To understand what all this means, let's say that Netflix has made two strategy choices: one, to enter the content production and streaming businesses, and two, to exit its original mail-order business. To put those choices into effect—to implement them—Netflix leaders must, for example, either create relationships with content producers or hire their own, hire or redeploy software engineers to write new software, and create and finance a budget for content production. It might have to close down warehouses that held movies formerly shipped by mail, revamp its website and user interface on the TV screen, and ensure extra bandwidth to accommodate the content that once went through the mail. All this is not strategy—it's *implementation* of strategy choices that only the company's leaders could make: to enter new businesses (content production and streaming) and then to leave another (mail order).

Meanwhile, Netflix has to be doing things to help it succeed in both its content and its streaming businesses. That might include creating a vision or goal to inspire and guide the organization; setting targets and tying rewards to meeting those targets; evaluating content failures and successes; making decisions about what content to green light; and on and on. Those are all activities designed to help Netflix perform well in both content production and streaming. This is execution.

To summarize, here's a pertinent table:

Where does strategy stop, implementation begin, and execution fit in?		
Strategy	**Implementation**	**Execution**
• Particular choices that only leaders make (see chapters 2 and 3). • The job of leaders, though they should seek input, challenge, and inspiration from others (see chapters 51-54). • Determines the ceiling of a company's potential.	• To put into effect the strategy choices leaders have made. • Everyone's job, with leaders guiding it. • Primary purpose of plans (see chapter 4). • Affected by quality of leaders' strategy choices (see chapters 2, 3, 8, and 26).	• To perform—achieve business results. • Everyone's job; leaders' ultimate responsibility. • Primary purpose of plans and business models (see chapter 4). • Affected by quality of leaders' strategy choices *and* the implementation of those choices.

To be clear, these distinctions are *not* between thinking and doing, nor analyzing and acting, nor creating and decision-making, nor planning and producing. All of these are involved in all three of strategy, implementation, and execution. When business leaders make such false distinctions, they often end up conflating strategy with their business model, plans, vision, mission statement, purpose, and goals (see chapters 4 and 5). When that happens, strategy is the first victim and, sooner or later, implementation and execution suffer.

Leaders should heed Lim Chow Kiat's and Charles Handy's advice by being thoughtful and explicit about what those leaders mean by strategy, implementation, and execution. Their people, customers, and owners will be grateful for the clarity and results it yields.[1]

---

1   This chapter began as a post for HBR.org (see appendix 2) that was subsequently adapted for chapter 2 of *HBR Guide to Executing Your Strategy*, Harvard Business Review Press, August, 2023.

30

What's the difference between tactics and strategy?

How to draw the line, and why to bother

When I ask board directors, corporate executives, management consultants, and leading business academics how they draw the line between strategy and tactics, it's surprising how strained and varied their answers are. It seems that one person's strategy and "strategic" moves are another's tactics and tactical moves. When I dig deeper, I find this is because of how they typically define "strategy."

One of the most popular definitions of the term is that it's a set of actions designed to achieve a goal or objective (see chapter 1). But a "tactic" is also an action aimed at a particular objective. Like strategy, it originated in a military context (see chapter 43). For example, a first strike is an action to gain a "tactical" advantage over the enemy, and sending out a surveillance drone or a scouting party is one tactic to learn what's out there.

In the business world, tactics are also aimed at achieving a particular business objective. For example, joining up with a competitor is a tactic to gain an advantage over other competitors. A marketing tactic is aimed at achieving awareness, consideration, purchase, or some other such objective. Leaders and their teams pursue tactics every day to recruit and retain customers and employees; to secure better terms from suppliers or a partner or an acquisition candidate; to out-maneuver competitors, influence regulators, or preempt politicians; and so on.

But herein lies the potential for confusion: If strategy is a set of actions designed to achieve a goal or objective, and if tactics are also actions to achieve an objective, are they simply a part of strategy? Or are there some actions that qualify to be part of strategy and others that are demoted to mere tactics? And if so, how is that line drawn?

Some leaders draw the line by treating strategy as the big initiatives undertaken by the company to achieve its corporate goals, and they effectively define tactics as everything else. But this is problematic, because it conflates strategy with plans, thus undermining the utility of both as leadership tools (see chapters 4 and 7).

Instead, leaders should treat strategy as a particular set of choices that they—and *only* they—should make for their company (see chapters 2 and 3). Tactics, then, are the actions they and everyone else undertake to reinforce, support, and implement those choices. This gives us the basis for understanding the role of tactics in strategy.

To see how, let's take a real-world example and dress it up a bit. In early 2019, Bob Iger, then-CEO of The Walt Disney Company, announced the company's entry into the streaming business. It's called Disney+. It was offered as a subscription service for $6.95 per month, about half the rate Netflix was charging at the time. Disney also promoted it as part of a bundled service that included Hulu, plus ESPN+, the streaming arm of its flagship sports programming business.

Now imagine that Disney's head of streaming was not yet convinced that $6.95 was the optimal price point for Disney+. So—and I'm making this up— he decides to market-test a lower price in the U.K. and a higher one in Australia, both of which have market characteristics that are similar to those of the U.S. in terms of consumers' viewing habits, demographics, internet connectivity, familiarity with Disney films and franchises, and so on.

Meanwhile (again, this is made up), the head of marketing for Disney+ plans to build awareness for Disney+ through a combination of onsite promotions at Disney's resort parks, leaflets in its retail stores and theater productions, and advertising on its national broadcast network, ABC.

Finally, imagine that the SVP for Disney+ content ties her team's bonus scheme to the number of five-star programs they produce over the next three years, and also set up a writers-for-Disney workshop program to develop a community of content creators versed in the Disney Way.

Using the Disney example above, here's what we can say about the role of tactics in strategy: Iger's decision to add a new business—streaming—is a choice that's integral to his multibusiness strategy for Disney (see chapter 3). The low price point, bundling option, and even the Disney+ name (because of what it conveys to consumers in the target market for Disney+) are integral to the *Why?* choice for the Disney+ business strategy (see chapter 2).

The rest of the example illustrates three types of tactics. One of these is Marketing's approach to building awareness. This is an implementation tactic (see chapter 29) because it's designed to help Disney establish a new-business addition to its corporate portfolio as well as to build the customer proposition for that business.

A second type of tactic is the bonus scheme and workshop program for content producers. These are execution tactics (see chapter 29) because they are designed to help Disney realize the best possible results from Disney+, once it and its customer proposition are established.

The third type of tactic is exemplified by the (hypothetical) idea to market-test various price points. This is a learning tactic, because it's designed to help leaders optimize the business model supporting their strategy for the Disney+ business. It's analogous to a drone-surveillance or scouting-party tactic used to optimize a battlefield strategy.

In sum, leaders should reserve "strategy" for the essential choices that *only* leaders can make for their company (again, see chapters 2 and 3). Beyond that, leaders and their company should identify a rich set of tactics designed to help them and their organization implement their strategy, produce the best possible results from it, and optimize it through testing and learning. And this should apply to all levels of their organization—from the board to the frontline and every level in between.

(31)

What comes first, strategy or goals?

Which is the horse and which is the cart?

Many business leaders subscribe to the definition of *strategy* as a set of actions designed to achieve an overall aim. In other words, they believe strategy starts with a goal. The bigger, hairier, more audacious the goal, the better.

But for leaders who found great strategies and implemented them successfully, that's not how it typically happens. Take Microsoft: Looking back, it may seem that Bill Gates followed a straight path from a big, hairy goal to dominate the software market for personal computers to building a trillion-dollar company. But Gates didn't start with that goal—it came later, after Microsoft was already well on its way.

First, there was Traf-O-Data, a business that Gates and his cofounder, Paul Allen, started in the early 1970s. It was based on a software program they wrote for Intel's 8008 microprocessor to analyze information collected by traffic monitors on city streets. After this went nowhere, Gates and Allen wrote a BASIC operating system for the Altair 8800, the first microcomputer produced for retail sale. Gates wanted to sell the rights to this program to MITS, Altair's maker. What happened next changed everything.

Much to Gates's initial anger (which caused him to write an open letter that he later recanted), hundreds of microcomputer clubs across the country began pirating copies of his operating system software. In the process, however, they made it a *de facto* standard of the microcomputer industry emerging in the 1970s. From that point on, the exploding population of PC companies came to Gates with their "pockets stuffed with money" when they needed a BASIC operating system for their products, as James Wallace and Jim Erickson wrote in *Hard Drive: Bill Gates and the Making of the Microsoft Empire.*

Suddenly, Gates had his big idea: software interoperability across all makes of PCs! Around 1980, roughly five years after Microsoft was founded, he changed his original strategy of selling software programs for microcomputers to licensing MS-DOS—Microsoft's Disc Operating System for personal computers. It was only later, *after* Microsoft was well on its way to implementing Gates's new strategy, that he was able to turn his vision of a computer on every desk into a tangible goal of having Microsoft software on *every* computer in *every* home and office.

That is how most winning strategies happen: first comes the big idea (see chapter 9); then a strategy is devised to bring that idea to market (see chapter 8); finally comes a visionary goal to crystallize an ambition, motivate the troops, and excite investors. Unfortunately, strategy development in most companies starts at the wrong end of this sequence—and when that happens, bad strategies result.

Two problems arise when goals come before strategy. The first is that they tell leaders very little about what their big idea is (see chapter 9) or what their strategy choices should be (see chapters 2 and 3). The broader, more aspirational the goal, the more this is the case. For example, if Gates's original goal was to dominate the software market for personal computers, why would he start with Traf-O-Data? Why didn't he seek to "roll up" the highly fragmented PC software boutiques that were popping up everywhere? Now fast-forward to today: PCs are becoming less central to home and office life, and so what fueled Microsoft's success over its first 40 years is becoming tired. It would be very tempting for Microsoft to set a big new goal (perhaps "become a five-trillion-dollar company"?), but that won't work without some new, big idea. And it says nothing specific about what the company's strategy choices should be or how they should change over time.

It turns out that Microsoft *does* have a new big idea: to transform into a cloud-based software services and subscriptions company (see chapter 20) —in essence, a streaming service for enterprises and (within gaming) for consumers. That idea calls for a gigantic change in the company's strategy (and business model). But neither that change in strategy, nor the big idea powering it, came from a big, broad goal.

The second problem with putting goals ahead of strategy is the opposite of the first. If visionary goals tell you little or nothing about which strategies to pursue, other goals effectively tell you too much. This happens when goals are expressed in terms of highly specific metrics—for example, to achieve a certain size, market share, growth rate, margin, rate of return, or net promoter score.[1] Where do such goals come from? In the end, they are arbitrary, no matter how much they might be informed by benchmarking or past performance. And they can have a profound—sometimes counterproductive—effect on the direction strategies take.

For example, growth-oriented goals drive companies to chase high-growth markets even if they haven't earned a right to win there. Companies with profit-oriented goals cut costs to increase margin without regard to the effect on their capabilities, and they chase high-margin businesses whether they exploit those capabilities or not. Market share goals create a static mind-set of the market, thus causing companies to miss opportunities and to react too slowly to disruptive forces (see chapter 44). And then there's Goldman Sachs….

For years Goldman's leaders have been bothered by the company's low "multiples"—its stock price divided by current earnings and its stock price divided by net asset value—compared to those of its peers, especially its long-time rival Morgan Stanley. Their "multiple envy" is stoked by the financial media, which seemingly can't say anything about the company without pointing to its "anemic" multiples.

Goldman's strengths are in investment banking, principal investing, and trading, all of which are inherently cyclical. Goldman is better than most, if not everyone, in these businesses. But they are extremely volatile from year to year, compared to plain-vanilla retail banking and wealth management. This explains the low multiple—all else being equal, a stable earnings stream is more valuable than a volatile one.

To "fix" this, Goldman's leaders made a huge bet on retail financial services in the hopes of reducing the company's earnings volatility. This is financial engineering (see chapter 6), not strategy (see chapter 3).

Goldman Sachs has a powerful brand, world-leading capabilities in investment banking, principal investing, and trading, as well as business franchises that are the envy of its peers. But how do consumers of retail financial services benefit from these? Do they even care?[2]

Some companies try to fix the problem of goal-driven bias in their strategies by having a "balanced scorecard" of targets for growth, profit, market share, customer satisfaction, staff engagement, innovation, and so on; but that just gives them a richer mix of arbitrary targets to distort their strategies. Other companies try adopting goals that are broad enough to minimize arbitrary effects on the direction of their strategies, though that just takes us back to the first problem described above.

As we saw in previous chapters, companies like Ford, GM, Disney, Berkshire Hathaway, Crown Cork & Seal (now Crown Holdings), and Starbucks transformed themselves or their industries with breakthrough strategies powered by a big idea. Neither their strategies nor their big ideas came from setting big, hairy, audacious goals or specific, measurable ones. Great strategies rarely do.

Does this mean that goals have no role in strategy? They certainly help leaders define and evaluate their progress in achieving its strategy; motivate and guide their organization to implement the strategy; and inspire financial and other stakeholders to support it. Moreover, having a big goal might spark leaders to see that they need a new or bigger idea to power their strategy. But big goals *aren't* big ideas; and they won't give you one, either. Goals are ambitions—and the more ambitious they are, the less likely they'll be achieved without a big idea and a great strategy to commercialize it.

---

1   Net promoter score is determined by subtracting the percentage of customers who are detractors from those who are promoters, both of which are defined by how likely they are to recommend a product or service to a friend.

2   A few months after I wrote these words, Goldman Sachs decided to quit its foray into consumer banking and financial services. One commentator said, "It was poor execution." Yes, it was. But poor execution was the outcome of putting goals ("boost our stock price multiples") before strategy and ending up with a strategy that did not fit well with Goldman's enterprise capabilities and culture. It was more financial engineering than sound multibusiness strategy. That almost always leads to "poor execution."

32

Does structure really follow strategy?

Or is it the other way around?

In 1977, Alfred Chandler of Harvard Business School published *The Visible Hand: The Managerial Revolution in American Business*. It was a seminal book on the history of companies like DuPont, General Motors, Standard Oil, and Sears Roebuck. In his book Chandler proclaimed "structure follows strategy." All aspects of an organization's design, from the creation of divisions and departments to the designation of reporting relationships, should be guided by the company's strategy. As an example, Chandler described how Alfred P. Sloan created divisions—Chevrolet, Pontiac, Oldsmobile, Buick, Cadillac, and others—to implement his big idea of "branded price points" (see chapter 9).

A logical extension of Chandler's proclamation is that "a change in structure follows a change in strategy." But this is impractical. Changing an organizational structure generates enormous uncertainty, upheaval, and stress for everyone. Leaders can't afford to do that every time they want to make a material change in their strategy. And yet they must adjust, stretch, and even innovate their strategies fairly frequently to keep them abreast of an ever-evolving context (see chapter 23).

If leaders had to change their organization's structure whenever they changed their strategy, most would not evolve their strategies materially or fast enough to exploit new opportunities and blunt unexpected threats. Fortunately, they don't have to.

Most businesses operate in three dimensions: functions (marketing, sales, finance, HR, legal, manufacturing, R&D, and so on); markets (global, regional, national, and local); and product or service lines. If a business also serves distinctively different types of customers (for example, consumers and enterprises), it lives in a four-dimensional world. But whether leaders live in a three- or a four-dimensional context, each dimension has to be managed. Every function, market, product line, and customer group *must* have a person or team looking after it. *This is true under any strategy for the business, and no matter how much or how often that strategy changes.*

To make sense of their multidimensional world, leaders have two alternatives, with many variants and hybrids in between. One is divisions (or "business units"), each of which has its own functions, markets, products, and customers. This is the approach Alfred P. Sloan took for General Motors. The second approach is having a matrix of product (or service) units that span multiple markets; a parallel set of geographic units with responsibility for market-specific sales, marketing, customers, product customization, and so on; plus a set of "corporate functions" (HR, finance, IT, legal, etc.) to serve the product and market units. GM was operating with this structure when it went bust in 2009.

Neither alternative is an easy solution. Each creates tricky challenges that need to be addressed if they are to work well. For example, the divisional/business unit approach pushes the problem down a level, where each business unit has to cope with its own multidimensional operating challenge. And the matrix approach creates overlapping responsibilities and multiple reporting lines where it's all too easy for no one to be—or feel—truly accountable for anything.

There are many ways to solve such challenges and make either approach work. One of the most important is to ensure that the way leaders organize their *strategy* is consistent with how they organize their *company*.

For example, a company whose leaders choose to organize into fully self-contained business units is, by design, a multibusiness enterprise. Their strategy should be governed by the choices that determine how it will be more than just the sum of its individual parts (see chapter 3); and the company's individual businesses must have strategies that answer the essential questions that guide how their leaders build a thriving base of customers (see chapter 2).

If, instead, leaders have chosen a matrix for its organization, by definition it has no individual businesses. Every organizational unit—each product, market, and functional unit—is part of a single, bigger business that should be governed by the strategy choices governing any business (see chapter 2). Thus, the way leaders organize their strategy depends a great deal on the way they organize their company. In other words, *strategy follows structure,* not just the reverse.

The problem for many companies, though, is that they operate in a murky middle between a business unit and a matrix structure. For example, P&G circa 2020 had ten global business units ("GBUs"), each with "full decision-making authority for their businesses." That sounds a lot like a business unit structure. But it also had a set of units called Selling and Market Operations ("SMOs") that were "responsible for developing and executing go-to-market plans at the local level" in six regions around the world, as well as a "Global Business Services" (GBS) organization that "operates and supports the infrastructure, operations, systems, and shared services that run P&G"—plus a set of "Corporate Functions" that "provide company-level strategy and portfolio analysis, corporate accounting, treasury, tax, governance, human resources, information technology, and legal." This is more like a three-dimensional matrix structure with product units (the GBUs), market units (the SMOs), and functional units (GBS and Corporate Functions).

In effect, P&G was operating as *both* a multibusiness company with ten global businesses *and* a single-business enterprise with multiple products, markets, and functions. As a result, it had neither a clear multibusiness strategy nor a discernible single-business one, and its GBUs likely operate with far less decision-making authority than they need to be fully accountable for their own strategies. This murkiness was bound to undermine P&G's organizational effectiveness (see chapter 28) as well as to compound the difficulty already inherent in running such an enormous, complex company.

With some urgency imposed by the high-profile attack of an activist investor, P&G worked to tackle its ambiguous structure known internally as "the thicket." But until it decides whether it wants to operate as a multibusiness or a single-business company, the improvements will be marginal, and its strategy will show it. In other words, P&G's strategy will follow its structure into a bit of muddle.

What, then, do leaders mean when they invoke the mantra "structure follows strategy"? Most of them really mean "structure follows priorities." Thus, if "accelerate adoption of digital technology" is a big priority, a chief digital officer might be called for. If "eliminate duplication" is deemed a corporate priority, they might pull the HR, IT, R&D, sales, manufacturing, or other such functions out of the business units and into corporate groups to "leverage scale economies." Or if "sharpen accountability" is the priority because these functions are already centrally grouped and considered overly bureaucratic, leaders might go in the opposite direction and "decentralize" them by giving each business unit its own HR, IT, Sales unit, and so on. If priorities like these are necessary to effect a change in strategy, and if acting on such priorities requires a change in structure, then structure is indeed following strategy. But if they have little to do with leaders' essential strategy choices (see chapters 2 and 3), and if they make an organizational change on behalf of those priorities anyway, they will create a disconnect between their strategy and structure—and surely undermine the effectiveness of both.

33

What purpose should purpose have in strategy?

Which should inform which?

Dov Siedman—an author, columnist, and founder of LRN (an ethics and compliance management firm)—was quoted in *Fortune* magazine saying, "The business of business can no longer just be business. [It] is society. Mission and margin, profit and principle, success and significance are now inextricably linked."

Echoing Siedman, the authors of an April 2020 article in *McKinsey Quarterly* wrote as follows: "Business…has an opportunity, and an obligation, to engage on the urgent needs of our planet, where waiting for governments and nongovernmental organizations to act on their own through traditional means such as regulation and community engagement carries risk." In the same article, the authors report that 72% of surveyed employees agreed with this statement: "Purpose should receive more weight than profit." The authors also point out that "contributing to society" made the top two of those employees' priorities.

And then there is Larry Fink, chairman and chief executive of BlackRock, the world's chief money manager. Fink publishes an annual letter to chief executives of companies in which his company invests. In his 2018 edition he asked them to "clearly embody purpose in their business models and corporate strategies." He referred to a survey of millennials in which 63% said that the primary purpose of business is "improving society," and goes on to suggest that "society is increasingly looking to companies…to address social and economic issues… from protecting the environment to retirement to gender and racial inequality….."

Fink's perspective at the time (it has since evolved) was supported by surveys such as an annual global survey from the Edelman Trust Barometer, which has been running for over two decades and covers more than 30,000 people in almost 30 countries. Edelman reported that 69% of workers say a company's social impact is a "strong expectation" for them when considering a job, while 63% of consumers say they will "buy or advocate for brands based on my beliefs and values."

Meanwhile, across the Atlantic, in April 2019, the French Parliament approved a corporate governance framework called PACTE[1] that was partly inspired by a report coauthored by Jean-Dominique Senard. He is the former CEO of the tire company Michelin and chairman of Renault and the Renault-Nissan-Mitsubishi alliance. In a July 2019 interview with *Strategy+Business*, he called for "reasonable, sustainable capitalism" and as part of that, asks corporate leaders to define their purpose, which he defines as "their approach to social and environmental responsibility…beyond making a profit."

Fink and Senard (as well as Siedman) are emblematic of the movement called "purpose-driven enterprise." They are essentially asking companies to define their social purpose, and they distinguish this from an economic purpose to generate profits and a commercial one to, as Peter Drucker put it, "create a customer."

Fortunately, both Fink and Senard separate strategy from purpose. But sadly, neither of them defines what he means by "strategy," leaving leaders with little guidance on how strategy and purpose should relate to each other. Nevertheless, Senard's former company gives us a great example of how social purpose can play a healthy role in strategy.

At Michelin, Senard defined the company's purpose—what he called its *raison d'être*—as to make environmentally friendly products and reduce CO_2 emissions. Guided by this purpose, he poured massive investment into technology and materials to ensure that Michelin's tires are still very safe at the end of their life even though they are "worn." Other companies sell less-expensive tires that wear out more quickly and are more dangerous when worn down. To achieve the same outcome for their tire customers, these companies have to produce many more tires, and thus use much more energy and raw material.

Michelin chose to make tires that are roadworthy longer. The profits come from offering longer-lasting, safer tires that justify a price premium while also helping the environment.

Senard's purpose for Michelin played a big role in leading him to a compelling customer proposition that sits at the heart of any great strategy (see chapters 2 and 8). But skeptics might suggest that Michelin's economic and commercial success was the result of a compelling product offering, not Senard's social purpose; that he didn't need a purpose to land on the customer proposition he chose for his strategy; and that the leaders of *any* tire company could have chosen the same strategy to differentiate its products, whatever their social purpose.

Nevertheless, if Fink is right, customers and employees will increasingly gravitate to companies that commit to solving particular social issues. Leaders can respond in one of two ways. The first is to **have social purpose inform strategy.** This starts with leaders spelling out the social issues they want their company to target, and then to create products and services that serve those issues and build the capabilities to market, sell, produce, and deliver those products and services. Purpose is explicitly built into a company's customer proposition and leading capabilities. This was Senard's stated approach at Michelin.

Another example of this social-purpose-informs-strategy approach is Gotham Greens, a hydroponic farmer. The leaders' stated purpose is to produce local food for a sustainable future. A critical element of its promise to customers is eco-friendly packaging. This led leaders to research alternatives to single-use plastic, compostable fiber, and compostable plastic, all of which undermined both their customer promise and social purpose.

The second approach is to **have strategy inform social purpose,** first by spelling out the particular social issues that are served when customers buy a company's products and services, and then by defining the company's purpose to embody those issues. For example, at the heart of Walmart's customer proposition is "everyday low pricing." Based on that, the company's social purpose could be "to make life better for all" (especially those on the lower rungs of the economic ladder).

Another example could be WeWork, the now-bankrupt shared-office-space company for startups, small businesses, and freelancers. Its strategy was based on offering benefits that included access to health insurance, an internal social network, social events and workshops, and an annual summer retreat for its 100,000+ members. Its social purpose could have been stated as "to facilitate small-business formation and the jobs and prosperity it brings, while fostering community-building to bring the world closer together."

Either approach—social purpose informing strategy, or vice versa—offers a path to Larry Fink's "sustainable, long-term growth and profitability," because each entails a compelling strategy, whether informed by a social purpose or at least consistent with one.

However, leaders should beware the risk of conflating strategy and purpose. That is, making a company's purpose—"we tackle social issues X, Y, and Z"— the primary reason that people should buy its products and services. For example, making cookies without palm oil might support a social purpose of promoting public health, but those cookies had better taste just as good as the alternatives that customers might consider! People and companies rarely choose inferior offerings because the company that provides them has a compelling social purpose. This was a hard lesson learned by Allbirds, the soft-shoe company loved by techies, when its "sustainable" products developed a reputation for wearing out quickly.

Instead, a more-realistic scenario is social purpose acting as a tiebreaker. For example, the leaders of Buhler, a manufacturer of high-end milling, grinding, sorting, and die-casting machines, are wholly committed to its sustainability purpose. They promote this to distinguish their offerings, but only after establishing their products' bona fides in terms of quality, durability, and value. The idea is to nudge prospects over the finish line by giving them a chance to save the world when they choose Buhler's products over someone else's products that may be good enough but whose sustainability credentials are inferior to Buhler's.

More generally, in a survey conducted by McKinsey, the firm claims that 70% of respondents said they would pay an additional 5% for a green product but only if it met the same performance standards as a nongreen alternative.

To be clear, no matter how strong their social purpose, companies cannot escape their economic and commercial purposes. Those that fail to successfully prosecute them will lack the wherewithal—financial and otherwise—to sustain their social purpose. For example, a poster child for the purpose-driven movement is Unilever PLC, the global consumer packaged goods (CPG) company. It was revered for its commitment to social purpose until its profit growth faltered, at which point its commitment to purpose was seen as a distraction. Another example is Etsy, the online arts and crafts marketplace. In 2012, its then-CEO adopted a purpose "to reimagine commerce in ways that build a more fulfilling and lasting world," and to support that, he converted the company to a certified B corporation (a designation given to companies that meet strict environmental, social, and governance standards). It worked to attract top talent to Etsy's social purpose, but it crushed the company's profits. The next CEO let its B-Corp designation lapse, not to cancel the company's social purpose, but rather to make it economically sustainable.

A second risk that leaders should beware of is conflating their company's purpose with social activism. Speaking out on social issues—especially if they have nothing to do with a company's purpose—is courting disaster. The beer company AB InBev fell into this trap when it sent trans influencer Dylan Mulvaney a few cans with her face on them. Disney did the same with its attack on Florida's so-called "Don't Say Gay" law. And even Major League Baseball got into trouble when it pulled the All-Star game from Atlanta in protest over its voter restrictions law. It doesn't really matter whether all three companies were right or wrong in the stance they took. What matters is whether those issues had anything to do with their enterprise purpose, whether their purpose makes them more attractive to their customers, and whether speaking out on certain social issues amplifies or dilutes their purpose.

The third risk is perhaps the biggest one of all: for leaders to wrap their company around a social purpose and then contradict or undermine it in their strategy and tactics. An example of this is a company's promoting a "health-and-wellness" purpose while filling grocery shelves with sugary drinks and fatty, salty snacks. Or when Volkswagen's leaders said in 2010 that their goal was to have it become the most ecologically minded car company in the world, while their engineers were busy rigging millions of cars to cheat on emission tests. Or when the chairman of Ford Motor Company stresses his company's green credentials and then approves a shift away from selling low-margin cars to more profitable—but gas-guzzling—SUVs and pickup trucks. Even BlackRock found the hotseat for things like exercising its proxy voting rights in support of a campaign that forced Exxon to exit certain oil fields that could then be acquired by PetroChina, one of BlackRock's own investments.

Adopting an explicit social purpose may seem a savvy and worthy thing to do. That's especially so in today's political climate, where many consumers and employees think businesses should play a leading role in addressing social problems, lots of young adults have reservations about capitalism, politicians are attacking big-company cronyism, and some of the best and brightest business leaders have decided they need to save capitalism from itself. But it's not risk-free. It puts a company into a whole new ball game that can be easy to lose, because as Yuval Noah Harari says in his book *21 Questions for the 21st Century*, "Historically, corporations were not the ideal vehicle for leading social and political revolutions. A real revolution sooner or later demands sacrifices that corporations, their employees, and their shareholders are not willing to make."

In a fascinating twist, Tariq Fancy, the former chief investment officer for sustainable investing at none other than BlackRock, echoed Harari when he argued that trusting companies and investment fund managers to make the right judgments for society will ultimately fail, because their views (and actions) will necessarily be driven by profits for companies and investment returns for fund managers.

Perhaps Harari and Fancy would cite McKinsey, the world's most prestigious consultancy, as an example. McKinsey tied its mast to the stakeholder capitalism movement by signing the Business Roundtable's 2019 manifesto (see appendix 1). Shortly thereafter, Phil Weiser, Colorado's Attorney General, noted that McKinsey had been advising governments on how to deal with the opioid epidemic at the same time it was advising Purdue Pharma on how to turbocharge sales of OxyContin. As he put it, "The partners…tried to cover up their actions [and] placed profit over [socially] responsible behavior." New York's Attorney General, Letitia James, added, "McKinsey's cynical and calculated marketing tactics helped fuel the opioid crisis." Companies *will* make mistakes. But those mistakes are amplified when they put themselves forward as solving the world's social problems.

So, where does this take us? In his 2018 annual letter, BlackRock's Fink equates purpose to "a company's fundamental reason for being." He argues it should be a social purpose because this is necessary for companies to successfully prosecute their economic and commercial purpose. Maybe so. That's up to leaders—working with their board and investors—to decide for their company in its particular context. And if they do adopt an explicit social purpose, they should tie it directly to their strategy in one of the two ways suggested above. This is the only way for leaders to keep themselves from having to trade off purpose or profit for the other.

The hard question that leaders should ask themselves is *not* "Are we committed to mission *and* margin?" Rather, it's "How do our social, economic, and commercial purposes serve each other?" Good leaders are both visionary *and* practical. They will respond to the tougher challenge of making purpose and profit multiply each other instead of pulling against each other. If they don't, as sure as night follows day, profit or purpose—or both—will become a constant thorn in their side.

---

1   PACTE stands for Plan d'action pour la croissance et la transformation des entreprises.

34

How should "doing good" figure into a strategy?

Which path to making a positive social impact is best?

In Milton Friedman's 1962 book, *Capitalism and Freedom*, the Nobel Prize–winning economist declared, "There is one and only one social responsibility of business—to use its resources and engage in activities designed to increase its profits…while conforming to the basic rules of the society, both those embodied in law and those embodied in ethical custom." But in a 2019 poll of CEOs by the business magazine *Fortune*, only 5% of the respondents agreed with the following statement: "I believe my company should mainly focus on making profits, and not be distracted by social goals." It seems that few business leaders agree anymore—if they ever did—with Friedman's dictum.

In that same poll, more than half said they see charitable activities to address social problems as part of their companies' responsibility. Another 44% went even further by agreeing that their companies should actively seek to solve major social problems as *part of their strategy*. These very different views on the link between strategy and "doing good" give leaders a lot to unpack in order to develop their own view on the best path for their companies to have a positive social impact.

Here's my recommendation: First, leaders should remember that in genuinely competitive product and labor markets, customers and employees have real choices. In such markets, underserving customers and treating employees poorly will encourage them to go elsewhere. This means that businesses can do well *only* by having good strategies, including a sharply defined ideal customer; a promise of benefits that compel customers to willingly, if not enthusiastically, part with their hard-earned money; and prioritized capabilities—powered by highly motivated, loyal people—to market, sell, and meet that promise better than anyone else. There's no getting away from these essential choices for every strategy.

To be sure, corporate misbehavior makes for unsustainable enterprises. Sooner or later, the cost of bad press, social media attacks, customer boycotts, employee revolts, government interventions, and other factors will become too high to bear. For example, when the mining company Rio Tinto downplayed its destruction of a 46,000-year-old sacred Aboriginal site in Australia, it cost the company its chief executive. And after years of skimping on safety, BP experienced the Deepwater Horizon oil spill, which ultimately cost the company $70 billion for one of the worst environmental disasters ever recorded.

On the flip side, "doing good" can be good for workplace morale, commitment, and skills development. For example, LEGO claims that programs such as one that unites dozens of children in rural China with their working parents played a big role in beating its targets for employee motivation and satisfaction by 50%. And according to Sodexo, the French food services and facilities management company, its program to encourage gender balance among managers increased retention by 8%.

But do-gooding companies with bad strategies are unsustainable, too. Eventually, the costs of misallocating their resources and disappointing their customers and shareholders will bring them down.

Next, leaders should recognize that businesses do a lot of good when they do well. Another Nobel winner, William Nordhaus, quantified this in a 2006 paper for the National Bureau of Economic Research. To paraphrase: Yes, entrepreneurs, innovators, and business leaders generate wealth for themselves, but that is only a fraction (4%) of the value they create for society. This is because businesses with great strategies can offer attractive jobs, provide more than just a living wage, pay taxes that support governments and their programs, fund retirement savings, generate capital for investing in the real economy, and create wealth for the philanthropically minded. These are fantastic social goods. Even if leaders don't explicitly seek to produce such goods, they do just that by devising strategies that enable their companies to do well.

This is what Milton Friedman meant. He knew that sustaining profitable growth in competitive markets is not easy. It can only be achieved by serving customers well, being a good employer, innovating, investing for the long term, avoiding waste, being safe, acting responsibly, and establishing habits such as honesty, trustworthiness, and self-discipline. Friedman also argued that it's the responsibility of a "government by and for the people" to set the guardrails for businesses, ensure level playing fields, help those who are left behind, and steer all members of society (citizens, charities, churches, global and local institutions, and, yes, companies) to work together on solving the world's problems, social and otherwise.

As my third recommendation, leaders should consider the example of companies that are showing that doing good can also be a path to doing well, not merely a result of it. For example, the Brazilian company Natura is the world's fourth-largest freestanding beauty company. Its leaders have always pursued social and environmental goals, such as sustainable sourcing of tree oils from the Amazon. This has become a galvanizing appeal of its proposition to those who buy its products.

Other examples come from Novo Nordisk, the specialist in treatments for diabetes, and Unilever, the CPG company. According to Novo Nordisk, its funding of programs to educate physicians and improve patient outcomes in China increased its market share and sales. And Unilever claims that its products designed to save on water consumption, such as Sunlight dishwashing liquid, outpace category growth by 20% in certain markets.

And then there's Dave's Killer Bread, a company based in Milwaukie, Oregon. The following is prominently displayed on all its packaging:

15 years in prison. That's a tough way to find yourself. Dave Dahl realized he was in the wrong game and knew he had more to offer. His brother, Glenn, saw a change in him and gave Dave a second chance by welcoming him back to the family bakery. Dave set out to make a loaf like no other—the most nutritious, organic whole grain bread— and the result is what he called "killer" bread. Dave's Killer Bread is built on the belief that everyone is capable of greatness. What began as one man's journey has turned into so much more. Today, one-third of

*our employees at our Oregon bakery have a criminal background, and
we have witnessed firsthand how stable employment sparks personal
transformation. "Just refuse to eat any other kind of bread. Period," said
[one of our customers]. We couldn't have said it better ourselves.*

Dave surely promotes the superior taste and nutrition of his product, but his pitch includes another important benefit: supporting a good cause when you buy his products.

Many other great examples can be found to echo Dave's Killer Bread motto. These include MoD Pizza, which calls itself a "second chance employer" by offering employment opportunities to ex-cons, individuals with disabilities, 16-to-24-year-olds who are not in school, and those who have struggled with homelessness or are recovering from addiction.

Yet more examples are the Italian company Aquafil, which makes a recyclable fiber from nylon waste, and Fair Harbor in New York State, which offers swimsuits made out of recycled plastic bottles.

Yet more examples include the Swedish company SSAB, which has committed to making "green steel" by using hydrogen in its production processes to replace its CO_2 emissions with water vapor; Ecotricity, a U.K. energy company, which supplies over 200,000 people with its fleet of wind turbines while also operating a network of electric vehicle (EV) charging points; and Koka Networks, a company in sub-Sahara Africa that supplies clean cooking fuel made of bioethanol that is bought via a mobile app and delivered through refillable cannisters at vending points.

There's also the plethora of buy-one-give-one companies like Warby Parker, which donates a free pair of glasses for every purchase of its eyewear; Bomba, which does the same with socks; and the beer company Patagonia (no tie to the outdoor clothing company), which plants a tree for every case of *cerveza* it sells.

These are all examples of companies seeking to do good in ways that will help them do well by making their offerings stand out with their target customers and thus win more of them.

In addition to differentiating themselves by "doing good," leaders can do the same with their leading capabilities. Examples abound, including 3M, which counts $2.2 billion of cumulative benefit from adding "pollution prevention" to its product development capability, and FedEx, which claims massive reduction in the cost of its last-mile delivery capability from its ongoing conversion to electric or hybrid-powered transport.

Finally, leaders should know that other companies are taking another, third path to doing good. For example, IBM runs a program called P-Tech to train disadvantaged youth for technology jobs, and also provides free, web-based business management resources to small and midsize companies; Microsoft funds efforts to combat housing issues in its local communities; Google offers a free suite of education tools for teachers in underserved communities; USAA set up initiatives to support education, job growth, and economic mobility for Black and brown communities that represent over 50% of USAA's target market (see chapter 65); and Kind, a maker of snack bars, which sponsors the "Kind Movement" with the objective of creating a community of people who choose kindness and make it a state of mind.

Some companies are even joining forces with each other to solve social challenges, such as apparel giants H&M, Kering, Nike, and PVH. All four have partnered to create Global Fashion Agenda, a nonprofit that promotes "sustainable fashion," which it defines as the efficient use of resources, safe and secure work environments, and closed-loop recycling.

These are examples of *doing good* with the spoils these companies gain from *doing well*. And each action can be considered a good strategy if it attracts more customers to their products and services, enhances their promise of benefits, or somehow fortifies their leading capabilities—for example, with a more-motivated workforce or greater productivity-boosting cost savings.

All of this can be distilled into three paths that leaders should consider for their strategies:

- Path 1: Do good by doing well.
- Path 2: Tie the purchase of their products and services directly to support for a particular social cause.
- Path 3: Use some of the company's profits to support a specific worthy social cause.

Taking path 1 does not make leaders bad people or their business an evil enterprise. But even Milton Friedman acknowledged paths 2 and 3 when he wrote: "It may well be in the long-run interest of a corporation to devote resources to providing amenities to [its] community or to improving its government. That may make it easier to attract desirable employees, it may reduce the wage bill… or have other worthwhile effects." He surely would have agreed that it would be highly irresponsible for leaders to forego path 2 or path 3 if one of them offers the opportunity to either elevate their strategy or improve their ability to succeed with it.

35

What role should "shareholder value" have in strategy?

Where ends and means fuel each other

Two versions of "shareholder value" have been floating around for some time. One is "current stock price." The other is what finance professors call "net present value" or what Warren Buffett, the long-time chairman and CEO of Berkshire Hathaway, calls "intrinsic value."

In the second version, shareholder value is "the value today of all cash flows that a business is likely to generate *for the rest of its life*." And "maximizing shareholder value" means choosing the strategy that is most likely to yield the greatest cash flow value for the business. It also means that leaders can never stop looking for better strategies, because they can never know with absolute certainty if there are higher-value ones than those they've considered so far.

Maximizing shareholder value demands that leaders avoid two common problems. The first is well known: so-called "short-termism." This means taking actions that boost near-term results without regard for the impact on a company's future cash flows. It can include, for example, cutting productive R&D or buying back shares to hit an earnings-per-share target; or offering distributors special discounts at the end of a quarter so managers can hit their sales targets; or selling well-running businesses to boost profits with the one-off capital gains;

or negotiating one-time cash payments from suppliers in exchange for guaranteed future business. One factory manager even cut down trees in the forest adjoining his factory and sold the lumber to make his numbers.

Sadly, in a survey of executives and board members commissioned by McKinsey with the Canada Pension Plan Investment Board, most respondents "cited their own executive teams and boards (rather than investors, analysts, and others outside the company) as the greatest sources of pressure for short-term performance."

The second, less-recognized problem is the opposite of short-termism and just as deadly: "long-termism." This means the tolerance of luxurious investment, lax overhead, and low-balled targets. Such behaviors put a company's long-term health at risk, because they sap the profits needed today to invest in boosting and fortifying the company's future earnings power.

As a former Honeywell CEO, David Cote, put it, the cures for long-termism are to "invest in the future but not excessively," followed by "grow sales while keeping fixed costs constant" (in other words, keep fixed costs fixed!). By doing this, he stated, "you're bound to generate the savings that both fuel new investment [for the long term] and increase quarterly earnings [in the short term]." Cote was described by one lieutenant as "a big annoying bear threatening the livestock" in relentlessly ensuring that each business was adding sales faster than attracting people *and* was investing sufficiently in long-term projects.

By explicitly adopting shareholder value as a north star for their strategy, leaders don't settle for making trade-offs between winning now and winning later. They commit to doing both—to funding tomorrow's hits by bolstering today's profits. Here's how:

- They promise not to skimp on safety, not to make expedient decisions just because their peers are doing so, and never to use accounting or financial trickery to boost short-term profits.
- On the flip side, they mean it when they tell each other (and their own people) that they will be disciplined investors of capital, intolerant of unproductive overhead, and champions of performance targets that demand the best of themselves and their teams.

Adopting practices and behaviors like these is not the only commitment leaders make when they choose maximizing shareholder value to guide their strategy. They also promise each other and their organization that providing competitive value for customers, employees, and other so-called "stakeholders" will guide their strategy choices and how they implement them (see appendix 1). This is not merely a means to the end of securing the company's future earnings power. It is also the *result* of meeting that end: companies with strong earnings power are more able to offer competitive value to all its stakeholders.

In other words, there's a virtuous circle between maximizing shareholder value and offering competitive stakeholder value. For example, McKinsey wrote in its article "The Real Business of Business" that maximizing shareholder value "builds stronger economies, higher living standards, and more opportunities for individuals." But all these things help businesses maximize shareholder value, too. The cause and the effect go in both directions. The end (shareholder value) and the means (stakeholder value) fuel each other.

Moreover, if leaders choose to adopt a social purpose for their company (see chapter 33), then committing to the objective of maximizing shareholder value means they seek strategies that deliberately make "purpose" and "profit" fortify each other. Buffett gives us a good example of what this looks like in practice. In his 2016 letter to shareholders, he wrote that renewable sources would grow in importance, and that was why Berkshire's energy subsidiary chose to invest in them. "[This] will make great sense, both for the environment and for Berkshire's economics."

To be sure, the language of "shareholder value" has become politically loaded. Leaders have to be very careful with the language they use, lest they become the devil incarnate themselves. By contrast, shareholder value gives leaders an indispensable compass for steering their strategy and its implementation through the choppy waters stirred up by the many other masters that a business must serve.

For example, given a choice between stretching their strategy in one direction versus another (see chapter 18), which criterion should leaders use to make the choice? Is a million dollars more wisely spent on a company's social purpose than on a new plant or employee training? Is it better to build a financial safety net or to take on more risk? In deciding whether to relocate a plant, how should leaders weigh the ill effects on current workers against the positive effects on the new plant's employees and community? Are the benefits of replacing workers with robots worth the investment required, the reputational risk, or the potential of alienating customers? If a company hits a bump in the road, are suppliers, creditors, employees, or customers more important?

Leaders are confronted with an unending stream of such choices, all involving a complex web of trade-offs where the interests of different groups conflict. Prioritizing shareholder value—a.k.a. the company's future earnings power—is the best true north for navigating the trade-offs. No other decision criterion can help leaders navigate them as consistently and fairly over time as this one does.

Again, Buffett exemplifies the power of maximizing shareholder value in practice. He's been a tireless promoter of "intrinsic value" as "the only logical way to run companies and invest in them." He cares little about next quarter's earnings per share or day-to-day movements in Berkshire's stock price. He focuses on growing intrinsic value—a.k.a., maximizing shareholder value—and he chooses and lauds executives who use that lens for developing their own strategies. As he wrote in the 2019 edition of his annual shareholder letter, "In representing *your* interests, [our directors] will…seek managers whose goals include delighting their customers, cherishing their associates, and acting as good citizens of both their communities and our country."

Though Warren Buffett may seem like a rare example, he's not the only one. From my own firsthand experience, I can name at least three others: Roberto Goizueta, who revitalized the Coca-Cola Company during the nearly two decades he served as CEO. (He became one of Buffett's favorite leaders, and Coke became one of Berkshire Hathaway's largest and longest holdings.) Sir Brian Pitman did the same when he ran Lloyds Bank (now Lloyds Banking Group PLC) for more than a decade (see chapter 26). As did Franz Humer when he remade The Roche Group into the world's leading life sciences company by prescription sales (see chapter 61).

These leaders had to make some extremely tough decisions that weighed heavily on them personally, from which customers to leave behind to which businesses to jettison, which communities to exit, and more. They didn't always make the best decisions. And they often took a lot of political flak for their decisions. But they left their companies—and all of their many stakeholders who stuck with them—better off by orders of magnitude. Much of their success can be attributed to the practice of maximizing shareholder value, as described here. I know because I was there, working personally with Pitman and Humer and, in my younger days, on a team that worked with Goizueta.

36

What place should "stakeholder value" have in strategy?

How to navigate a complex web of interested parties

The word "stakeholder" was coined at the Stanford Research Institute in 1963.[1] Stakeholders were defined as "groups without whose support the organization would cease to exist." Six groups were called out: shareowners, employees, customers, suppliers, lenders, and society.[2]

By 1983, however, the notion of "stakeholder" was broadened to include "any identifiable group or individual who can affect the achievement of an organization's objectives or who is affected by the achievement of an organization's objectives…[or] on which the organization is dependent for its continued survival."

With such a broad definition, it was inevitable that the number of groups to be counted as "stakeholders" would balloon. For example, the latest Wikipedia entry includes more than 25, which, for reasons that will become clear, I have put into four camps:

Camp 1	Camp 2	Camp 3	Camp 4
Current, prospective customers	Current, prospective employees, managers	Governing authorities (tax, regulatory, legislative, etc.)	NGOs; other advocacy groups
	Suppliers, distributors	Labor unions	Schools
	Financiers, creditors	Communities—local, national	Competitors
	Shareholders, investors, owners	People at large (global community)	Analysts, media
	Trade groups, professional associations	Future generations	
	Research centers		

These stakeholders create an enormously complex web of interested parties that leaders must account for in their strategy. To navigate that complexity, leaders will find it helpful to assign each type of stakeholder to one of the four camps, as indicated above.

Customers are in their own camp—Camp 1—because they take front and center in the three choices that constitute a strategy (see chapter 2).

Camp 2 includes stakeholders who have a voluntary relationship with the company that typically—though not always—involves a monetary exchange. For each group in this camp, leaders must answer two questions:

- Who are the ideal members of each stakeholder group to help us build the leading capabilities we have chosen for our strategy?
- Why should they choose us over their perceived alternatives?

That second question just above can be reframed with the jargon *du jour* of "stakeholder value," which might read thus: "What is the stakeholder value we should offer that will compel stakeholders in this camp to choose us over their perceived alternatives?"

In this context, stakeholder value is the balance of benefits and costs that stakeholders perceive in their experience with a business. The benefits typically comprise a mix of financial and nonfinancial value. Financial value includes, for example, good pay for staff, attractive margins for suppliers, and the prospect of superior returns for investors. Examples of nonfinancial value include purpose, societal impact, working conditions, or career development for employees; as well as trustworthy or friction-free relationships for suppliers;

plus reputational "halo" or learning opportunities for investors.

Of course, these benefits—both financial and nonfinancial—have to more than justify perceived costs, such as long hours for staff, tight deadlines or stringent quality standards for suppliers, and lack of liquidity for investors.

This brings us to Camp 3. Having a relationship with stakeholders in this camp is often not a choice, since their support is required for any business to at least have the license to operate and maybe even to succeed. For example, governing authorities are more likely to award access, approvals, and licenses to companies they trust.

Here, leaders have to answer two different questions:

- What support do we need from stakeholders in Camp 3 to fortify our leading capabilities? For example, if local energy costs are essential to one of our mission-critical capabilities, how can the communities in which we operate help us with those costs? Or if an aging workforce threatens a leading capability, how can we gain the support of future generations to avoid a critical workforce shortage? Or if permission to open a plant, explore for natural resources, or build critical infrastructure in a certain location will make or break a leading capability, how can we motivate the regulatory action needed to win permission?

- What can and should we do to earn the support of stakeholders in this camp? In some cases, such as with regulatory agencies and tax authorities, it's just a matter of being a good, rule-following corporate citizen that is easy to work with. But in other cases, leaders have to think harder about the benefit–cost equation ("stakeholder value") that is necessary to earn the support of Camp 3 stakeholders.

In Camp 4, we have stakeholders where the relationship is typically voluntary and could involve a monetary exchange but often does not. These stakeholders are important to the degree they can materially inspire other stakeholders such as customers, employees, and communities, all of whom are critical to marketing, selling, or meeting the promise of a product or service offering.

Here, the questions are:

- Which influence from stakeholders in Camp 4 would best serve our leading capabilities to market, sell, or meet the promise of our offerings? This could range from validation to endorsement, testimonials, regulatory change, permission to do business in certain countries, access to particular customers, suppliers, or potential employees, and so on.

- What *can* and *should* we do to earn the positive influence of the stakeholders in this camp?

It's worth emphasizing here that relationships with Camp 4 stakeholders should be earned, not bought. They should all be mutually beneficial relationships that do not require a monetary exchange to produce value for both parties. Customers, employees, and investors will see right through Camp 4 relationships that are purely financial and transactional, which will defeat the purpose of having them.

Here's a table that summarizes the questions leaders must address for each type of stakeholder:

Camp 1	Camp 2	Camp 3	Camp 4
Having a relationship is a mutual choice and always involves a monetary exchange.	Having a relationship is usually a mutual choice that often involves a monetary exchange.	Having a relationship is typically not a choice, and is essential.	Having a relationship is normally a mutual choice and could involve a monetary exchange, but often does not.
Who are the ideal customers for our offerings? Why should they choose us over their perceived alternatives? What capabilities should we prioritize and nurture to be the best at marketing, selling, and meeting the promise of our *Why?*	Who are the ideal members of each stakeholder group in this camp to help us build our leading capabilities? Why should they choose us over their perceived alternatives?	What support do we need from stakeholders in this camp to fortify our leading capabilities? What can and should we do to earn the support of stakeholders in this camp?	What influence from stakeholders in this camp would best serve our leading capabilities to market, sell, or meet the promise of our offerings? What can and should we do to earn the positive influence of the stakeholders in this camp?

Leaders can use this framework to account for any stakeholder in their strategy choices, including those not included in the Wikipedia list further above, such as board directors (Camp 2), beneficiaries of the company's pension plan (Camp 3), and the families of employees or customers (Camp 4). But leaders should not attempt to account for every conceivable stakeholder in their strategy unless they want to wrap themselves around the proverbial axle.[3]

Yes, companies must earn the trust and active support of anyone and everyone who can materially influence their success. Yet when it comes to strategy, leaders should consider only those stakeholders that play the most important role in the leading capabilities they choose for their strategy. This will *always* include at least employees, suppliers, and partners. Who else to include is necessarily a judgment call for leaders that depends a lot on factors like their company's industry, geography, and scale.

It also depends a lot on their strategy. That means starting with Camp 1 and then prioritizing within and across the other three camps, using the questions in the table above. In short, the role that "stakeholder value" should play in a strategy depends a great deal on what that strategy is in the first place.

---

1   See "Stockholders and Stakeholders: A New Perspective on Corporate Governance," by R. Edward Freeman, California Management Review, Spring 1983.

2   Note who comes first in this list (shareholders), compared to who comes last (shareholders) in the Business Roundtable's now-famous declaration in August 2019 on "The Purpose of the Corporation" (see appendix 1).

3   This is where critics of "stakeholder capitalism" have a field day. Asking leaders to be accountable to so many self-interested parties is effectively the same as having them be accountable to no one.

37

How should stock price influence strategy?

A signal, not a goal or objective

A few years ago, an activist investor proposed that General Motors split its common stock into two classes—one that pays a dividend stream to attract "yield investors" and another designed for "growth investors" that would appreciate as GM's earnings increase. The catalyst for the activist's proposal was GM's stock price, which as a multiple of its profits was then far below the market average and materially less than other auto companies' valuation. The idea was to boost the price of GM's stock by making it more attractive to two types of investors: those more interested in GM's current dividends stream, and others willing to bet on the company's future growth.

Fortunately, GM's board saw the proposal as nothing more than hocus-pocus for conjuring a higher stock price out of thin air—financial engineering at its worst (see chapter 6). Fiddling with the company's stock structure would not change the company's fundamentals—namely, leaders' strategy, their ability to implement and produce results from it, and their industry context. GM's directors rightly concluded that the proposal would have zero impact on its future earning power, its wherewithal to pay dividends, and its overall capacity to invest, innovate, and grow.

However, the board still had to grapple with the reality of GM's anemic stock price. A company's stock price is the result of what people with something real at stake (their money) are willing to pay for a bet on its future. GM's very low share price relative to its current earnings indicated that a lot of people in the stock market were unwilling to make that bet. That suggested they had little confidence in GM's strategy or its ability to implement that strategy. This can shorten the leash on leaders and strangle their time, options, and freedom of action to fix whatever's driving investors' lack of confidence in the company. And sadly, this will further encourage such activist investors—some with strange notions of the solution—to heap even more pressure on leaders and their board.

But instead of railing against "short-termism" and misguided investors, companies with a stagnating valuation need to take a long, hard look at two possible explanations. One is that the market is missing something. "The market" is made up of various actors whose collective behavior is adding up to a languishing stock price. This includes investors who've chosen to hold shares and others who decided to avoid them; and it includes investors who are in a particular stock for only the short term and others who are in it for the long haul. Leaders should ask investors in each category about the strategy that leaders have for their company: What is it, and what barriers do investors see to implementing it? Is it specifically differentiating enough (see chapter 8)? Are there ways to stretch that strategy to enhance the company's future earning power (see chapter 18)? Is the big idea (see chapter 9) behind the strategy clear and compelling, or is there a need to revitalize or replace it (see chapter 16)?

Leaders should ask themselves whether investors' answers to these questions are compelling or perhaps just ignorant. If the latter, leaders must put on their agenda the need to educate investors and convince them. But if leaders hear some compelling answers, they should face up to the possibility that the market sees something they can't ignore. Then it's time to go back to the drawing board and objectively consider whether developments in the company's world are making obsolete some aspect of leaders' strategy or the big idea that supports it.

Sometimes outsiders have clearer eyes than insiders, and the market is collectively saying that it sees something leaders don't. If the market is correct, whatever leaders are missing will eventually weigh heavily on their company's future earnings power, flexibility to hand out dividends, and ability to invest, innovate, and grow.

The GM example tells us that, though a company's stock price is not the goal or objective of strategy, it *can* be an important signal to leaders. It contains valuable information about whether the company's strategy is well understood or needs a rethink. It represents the balance of views—from those who have real skin in the game—on the company's future prospects, both tomorrow and for the foreseeable future. Leaders ignore that signal at their own peril.

However, leaders should never let their company's stock price be the dog that wags the strategy tail. Companies get the investors they deserve. Most companies have tens, hundreds, thousands, and even millions of shareholders, who can have very different wishes. Some want a quick return, others want share buybacks, some want dividend increases, and yet others want a company to grow faster or slim down. It's impossible to appeal to every wish of every shareholder all the time. Instead, leaders should be crystal clear on what their strategy is, how they are implementing it, and how they will realize the best possible results from it. And they should let shareholders self-select, based on what they hear and see from leaders.

Kenneth Frazier, a former CEO of Merck, the life sciences company, tells a good story about how he got the investors he wanted by dropping the company's five-year earnings-per-share guidance. As he said in *Leadership Next*, which is a podcast helmed by Alan Murray, CEO of Fortune Media, "the stock plummeted [when I cancelled the guidance] and every time a share of Merck stock got sold, somebody bought it, and the people who bought it were patient, long-term shareholders for a company that would invest in R&D."

All this goes to say that leaders who try to boost their stock price with financial engineering and empty promises mostly lack conviction in both their strategies and their ability to implement and execute with them. Leaders having strong convictions want only those investors who believe in the path that those leaders have set out for the company *and* in their ability to stay on it. Self-assured leaders are willing to change their convictions if their company's valuation suggests investors are unwilling to bet on it other than at a knock-down price. And if their company's valuation is subpar, they are able to acknowledge that perhaps the market is making a point. They are willing to find out what that point is, and then to act on it.

38

What is the role of brand in strategy?

How to harness the power of a valuable asset

In 1931 Neil McElroy, an executive at Proctor & Gamble, wrote a memorandum about "brand management." This called for creating a new role—the "brand manager"—with responsibility for overseeing all aspects of a branded product, including pricing, packaging, manufacturing, distribution, and, of course, marketing. McElroy made no distinction between a brand and a business. He thought of *Ivory*—P&G's soap brand—as a business and its "brand manager" as the person who coordinates all aspects of the *Ivory* business.

But sixty years after McElroy sent his memo, David Aaker published the book *Managing Brand Equity*. He defined brand equity as "the commercial value derived from consumer perception of the brand name of a particular product or service, rather than from the product or service itself."

Aaker's book popularized the notion of "brand equity" as a discrete asset that has attributable value in its own right, like factories, inventory, patents, and working capital. In other words, unlike McElroy, Aaker defined a brand as an asset of the business rather than the business itself. The more "equity" a brand has, the more valuable it is to the business that owns it. Inevitably, the separation of brand from the business (or product) to which it's attached has led to "brand" becoming yet another modifier of strategy, as in "brand strategy."

Brand strategy starts with the idea that people form human-like relationships with a brand—from love, infatuation, and respect to hate, boredom, and disdain—that affect their purchase behavior toward the brand, including consideration, usage, preference, and advocacy.

In turn, these relationships are determined by the "positioning" (promise) it occupies in the minds of a target audience; and a brand's positioning is "activated" (influenced) by all the touchpoints that consumers have with the brand, such as its products, promotions, sponsorships, customer support staff, availability, and advertising.

Thus, "brand strategy" comprises three choices:

- Who should be the brand's target audience?
- What should be the brand's positioning with that audience?
- What touchpoints should be prioritized and nurtured to activate the brand's positioning in the best possible way?

Readers of chapter 2 will see that these questions line up with the *Who? Why?* and *What?* of business strategy:

- *Who* should be our target customer?
- *Why* should our target customer choose us?
- *What* capabilities should we prioritize and nurture to make us the best at marketing, selling, and living our *Why?*

This does not, however, make brand strategy the same as business strategy. The governing objective of business strategy is to grow future earnings, while for brand strategy it's to grow brand equity. But here's the rub: brand equity only matters if it contributes to the earnings power of a business in an attributable, identifiable, and quantifiable way. Thus, brand strategy must complement and fortify business strategy or as sure as night follows day, there will be friction.

For example, if the brand positioning for an AIDS medicine is "trusted to make your virus undetectable," the product's molecule may need further development to meet this promise, faster and in more subpopulations (as in patients who are more difficult to treat). But if the business strategy calls for a *Why?* that does not include this promise and if the business plan doesn't prioritize resources for such development, the brand strategy cannot be implemented.

More generally, the benefits that are prioritized for a brand's positioning—from functional and experiential to emotional and purpose—must mirror and amplify the *Why?* that leaders have chosen for their business strategy. Otherwise, a brand's promise to consumers in its target audience will be different than what they actually experience with the brand. This is a recipe for baking all kinds of implementation and execution challenges into both the brand and the business strategies.

Likewise, if the business and brand strategies are aimed at different target audiences, there will almost certainly be a disconnect, such as between the focus of sales resources and marketing spend, respectively. Such disconnects inevitably produce execution problems due to inefficient—even contradictory—investment.

Finally, if the marketing team's brand strategy prioritizes touchpoints that require enterprise capabilities that are not prioritized by enterprise leaders, the gap will create execution barriers. For example, if the brand's positioning emphasizes "easiest to find and buy," the business strategy had better call for a superior distribution capability to meet that promise.

All this goes to say that if leaders see their brand equity as a true asset, and want their marketing team to have a strategy for increasing it, the marketers should start with the *Who? Why?* and *What?* that leaders have chosen for their business strategy. In other words, business strategy should be the dog that wags the brand strategy tail.

But what about companies like P&G that have multiple brands? Is brand strategy for them just an aggregation of the strategies for their individual brands? No. They need a multibrand strategy, much like why companies with two or more businesses require a multibusiness strategy.

Readers of chapter 3 will recall that multibusiness strategy entails three key choices:

- What should be our unique way of contributing to the future earnings power of our individual businesses?
- What capabilities should we prioritize and nurture to make us better than anyone else at our way of contributing to the future earnings power of our businesses?
- What businesses should we own because they fit best with our way of contributing to their future earnings power?

This is where Chief Marketing Officers can play a difference-making corporate role, rather than just their traditional functional role. Here's how:

Leaders can think of their brands as a contributor to the earnings power of their businesses, and if they do, they should charge their CMOs with proposing answers to these three questions:

- What should be our unique way of contributing to the positioning and activation of our brands?
- What capabilities should we prioritize and nurture to make us better than anyone else at our way of contributing to the positioning and activation of our brands?
- What brands should we have in our portfolio because they fit best with our way of contributing to their positioning and activation?

The answers to these questions are the active ingredients of a multibrand strategy. They should both inform a company's multibusiness strategy and be informed by it.

For example, if a company is particularly good at the emotional positioning of brands, its multibusiness strategy should—all else equal—call for businesses in which it's more difficult to unlock customer willingness to pay on functional and experiential grounds alone. This reminds me of a friend who once told me that he's willing to pay $40,000 for a car to haul his family around reliably and safely, but he'd be prepared to pay much more if it made him feel excited, young, or cool to drive that car. He would buy the car either way, but if the car's branding could create that emotional connection for him, it would open up more of his wallet.

Another example could be for a company that has a leading capability in distribution. Its multibrand strategy could prioritize businesses in which physical availability is an important contributor to consumer preferences for the brands they own.

These examples suggest that multibusiness and multibrand strategies should be two sides of a single coin. If leaders and CMOs don't manage accordingly, execution challenges will surely arise, and that won't be good for their businesses or their brands.

This takes us to a final point— about the role of "brand architecture" in strategy, an issue that often pops up at many companies. A typical question is, "Are we a house of brands akin to Procter & Gamble and Newell Brands, or to a branded house such as Apple and Google, or to something different like the Endorsing Brands model?"[1]

Two critical inputs are required to answer this question as objectively as possible:

- An explicit, coherent multibrand strategy with clear and compelling answers to the three questions just above
- Robust metrics on the relative strengths and weaknesses of a company's brands as perceived by their key stakeholders, starting with the end user or consumer, but also including intermediaries, staff, regulators, and even investors

As many companies are missing either or both of these two inputs, they often default to "I say, you say" debates in which the loudest voice, the most senior voice, or the expert-in-the-room wins. A typical outcome is that brand architecture becomes the company's *de facto* brand strategy rather than the result of a deliberate one.

---

1   The Endorsing Brands model is often communicated with "a powered by" or "brought to you by" tagline. Marriott International uses this model to support its many hotel brands with the endorsement of Marriott's corporate brand.

PART VIII

What Are the Right Guideposts for Strategy?

What to look for—and be
wary of—to stay on track

39

Should strategy be stable or dynamic?

Yes, and leaders have to manage that apparent contradiction

The Prussian general and military theorist Carl von Clausewitz wrote: "No battle plan survives first contact with the enemy." Centuries later, former heavyweight champion Mike Tyson must have been channeling Clausewitz when he remarked, "Everybody has a plan until they get punched in the mouth." Like battle-tested generals and boxers, good leaders know their strategies must be adaptable, dynamic, and flexible. That's because every strategy is contingent on an unpredictable future and each day brings new learning about how the future might unfold. Technology; politics; regulation; competition; customer expectations; organizational turnover—all these forces, and more, conspire to render strategies irrelevant, out of date, and off the mark. This is true even for the most data-driven, scenario-tested, and thoughtful strategies.

Moreover, the leaders of every business are confronted by a constant stream of new challenges and opportunities that could—or should—require changes to their essential strategy choices (see chapters 2 and 3). Thus, the work of strategy is never done.

Nordstrom, under its former chief executive, Blake Nordstrom, is one company that institutionalized strategy as a continuous, dynamic, and living leadership tool. When the board came in for its regular board meetings, Blake carved out separate time for the executive team and directors to work on their strategy. This time was organized around specific topics that could demand a material change of strategy, such as whether to create a new young-women's fashion department, how to participate in the e-commerce revolution, and how to digitize its retail floor operations. To be sure, leaders and directors of most companies do plenty of talking about strategic issues and how to respond. But Blake's approach was much more rigorous.

Each challenge had to go through four nonnegotiable steps. First, what, exactly, is the issue or opportunity? Then—because there is always more than one way to skin a cat—what alternative solutions to the issue or opportunity should we short-list for deeper evaluation, *and* what criteria will we use to evaluate them? Next, given our evaluation of the short-listed alternatives, which should we choose? Finally, given that choice, how should we accordingly adjust our strategy and plan?

Each question was treated as a consequential decision. No question came into focus until there was sufficient agreement on the previous question. This could take anywhere between two to four separate board discussions, depending how big the issue or opportunity as well as the stakes of getting the decision right the first time. Each discussion was set up to invite constructive disagreement and bring differences to the fore that would normally stay hidden under the surface. Blake believed this was the *only* way to forge genuine agreement on what to do about the most important challenges for his strategy, as well as to minimize strategy talk-shops that produced vaguely dissatisfying results.

When challenges were resolved in the Nordstrom board, they were replaced with new ones that relentlessly roll over the horizon (as they do for every company). This approach made strategy a living, ever-adapting tool for raising the company's metabolic rate of decision-making and execution. And it helped the board actively contribute to strategy in a consequential, collaborative manner (see chapter 52).

As a rule of thumb, leaders and their board can make two to three big strategy decisions per year. Each can be worth 5% to 10% of a company's enterprise value. Thus, over any five-year period a strategy might turn over completely—though certainly not all at once. Does this mean that strategies should be 100% variable? No. While a strategy should continuously evolve, its foundation should not.

A multibusiness company can spend years building a distinctive, proprietary way of contributing to the health and strength of its businesses, along with a portfolio of businesses that fit with that approach. This is why Berkshire Hathaway steers clear of high-tech companies it doesn't understand, why Procter & Gamble exited food, and why the Roche Group got rid of its Consumer Health business. Leaders may be able to turn over their portfolio rapidly—even within a few months—but it takes years to change their company's way of contributing to its businesses and the capabilities that support it. For example, Frito-Lay's direct-to-store delivery capability (see chapter 14), Inditex's fast-fashion supply chain, and Toyota's production system took many years to hone into true sources of enterprise differentiation. The foundations of a multibusiness strategy need to be stable enough for long enough to let it work.

Likewise, for a single-business strategy, it takes time to implement both a compelling offering of benefits and the capabilities to perfect it. An organization can't keep up when leaders frequently or suddenly change their *Who?* or *Why?* Consider JC Penney under its former CEO Ron Johnson. Both its customers and its capabilities system were put into shock with his sudden switch from promotion-based selling of mostly own-branded apparel to everyday-low-pricing of store-within-store branded merchandise. The dramatic change in JCP's offering confused customers and upset a capabilities system that had been honed over decades. Supply chain, merchandise buying, in-store merchandising, service staff training—all these capabilities were suddenly disrupted.

Consider the difference between how the two clothing retailers Nordstrom and JC Penney managed their strategies. At Nordstrom, leaders continually challenged the merchandising, service, channel, and all other dimensions of their strategy in a way that took advantage of the foundational choices that underpin it. In contrast, JC Penney's leaders pulled the rug out from beneath the foundation itself.

Effective leaders adapt their strategy as their situation changes. But the ability to do that is based on having a strong foundation. If your company is clear and consistent about how it brings benefits to its businesses, leaders will make better decisions about the shape of their portfolios. If leaders understand their company's handful of special capabilities, they'll prioritize more smartly their growth priorities to exploit and enhance those capabilities.

Likewise, when leaders of the individual businesses within a company are sharp and consistent with regard to their essential strategy choices—*Who? Why?* and *What?*—their people will make smarter decisions, from which markets to prioritize and de-emphasize to how to sell into those markets, how to manage new product development, how to manage costs, where to invest, and all the other decisions that are inherent in turning a winning strategy into a winning business.

A strategy *must* be dynamic, or it will fail to keep up. But much of it also needs to be stable, otherwise all those decisions and actions an organization takes will be diluted by their lack of direction and coherence. Leaders have to reconcile and manage this apparent contradiction. In doing so, they will increase by leaps and bounds the pace and quality of their company's decision-making and execution.

40

What mix of continuity and innovation should a strategy have?

Great strategies have a lot of both.

Strategy continuity is a hallmark of many companies that have sustained great execution for decades. For example, Southwest Airlines' decades-old strategy of short-haul, high-frequency, point-to-point, low-fare service-with-a-smile has produced one of the best-performing companies in any industry over the last half-century (see chapter 8). Likewise, for over 50 years, Walmart has pursued a strategy of offering the broadest, deepest range of everyday goods at the lowest "everyday" price so that people "can live better" (see chapter 62). And the essence of Walt Disney's original strategy for The Walt Disney Company remains intact today: to have a range of leisure and entertainment businesses—from animated film to fun parks, TV, streaming, retail, cruise ships, and more—featuring a group of engaging, family-friendly characters (see chapters 3 and 10).

Yet the corporate landscape is also littered with companies whose strategies became obsolete faster than their leaders could reinvent them. For example, deregulation killed off icons in the airline business such as Pan Am and TWA. Digital technology famously overwhelmed Kodak's once-formidable business in chemistry-based photography. Electronic commerce obliterated Borders, Circuit City, and Blockbuster. Smartphones destroyed Blackberry's consumer business.

For these companies, lack of sufficient, timely strategy innovation hastened their demise. They needed *strategy innovation,* not continuity.

The two sets of examples above confirm what experienced leaders intuitively know: that sustaining great execution requires both strategy continuity and innovation. But how can they achieve that without having to sacrifice one or the other at any point in time? Answering two important questions will help:

- What capabilities set our company apart from everyone else?
- Are there changes in the world—or to our *Who?* or *Why?*—that will make those capabilities obsolete or insufficient?

Strategy continuity demands that leaders be clear about the first question—the capabilities that make their company special. Prime examples are Microsoft's expertise in engineering highly complex software at enormous scale; GE's former ability to develop general managers; and Nordstrom's sales-floor service capability. Such capabilities are a foundation of sound strategy (the other is having a big idea—see chapter 9).

But like Rome, leading capabilities aren't built in a day. While leaders can change their *Who?* and *Why?* relatively quickly, capabilities take much longer to change (see chapter 39). Without a degree of continuity in their strategy, leaders can't allow their company the time it takes to turn certain capabilities into a durable advantage.

However, at the same time, leaders must regularly ask whether their company's best capabilities are still relevant. For example, in an increasingly digital world, will Nordstrom's sales-floor service capability still be a difference-maker in the future (see chapter 62)? Is developing general managers still a differentiating capability for the new companies that were created when the General Electric Company split itself into three pieces? And what is the open-software movement doing to the value of Microsoft's in-house, closed approach to software (see chapter 20)?

It's hard to find an industry in which capabilities are *not* demanding innovation. Take credit card companies and the emergence of digital commerce. In the traditional payments business, their success was tied to driving card usage, because that generated transaction fees; but in digital commerce, an essential capability is generating, analyzing, and using consumer data to drive sales and loyalty for their primary customer: the merchants who accept their cards.

Another example can be found in big-box retailing. Most players—such as Tesco in the U.K., Carrefour in France, and Walmart in the U.S.—have run out of locations in their home markets for laying down more superstores. They are all seeking growth by using a small-store format to penetrate pockets of geography that their bigger stores cannot reach. But the capabilities—from merchandising to managing store staff and operating the supply chain—are very different for a small-store format.

In U.S. health care, the push for more-accountable care requires some degree of risk sharing with insurers. Such models will demand capabilities—such as risk underwriting and contingent revenue management—that are currently alien to most health care providers.

And in the energy sector, oil-&-gas companies are having to grapple with a world demanding fewer CO_2 emissions. Many have tried to envision themselves as "energy" companies to assert their permission to enter wind, solar, tidal, algae, and other such businesses. But the difference-making capabilities to win in these businesses are nothing like the capabilities they've spent decades perfecting.

Leaders of any company operating in credit cards, big-box retailing, health care, or oil-&-gas should be saying to themselves, "Yes, changes happening in our world *are* making our capabilities insufficient, if not obsolete. Strategy continuity is not enough right now; we need strategy innovation to shore up and bolster the foundation of capabilities that will underpin great execution from what we will have in the future, not just what we have today."

If leaders correctly identify the capabilities that make their company great and build their strategies around those capabilities, and if leaders act smartly on the enhancements or additions to those capabilities that their changing world or strategy requires, they will achieve the benefits of strategy continuity and innovation without having to sacrifice one for the other.

Phil Knight transformed Nike from a sports shoe company to a sports licensing company. Reed Hastings led Netflix through a dramatic and traumatic pivot from direct mail-ordering to online streaming. And Satya Nadella put Microsoft into the cloud (see chapter 20) and transitioned to more open-source software development through his GitHub acquisition. The strategy innovations at these companies meant adding new capabilities to those that made each company thrive in the first place. Their leaders were able to maintain an important degree of stability in their strategies without causing them to fall behind the changes happening all around them.

The CEO of a Fortune 100 company once asked one of my teams to help him assess his strategy for an upcoming board meeting.[1] He wanted to know if it had any "sinkholes." The team framed its assessment around those two questions above. His feedback: "The best strategy discussion I've ever had with the board."

---

1   This showed great leadership and confidence. Strategy is a lot like IQ for many leaders: to challenge their strategy is to question their intelligence.

41

What is the optimal mix of organic and inorganic[1] growth for a strategy?

The combination that's required to implement it

Every so often leaders think they need to develop a "growth strategy." Or sometimes they are asked by their board or pressured by certain investors to create one. In either case, they often frame their task with these three questions:

- How much growth should we target?
- How much growth will our company produce on current course and speed?
- What mix of organic and inorganic growth should we pursue to close the gap?

Readers of chapter 31 know what to think of the first question. It's the wrong place to start. Leaders cannot analyze their way to an objective answer. The answer is ultimately arbitrary. It can bias the essential choices that a strategy comprises (see chapters 2 and 3). It also puts the target cart before the strategy horse (see chapter 31).

The second question seems straightforward, but it's not. Does "current course and speed" include planned investments in, say, product development, new-market entry, sales force expansion, marketing spend, or next-gen plant and equipment? If not, are leaders saying that their company can grow without such investment? Or do they have to draw a line between "current course and speed" investment and "incremental new" investment? And if so, how do they draw that line? What is "incremental new" versus "current course and speed"? Like the first question, this second one has no objective answer. It's ultimately an arbitrary one, no matter how much analysis is commissioned to produce it.

Even putting aside such issues, answering the first two questions doesn't resolve two opposing views that often turns the third question into an endless debate: one, that organic investment is a slower path to growth than acquisitions, often negatively hitting the bottom line faster than it positively contributes to the top line; and the other that buying companies is expensive, tends to produce a lower return on capital than organic growth, and involves a lot of risk in coordinating—if not integrating—different operations, organizations, and cultures. Each view is valid; and each sends leaders in the opposite direction from the other, setting up an impossible trade-off.

The only way to resolve this debate is to start with a different set of questions:

1. For our company to grow, how should we stretch our strategy?
2. What companies, products, IP, technologies, or other such assets could help us implement our most-promising strategy stretches?
3. Could we acquire any of those companies cost-effectively, partner with any of them productively, or replicate what they have ourselves?

Leaders have chosen a "growth strategy" when they can answer the first question. Chapter 18 can help them find their answer, and chapter 19 can steer them clear of the pitfalls in answering it.

The next two questions concern how to implement the growth strategy leaders have chosen with their answer to the first question.[2] For example:

- When IKEA chose to enhance its offering with a service to help customers assemble their furniture, it bought the handyman site TaskRabbit to implement that choice.
- Well before IKEA bought TaskRabbit, Best Buy bought Geek Squad to implement an improvement in its proposition for customers needing technical support associated with its products.

- Walgreen's, the pharmacy giant, acquired the health & beauty company Boots Alliance to enhance the customer proposition that Walgreen offered with its highly successfully range of Boots Alliance's own-branded and own-made beauty and personal care products, such as the cosmetics line No. 7.
- Otsuka, the Japanese drug company, is making a big push into a wide range of digital technologies to enhance the benefits of its drug therapies. To help them implement that strategy, they partnered with—and then purchased the assets of—a company called Proteus Digital Health to embed an electronic sensor in every dose of its drug for bipolar disease and schizophrenia. (That makes it easier for patients and their caregivers to know whether prescriptions are being taken in the right dose at the right time, thus increasing adherence and reducing the complications of nonadherence.)
- Adding open software development to Microsoft's capabilities became a big part of CEO Satya Nadella's growth initiatives for the company (see chapter 20). To help the company implement that strategy, he acquired GitHub for $7.5 billion.
- To help the Roche Group implement his "personalized medicine" strategy (see chapter 61), CEO Severin Schwartz bought Ventana for its tissue-testing capability that facilitates diagnosis and treatment of cancer tumors based on their genetic composition.
- After Mars, the confectionary company, made the choice to add pet care to its pet food business, it bought Banfield Pet Hospital and then made a string of veterinary services acquisitions in both the U.S. and Europe.

Leaders of these companies decided that acquisitions were the most cost-effective way to implement their strategy. First came their strategy choices—question 1; then consideration of companies that might help them implement their strategies—question 2; and finally, a decision on whether to buy, borrow (partner with), or build (through organic investment)—question 3. In other words, the particular mix of organic and inorganic growth that leaders choose for their company is *not* a growth strategy; rather, it's an outcome of a plan that spells out what's required to implement a strategy stretch.

To be sure, leaders have no shortage of advisors—bankers, their own corporate development staff, consultants, board directors, and on and on—who will pitch acquisitions that leaders should make. Indeed, many of the examples cited above may have started this way. When that happens, leaders should ask how a proposed acquisition could help them stretch their strategy and why that would be the best way for doing so. At a minimum, this will help them separate the wheat from the chaff when confronted with acquisition opportunities. More important, it will help them get the most out of their partnerships and acquisitions.

---

1   "Inorganic" growth is the term commonly used for growing through a merger or acquisition. It is often referred to as "M&A."

2   See chapter 29 for what "implement" means in this book.

42

What is the right time frame for strategy?

The time required to implement it

When I work with business leaders on their strategies, they often ask me about time frame. Most of them think that strategy is about the long term, but they wonder how long that should be. Many feel that their industry should dictate their time frame. For example, it can take decades to discover and commercialize a new drug or oil well, whereas it only takes a year, or even less, for trends to change in the clothing and toy businesses.

But most leaders tend to pick a time frame that feels natural to them— three or five years. Or they land on a calendar milestone that's just ahead. For example, in the mid-1990s, "Strategy 2000" was a common choice; a few years ago, "2020 Strategy" was a favorite. Or leaders may choose a time frame based on a milestone that's specific to their company. I know of one 80-year-old company whose board has asked management to develop a 20-year strategy in anticipation of its 100th year of operation.

If that feels too far "out there," consider the example of Ingvar Kamprad, the late founder of IKEA, the world's largest furniture retailer. He once reportedly said to a group of managers that it was important to "think about where [we should] be in 200 years." As the story goes, the managers asked Kamprad if that wasn't too much time. "Yes, of course," he responded, "but then you make the short-term plan: That means the next 100 years."

But giving strategy a time frame, *a priori*, is the wrong way around. Instead, the time frame should depend on the strategy. To be clear, "What time frame should we have for our strategy?" is the wrong question. The better question is, "What changes does our strategy need, and how much time do we need to implement them?" In other words, leaders have a five-year strategy if the changes they want to make to their strategy will take five years to implement. IKEA could someday devise a new strategy that would take 200 years to implement, but that seems a stretch. The better way to interpret Kamprad's guidance is that he wanted his leaders to be thinking far into the future as they considered the changes IKEA's strategy might need *today*.

All of this means that the right time frame for a strategy depends more on what changes leaders want to make to it than on the business they are in. For example, in 2014, Microsoft CEO Satya Nadella began replacing the foundation upon which the company's strategy had stood for 40 years (see chapter 20) by putting cloud computing (*Azure*) at the heart of its business and making its *Office* products suite available as a subscription service called "Office 365." Whether that's a three-year, 10-year, or even longer-term strategy depends more on how long it takes to realize the transition than on the business Microsoft is in.

Coming back to IKEA: At one point, its leaders found themselves considering two significant changes to the company's strategy. One was to offer customers the option of leasing their furniture rather than buying it. Perhaps they landed on this idea by trying to really look 200 years into the future and envisioning a world of prematurely discarded furniture clogging up our oceans and landfills. But rolling out a leasing strategy across all of its stores around the world—if that's what the company decides to do—would be a multiyear effort, not a multi-century one. So, it might be a five-year strategy informed by a 200-year perspective, but it's definitely not a two-century strategy. And whatever the time frame is, it's not all that dependent on IKEA's being in the furniture retail business. Businesses in many industries could choose to pivot toward a leasing or subscription model.

The second change leaders came together to consider is whether to enter a new business by building an e-commerce platform that would be available to both IKEA and other furniture retailers. Again, they may have peered ahead 200 years and concluded that the world would only have room for one online furniture retailing platform, and it might as well be them. But that doesn't make this potential change a 200-year strategy. Nor is the time frame for this strategy determined much by the industry in which IKEA operates.

To be clear, leaders should consider the long-term future when considering their strategy choices. But equating that to the time frame their strategies should have is a recipe for strategies that are merely a set of sweeping generalizations. Because the further out you look, the fuzzier things get.

Great strategies comprise sharply differentiating choices for *Who? Why?* and *What?* (see chapter 8). It's impossible to know with much specificity what these should be a decade from now. Imagine how much water will pass under the bridge between now and then, let alone over the next century. Yet it's also impossible to change overnight the essential elements of a strategy in any meaningful way (see chapter 39). Choosing a time frame that's too short will force leaders into a mode of incremental strategy, which is an excellent recipe for failing to keep pace with a changing world (see chapter 40).

The bottom line is that whether their business is in life sciences, oil, toys, clothing, furniture, or any other industry, leaders should set the time frame for their strategy choices based on what they can see and foresee with a high degree of confidence. What's happening right now that will require particular changes to our strategy and how long will it take to implement those changes? Anything else is arbitrary or, worse: an attempt to tie one's fate to a prediction of an unknowable future that will emerge in some predetermined amount of time.[1]

---

1   In the 1990s, the software guru Martin Fowler published his "CHAOS report" about the awful success rate of software projects. Some 90% came in late, and up to 40% or 50% completely failed. Fowler wrote that the cause wasn't a failure of the project itself, it was a failure of the chosen time frame—of the time it would take to complete the project. Many projects, such as Windows 95, created enormous value despite being very late, according to their original (arbitrary) timetable. But many failed because they were held hostage to a timetable that made them infeasible. You could say the same for many strategies.

(43)

Is strategy for winning customers or beating competitors?

Business is neither war nor sport.

The original concept of strategy comes from the Greek *strategia*, meaning "generalship." Its root definition is "the science and art of military command exercised to meet the enemy in combat under advantageous conditions." In business, if the enemy comprises competitors, then the objective of strategy must be to fight them all with an advantage, if not crush them entirely. Indeed, to this day, when business leaders are asked about their favorite business books, they will often include *The Art of War*, written by Sun Tzu in the 5th century B.C.

Michael Porter gave academic standing to this way of thinking when he popularized the idea of "competitive advantage" with his best-selling textbooks, *Competitive Strategy*, published in 1980, and *Competitive Advantage*, which came out in 1985 (see chapter 44). A decade later, Microsoft gave corporate life to this "crush your competition" version of strategy when CEO Bill Gates very publicly went after Netscape as the dot-com era was just heating up.

Today, we see military language and metaphors used everywhere in business: corporate "missions," competitive "maneuvers," price "wars," and market share "battles." There are sales "tactics," marketing "campaigns," product "launches," and promotional "blitzes." Companies have "front line" staff in the "trenches" and "bullet points" in their PowerPoint presentations.

Equating business strategy to winning a battle or winning a match turns business into a game where players compete to win by beating each other and claiming market "territory." In fact, one of the more popular strategy courses at top business schools is on game theory, and one of the more popular books on game theory is *The Art of Strategy* (an apparent play on Sun Tzu's book). In that book, the authors define game theory as the "emerging science of strategy," and they define strategy as "outdoing an adversary."

But whereas war and sport are mostly what game theorists define as a "zero-sum game"—for someone to win, someone else has to lose—business is definitely *not*. If business is a game, it is a "positive sum" one, where "winning" lifts everyone—growing the total pie, not just one player's piece of the pie at the expense of everyone else. Or as Marc Pritchard, Chief Brand Officer of Procter & Gamble, put it, "the best brands…help markets grow. They don't steal share from other brands, they make the entire market bigger…so all boats rise. Market growth through innovation and creativity is the best growth—it's good for consumers, retailers, suppliers, employees, partners, economies, and communities."

This is not altruism; it's simply good business. Companies are disproportionately rewarded when they create new benefits for customers and new growth for everyone else. For instance, no one benefited more than Pan Am from its early adoption of the jet airliner, but that move also expanded the market for all airlines. The iPhone didn't just make Apple a leader in smartphones; it also greatly expanded the market for mobile voice and data telephony. Sierra Nevada's Pale Ale made it the first national—even global—brewer of craft beer while simultaneously reviving the market for premium beer. Thanks in large part to novelties such as the Frappuccino, Starbucks became a global icon in less than 20 years; but it also created millions of new customers for a slew of premium coffee purveyors like Blank Street Coffee in New York; Intelligentsia in Chicago; Blue Bottle Coffee in Oakland, California; and Blue Island Coffee in Dallas. And George Mitchell—seen by many as the father of fracking— injected new life into the U.S. oil-and-gas industry that benefited hundreds of companies, not just his own entrepreneurial efforts. In each case, creating new value for customers expanded the pie for everyone while giving the company a bigger slice of the pie. Business need not be a zero-sum game because there's no limit to creating new customer value.

On the other hand, when leaders think of business as a "war" with their competitors, they inevitably seek to beat their rivals in ways that don't meaningfully enhance customer-perceived benefits—such as with me-too products, product-feature frenzy, or predatory pricing. Such moves rarely grow the total market and almost always produce lower margins and losing products. This is what happened when GM and Ford engaged in a market-share war with the Japanese in the late 1970s and 1980s; when the mainstream airlines tried to beat JetBlue, Southwest Airlines, and Ryan Air with their own discount airlines (Delta's Song, United's Ted, and Air France's Joon); and when Airbus sunk billions into the gigantic A380 plane in order to attack Boeing's profit stream from the 747.

When strategy is about competitors, leaders lose focus on the unlimited opportunities to grow customer value. Even the revered Steve Jobs made a big mistake when he declared "thermonuclear war" on Google, pledged to destroy the Android operating system, and subsequently introduced Apple's own version of Google Maps, a clearly inferior product whose only real purpose was to inflict harm on the competition. His customers revolted, his successor was forced to apologize, and Apple's halo became a bit dimmer for a while.

Whereas making strategy about competitors can be highly destructive, making it about the *customer* encourages leaders to find ways to win without having to pay the price for their victories. Amazon is a popular example of an obsessive focus on the customer. A favorite mantra of its founder, Jeff Bezos, is: "Our customers are loyal right up to the second a competitor offers [something] better." Bezos intuitively understands that the greater the benefit Amazon can provide to customers, the more likely it can be profitable in the future on an enormous scale. Sooner or later, high customer benefit translates into high willingness to pay, and that's how companies earn their growth rather than having to subsidize it. Put another way, the more that leaders enhance the *Why?* of their products and services, the more willing customers are to pay for their company's growth.

Does this mean that leaders can ignore competitors when it comes to strategy? Of course not. Go back to that Bezos quote above. Again, he intuitively understands that customers are always judging a company's proposition relative to their perceived alternatives (see chapter 13). Understanding competitors' promised benefits is one effective way to generate new thinking on how to improve your own. For example, JetBlue systematically studied traditional airline offerings and what customers liked, disliked, and didn't care about them. This led to a strategy of "focus on what really matters [to our *Who?*]." Out went free meals and first-class seating. In came media consoles for every passenger; comfortable leather upholstery with more legroom for every seat; and multiple healthy or even indulgent food options for purchase. The idea was to give a "premium travel experience at a discount price." Fliers love it and have helped JetBlue penetrate a highly competitive market with formidable incumbents that have decades more operating experience.

As an inherently competitive species, we humans are greatly tempted to think of business as war or sport where one's gains can only come at the expense of our rivals—where winning means the other guy is losing. Or as Genghis Khan is often quoted as saying: "It is not enough that I succeed. Everyone else must fail."

Indeed, "Beat Coke" is a highly-motivating rallying cry if you are Pepsi, or "Buy Detroit" if you are Chrysler, or a "Wage Holy War with Google" if you are Apple. But such "strategies" will only be successful if they spur their organizations to bring a more compelling promise of benefits to their primary customers—especially if that grows the total market, not just one's share of it.

So, let's be clear: Business is *not* war or sport. Strategy in business is different than strategy in those two arenas. It's about winning customers, not beating competitors. It entails the choices for which only leaders can be responsible (see chapters 2 and 3); being specific and differentiating with those choices (chapter 8); and having a big idea to power those choices (chapter 9). It's that simple… and that difficult.

44

Is competitive advantage the central aim of strategy?

A potentially dangerous concept that's hard to pin down

In the early 1980s, Michael E. Porter, a professor at Harvard Business School, published two seminal books on business strategy: *Competitive Strategy* in 1980, and *Competitive Advantage* in 1985. In these books Porter puts four stakes in the ground:

1. The aim of strategy is "to establish a profitable and sustainable position in an industry."
2. This requires a "sustainable competitive advantage."
3. There are three types of advantage: cost leadership (enabling a lower price), differentiation (justifying a higher price), or focus (targeting a "segment" within an industry).
4. Strategy demands a decisive choice between cost leadership, differentiation, and focus.

Some thirty years later, in 2013, Rita Gunther McGrath, a Columbia Business School professor, published *The End of Competitive Advantage*. In her book she drives a different set of stakes into the ground:

A. "Sustainable competitive advantages have become a thing of the past."

B. Companies need to practice "continuous reconfiguration and disengagement."
C. This means "investing in new advantages and pulling resources from declining ones."
D. The goal of strategy is to "capture territory" and "maximize share of potential opportunity areas."
E. Strategy is a choice of what "arenas" in which to compete and of "the job to be done" for customers in those arenas.

Both McGrath and Porter cast "business" as a competitive game (McGrath likens it to the Japanese game GO), view "advantage" as being necessary to win the game, and consider "strategy" as being the choices leaders must make to gain an advantage—or to refresh or replace it over time.

The problem is, when leaders think of business as a game or military battle to be won, they tend to obsess over beating competitors. That can be highly destructive and lead to bad strategy (see chapter 43).

Moreover, while the concept of "competitive advantage" is intuitively easy to understand, it's really hard to pin down. Is it having a higher market share? If so, what's the market? LEGO chief executive Niels Christiansen describes his main toy business as having to compete for the time kids spend on video-games, YouTube, and other "digital distractions." Is LEGO the world's largest toy company or a medium-sized player in entertainment for kids? Bud Light has been the top-selling beer in America since 2001, and until recently (when it fell behind the Mexico beer brand Modelo), it had an enormous market share "advantage" over every other beer. Yet its sales volume has been falling for years. That's because Bud Light competes with more alternatives than just other beer brands—like hard seltzers, hard iced tea, hard liquor, and craft beer—that have been gaining ground.

Leaders have a lot of leeway when defining their market and share of it, and they will often use that wiggle room to put their companies in the best light possible. For example, The Boots Company, a pharmacy chain in the U.K., has seemingly forever been the leading retailer of health and beauty products in that country. Its leaders were taken aback when they saw a presentation from an executive at Superdrug, a U.K. retailer with a mix of pharmacy and nonpharmacy stores, in which he claimed that his company was the biggest seller of health and beauty products *through stores without a pharmacy.*

If market share isn't the way to think of competitive advantage, perhaps relative profitability is. This is how Michael Porter defines it in *Competitive Advantage*: a company is competitively advantaged if it has higher return on investment (ROI) than others in its industry. But again, "industry" defined how? With the advent of online video, are CBS, Google (YouTube), Apple (iPhone with Apple+), and Microsoft (Xbox in the cloud) in one industry or four? Having acquired Time Warner (rechristened Warner Media and then sold off shortly thereafter), should AT&T have measured itself against Verizon, Comcast, or Disney? If a company has the highest ROI in carbonated soft drinks, but these are losing out to energy beverages, bottled water, and coffee concoctions, does it have a competitive advantage in the "nonalcoholic drinks industry"? And what if a company has a higher ROI, but lower growth than others in its industry? Does it really have a competitive advantage, or is it just setting a higher price than others and giving up some volume in pursuit of more-attractive margins?

Nailing down competitive advantage is problematic because it's a relative concept. By definition, it involves leaders' arbitrarily choosing a particular measure—relative market share, relative growth or profitability, relative stock price multiple of earnings, relative shareholder returns, or some other measure—to compare their company to a group of companies that those leaders decide are in their competitor set. This can lead to what Theodore Levitt, a former professor at Harvard Business School, called "marketing myopia" in a famous article he wrote for *Harvard Business Review* in 1960. Levitt argued that leaders' field of vision is dangerously limited when they define their market and competitors too narrowly. As a result, they'll fail to see challenges coming out of left field and will miss out on opportunities to stretch or innovate their strategy (see chapters 18 and 21).

In Levitt's article, he cited railroads as an example of his thesis. He wrote that they fell into steep decline because they thought they were in the *train* business rather than the *transportation* business. As new forms of transportation like cars and planes took hold, the railroads let other companies seize those opportunities and steal away their passengers.[1] Looking ahead, Levitt warned that the big oil companies might experience a similar fate. They're in the "energy business," he argued, not fossil fuels, and so they'd better pay attention to alternative forms of energy that could undermine their core product (yes, he wrote that in 1960!). Today, he might point to the blurring of boundaries between traditional retail, online retail, and online auction sites. Or between television, telecommunications, and computers.

Rita McGrath echoes Levitt when she argues that "the most substantial threats to a given advantage are likely to arise from a peripheral or nonobvious location." Both she and Levitt remind us that, to spot challenges and opportunities for their strategy before it's too late, leaders should look far and wide at the strategies, innovations, actions, and performance of any and all companies—competitors or not—operating in *any* sphere (see chapter 21).

It may feel heretical, but when it comes to strategy, leaders should put aside the notion of competitive advantage. The aim of strategy is to build, sustain, and grow a thriving base of customers who are willing to pay for, use, and then recommend their company's products and services. Moreover, no strategy can stand still (see chapters 39 and 40). Thus, leaders should regularly revisit two questions:

- Is our strategy still underpinned by a big idea that remains a big one (see chapter 16)?
- Are our strategy choices still sharp and differentiating enough (see chapter 8) to foster effective implementation and excellent execution (see chapter 29)?

When the answer to both questions is *Yes*, leaders can be confident that their strategy is still a great one. But these questions are dynamic. The world and a company's place in it are constantly changing. A *Yes* to each question can become a *No*—sometimes abruptly, at other times imperceptibly.

Leaders must challenge, stretch, and innovate their strategy to maintain a *Yes* to those two questions above. That's how they sustain a great strategy. And while a great strategy is insufficient on its own, it's absolutely necessary for sustained success (see chapter 26)—and, dare I say, for sustainable competitive advantage, too.

---

1   While Levitt's warning to leaders about defining their business too narrowly is still relevant, they need to be careful about the other extreme. Being in the "transportation business" doesn't qualify a company to be in just any transportation-related business. It depends on its big idea, its distinctive capabilities, and which businesses fit best with those capabilities.

45

Is splitting up a strategy?

Or the result of a failed one?

In 2013, after a lifetime of corporate empire-building, Rupert Murdoch split News Corporation into two companies: one running its publishing properties, and another—named 21st Century Fox—holding its entertainment entities. Such events are usually heralded with messages like Murdoch's proclamation that the split would "unlock the true value" of News Corp's assets because "they are undervalued…." But there's usually much more to the story than that.

Corporate divorces are a bit like earthquakes: We know they'll happen; we just can't know exactly when or where. And they unfold in much the same way that earthquakes do: Pressures build over time until they are released by some triggering event that catalyzes a fracturing of the status quo.

Disappointing shareholder returns are often the source of pressure for companies to split. For example, in 2020, Dell Technologies announced that it was considering a spin-off of its multibillion-dollar stake in VMWare, the cloud-computing company it acquired when it bought data storage maker EMC in 2016. The reason, as described by *Financial Times,* was "to address a valuation shortfall that has plagued the company for years." That shortfall led to shareholder returns falling considerably lower than both the NASDAQ and S&P averages, and hence the perceived imperative to do something about it.

Once such pressure is great enough, all that's needed is a trigger to release it. This can be anything from a bad acquisition to an activist investor's taking a material shareholding, or a succession problem, or a power struggle, or any number of other things. For News Corp, the trigger was the phone-hacking and police-bribery scandal at its *News of the World* newspaper in the U.K. This was the "butterfly flapping its wings" that set off a chain reaction leading to the company's splitting up.

But pressures and triggers don't cause corporate divorce any more than they cause earthquakes. They are symptoms that emerge from deeper systemic factors. To be sure, companies change strategies all the time, and sometimes this makes formerly indispensable businesses suddenly expendable. Still, the more-common cause of splitting up is the lack of great multibusiness strategies (see chapter 3).

When a company's businesses are underperforming, they are likely suffering from some combination of negative synergies between them (channel conflict, resource competition, and so forth), an oppressive corporate center (dysfunctional bureaucratic processes that add little real benefit, wrong-headed one-size-fits-all compensation systems, poorly informed strategy guidance, top-down goal-driven "strategies," and more), plus a lack of distinctive enterprise-level capabilities that give each business a genuine edge in its respective markets.

And when a company's businesses are underperforming, then so is the company. This will inevitably lead to underwhelming shareholder returns, and that will ultimately raise questions about "the whole versus the sum of its parts." This forces companies into the argument that breaking up will "unlock" value. But will it?

Corporate divorce "unlocks value" only if investors expect it will lead to better performance from the company's individual businesses because they can do better either as independent entities or within some other company.

Take the 2005 split of Viacom into CBS and the "new Viacom." The old Viacom had no enterprise capabilities that were particularly important to its subsidiary CBS, and it had a bad habit of draining cash flow from that network to fund Viacom's programming businesses. CBS did indeed perform much better, once it was freed of the negative effects of old Viacom's internal governance. If breaking up old Viacom "released value," it wasn't because its businesses were undervalued relative to the performance they were able to achieve inside old Viacom. It was because CBS was able to perform better outside of Viacom, and thus deserved a higher valuation as a separate entity. The divorce was not a successful "strategy;" it was just the end of a bad strategy.

Coming back to News Corp, no multibusiness company is always firing on every cylinder all the time. Sooner or later, one of its major businesses will hit a big enough speed bump to slow the company down, and that will always bring out the calls for breaking it up. When that happens, leaders are left defenseless if they lack a sharply differentiating multibusiness strategy that gives them a compelling answer to "What makes your whole more than the sum of your parts?"[1]

Because News Corp lacked such a compelling multibusiness strategy, its split became inevitable when continuing underperformance of its businesses translated into chronically poor shareholder returns. All that was needed was a trigger to set things in motion. That turned out to be the phone-hacking/bribery scandal. When this broke, it empowered agitated investors to question News Corp's massive empire and all-powerful leader. Murdoch's hand was forced because he was unable to show tangible evidence of a strategy that was making a material, positive contribution to the performance of each business in his sprawling portfolio. He might have been right that splitting up would "unlock hidden value," but only because he lacked a strong-enough strategy to keep them together after scandal rocked the company. He would have been more accurate had he said that splitting the company would "unlock better performance" from the businesses parting ways. Though his corporate divorce may have been a good thing for shareholders, it was a financial-engineering tactic used in response to a bad strategy (see chapter 6).

And it didn't stop there. Six years later, in 2019, Murdoch went through *another* corporate divorce, this time selling off a big chunk of 21st Century Fox. To whom? Disney. Its CEO at the time, Bob Iger, was able to outbid everyone else for the film rights to properties including *X-Men*, *The Fantastic Four*, and others because those properties fit neatly into Disney's "corporate franchise" strategy (see chapters 3 and 8). Iger's distinctive multibusiness strategy enabled him to turn Murdoch's second corporate divorce into a marriage made in heaven for Disney.

Leaders should never stop asking "Are our businesses consistently outperforming in their respective markets, and if so, how much of that can be attributed to the company? If not, how much of that can be laid at the company's feet?" Chapter 15 gives leaders a way to address these questions with honesty and integrity. Such questions must be asked and answered when times are good. Once the pressures start to build, it's too late. The immediate interests of managers, investors, founders, and other stakeholders will be diverging ever more sharply. This is when companies are forced to split up.

News Corp is one example of the many corporate earthquakes that will continue to rumble around the world. New fault lines are building all the time for companies that lack robust multibusiness strategies. It's only a matter of time before they experience their own seismic event.

---

1   For the record, this is one of those questions that makes no sense when you think about it for more than a second. A "whole" is always exactly equal to the sum of its parts. What this question is really asking is: "Why are your businesses (the 'parts') able to perform better because they belong to your company (the 'whole') than if they were trading independently or belonged to some other company?" It doesn't trip off the tongue as easily, but it's the better way to frame the question.

46

Is cross-selling a strategy?

Or is it just putting the company before customers?

In 1981 the retail giant Sears bought both the residential real estate firm Coldwell Banker and the nationwide stockbroker Dean Witter Reynolds. Sears' vice-chairman at the time, Donald Craib, explained: "We're going to allow Coldwell and Dean Witter exposure to this tremendous customer base." The message was clear: Sears planned to "cross-sell" financial services to its retail customers. Eleven years later, this "strategy" was in shreds and both businesses were unloaded.

Then in 2016 Wells Fargo was fined almost $190 million for opening fake accounts and charging customers for them in order to meet sales quotas. This was the dark side of its much-admired ability to sell multiple products to existing customers—an aptitude that was the envy of retail banks around the world. Shortly thereafter, I received an investor letter from the CEO of a multibillion-dollar financial services company that's building out a larger product line for its current customers. In the letter, he wrote, "We have increased the number of cross-buy opportunities with our current customer base." He added, "Thanks to the bad press, I can no longer say 'cross-sell'!"

Almost overnight, "cross-selling" went from a ubiquitous practice imbued with positive connotations throughout the business world to a politically incorrect word that's redolent of corporate misbehavior. And that could be a wonderful thing if it causes companies to rethink their approach when they have more than one product for their customers.

Cross-selling is a concerted effort to sell multiple products to a company's current customers, and it's often accompanied by a goal to average some number of products sold per customer. That seems perfectly sensible. Why *shouldn't* leaders try to capture every part of a customer's wallet that is allocated to the kind of products their company offers? Many leaders think—or act as if they think—that promoting multiple products to the same group of customers leads to greater loyalty and lower selling costs. The problem is, it puts the cart before the horse: leaders' goals—more products per customer—ahead of the company's customers. As a result, cross-selling is not really a strategy at all and when it's conflated with one, trouble will follow sooner or later.

A customer buys multiple products (or services) from one company for only two possible reasons. One is because each product on its own provides the best benefits for the price. The benefits can be tangible (such as superior functionality, quality, and reliability) or intangible (brand, trustworthiness, status, and community). For instance, even though they come at a higher price, I purchase TaylorMade's driver and its golf balls because I think both are better for my game than alternative brands and, frankly, because Tiger Woods switched to them after Nike stopped making golf equipment. I don't purchase them because a salesperson from TaylorMade or one of its retail partners noticed that I bought its driver and pushed me to buy its golf balls as well.

In contrast, I hold a checking account with my particular bank because I can access it anywhere in the world, but I get wealth management services from a different company because its proposition is much better. Only a more compelling one from my bank would make me switch to its wealth management services, and no amount of cross-selling will change that.

The second reason a customer buys multiple products from the same company is that the combination itself yields some kind of a benefit, economic or otherwise. For example, as an iPhone user, I subscribe to Apple Music because of the convenience it affords me in buying, storing, sharing, and listening to music. I also have a savings account at my bank, in large part because the bank waives fees for my checking account when my savings balance meets a certain threshold. In other words, I buy multiple products from Apple for the benefit of convenience, and I hold more than one account at my bank for the benefit of cost savings, not because someone is cross-selling me.

With its foray into financial services, Sears utterly failed to create either of these two reasons—more compelling products in their own right, or a compelling bundle of products—for its retail customers to purchase its real estate and stock-broking services. In fact, it was worse than that: Dean Witter did *less* business in Sears' stores than it did in its own freestanding offices.

When leaders fall for cross-selling, they distract themselves from achieving the very outcome they want: their customers' buying all their company's products. Instead, they should stay focused on creating compelling propositions for each of their products, or for some combination of them, that will make their customers want to buy and pay for multiple products from their company. That comes from putting customers ahead of the company, and strategy before goals (see chapter 31). Pushing staff ever harder to foist more products on customers and meet some inevitably arbitrary target for products per customer is asking for trouble and will rarely work. That's why a recent study by McKinsey & Company found that fewer than 20% of companies achieved their cross-selling goals.

I recently received another letter from the CEO of that financial company I referred to above. In it he writes, "Our strategy is starting to play out…as [our customers] are showing strong demand for additional products with no incremental paid marketing…. [T]hese cross-buying activities are a result of organic behavior, given our integrated mobile app experience, as opposed to specific concerted efforts to cross-sell." At the very least, he has his language right.[1] You want your customers "cross-buying" because they find it in their interest to do so. The result is a triple win—greater customer loyalty, lower customer acquisition (and retention) costs, and, yes, more products bought per customer.

All of this goes to say that cross-selling is a result of having a good strategy in which cross-buying is motivated by a strong promise of benefits *and* the capabilities to back it up. At best, cross-selling is a plan for implementing such a strategy, not a substitute for it. For sure, leaders should know how many products their customers are buying, and compare their results to others'. But if they don't like what they see, leaders should worry about customer pull, not sales push. They should look outside, not inside. They should question the *Why?* for each of their products from the customer's perspective, then consider whether their sales and marketing are doing justice to them. Before trying sweeter carrots or harsher sticks to stoke more cross-sell, leaders should work on exactly how their customers benefit from buying multiple products from their company. Offering better propositions—with sharper, better customer-centric sales and marketing—is a more durable path to earning a greater share of customers' business and loyalty. As Amazon's founder, Jeff Bezos, liked to say, "Our customers are loyal right up to the second a competitor offers a better product."

---

1   Language is vitally important when one is leading an organization. Word choice matters. (No, this doesn't mean that leaders need a "Word Strategy"! See chapter 7.) "Cross-sell" and "cross-buy" may be aimed at the same outcome—multiple products per customer—but they suggest completely different ways of getting there. And one way is definitely better than the other.

47

When is diversification good strategy?

There are only two reasons to diversify, and neither is "diversification."

Diversification is often presented as a strategy choice: Should we have more or less of it? It's an unfortunate framing of the choice, because it can put companies on a time-wasting merry-go-round. For every CEO who touts her strategy to create a laser-focused company by narrowing its range of businesses, there's a successor waiting in the wings to launch a new era of growth and expansion by adding new businesses to his company's portfolio. And for every CEO attributing strength and stability to his company's wide-ranging portfolio, there's a future leader ready to usher in a period of what they tout as "focused profitability and growth."

Take Coca-Cola. Facing stalled growth in the 1960s and '70s, the company pursued a "strategy" of diversification—even going so far as to purchase Columbia Pictures in 1982. Only a few years later, management decided to "focus" by exiting "non-core" businesses (Coke sold its last stake in Columbia Pictures in 1989), which worked beautifully for its soft drinks business. A few decades later, the soft drinks business stalled again, so the company's leadership sought diversification into new businesses such as chilled juices, water, energy and sports drinks, retail coffee beverages, and potentially even "hard" carbonated beverages. "And around and around we go."

The good news, though, is that diversification—even the extreme kind—works well when leaders have instituted a strong multibusiness strategy (see chapters 3 and 8). That requires many leaders to rethink their notion of diversification and reasons for seeking it.

What really matters is not how broad or narrow a company's range of businesses is. What's critical is how its businesses materially benefit from the company's distinctive capabilities that make it better than any other at its particular way of contributing to the future earnings power of each business in its portfolio.

Even a narrow company operating in highly related markets can fail this test. Think of oil-&-gas companies, with their portfolios of exploration, production, refining, and retailing businesses, all from the same industry. Few if any of these companies have capabilities that are both distinctive and relevant to every one of those businesses. Although their portfolios comprise businesses operating in highly related markets, each business requires very different capabilities to win in its own particular market. That's why you see many successful "pure play" specialists in each market. And that why it's nearly impossible for the leaders of broad-based oil-&-gas companies to build a coherent handful of enterprise capabilities that confer real advantage to every one of these businesses.

An opposite case can be made about a broad company whose businesses compete in unrelated markets yet benefit a lot from being under its corporate roof. For example, as explained in chapters 3 and 8, most businesses in Berkshire Hathaway's empire benefit tremendously from its unique set of three mutually reinforcing corporate capabilities; Danaher deliberately goes after businesses that can benefit the most from its famous "Danaher Business System"; and The Walt Disney Company is a highly diversified media and entertainment company with a sharply distinctive multibusiness strategy. All three companies could be (and often are) called "conglomerates" because they own an enormous range of businesses operating in seemingly unrelated product markets. But they are highly focused in how they contribute to their businesses and also in which businesses fit best with that.

With this perspective in mind, there are only two reasons to diversify. The first is to use a company's particular way of benefiting its businesses and its distinctive capabilities to generate new avenues for profitable growth. This is what Berkshire, Danaher, and Disney are usually doing when they acquire a new business. They are *not* doing it for the reasons that too many other companies diversify: to enter "attractive" markets in order to improve their financial profile (higher growth rate, better margins, or lower volatility of earnings). This is financial engineering, not strategy, and it usually leads to trouble (see chapter 6).

The second reason is to strengthen one or more of a company's current businesses, by enhancing either their customer propositions or their leading capabilities. Disney's 2006 acquisition of Pixar is a great example of the latter because it addressed a hole in the capabilities of Disney's original business of animated-film making. This is the business that creates many of the characters that feed Disney's other businesses. It's the glue that holds the company together as well as the grease that lubricates its "corporate franchises" strategy. But the emergence of digital technology threatened this essential business, when companies like Pixar were able to drastically reduce the cost of animation and enhance what it could do. So, although Disney brought a lot to Pixar, Pixar helped Disney fortify a distinctive capability that brings economic coherence to its massive entertainment complex.

LEGO is an example of how diversification can enhance the customer propositions of businesses already in a company's portfolio. The company has had two big diversification drives in its recent history. The first, which ended in the early 2000s, was motivated by financial engineering (see chapter 6) and nearly bankrupted the company. The second started around 2004. This time around, every new area that LEGO entered—amusement parks, education, virtual model construction, movies, and more recently *LEGO Masters*, a TV game show—has helped to increase the engagement of children and adults with its original toy business, which was based on those ubiquitous plastic colored building blocks. The company had few capabilities to bring to these new businesses, but "diversifying" into them did wonders for LEGO's original business and for the company overall. It is now the world's largest toymaker by sales and profits, after having been on the brink of failure a little under two decades ago.

Alibaba, the online commerce giant in China, gives us an example of how diversification can enhance both the customer propositions and leading capabilities for a company's current businesses. It created Alipay for its e-commerce platforms—Taobao and Tmall—to provide a much-needed service to both buyers and sellers, and to help foster trust between them. Then, to exploit its transactions and user data capability, Alibaba launched a credit-rating system for its merchants and consumers through its financial services arm, Ant Financial. Information from that rating system allowed Ant Financial to issue short-term consumer and merchant loans with very low default rates. With those loans, consumers can purchase more products on Alibaba's e-commerce platforms, and in turn Alibaba's merchants can fund more inventory. Thus, each business makes every other business in Alibaba's corporate portfolio a better one for their respective customers.

When leaders identify the right reasons for diversifying, their moves to grow beyond their current business are much less likely to put them on the merry-go-round and turn their CEO's office door into a turnstile. Instead of diversifying *away from* their base, they'll diversify *for it*. Instead of diversifying to improve their company's financial profile, they'll diversify because it fortifies the businesses they already have. And instead of diluting what makes their company great, they'll enhance it.

48

When is vertical integration good strategy?

Why be your own supplier or customer?

Vertical integration comes in two forms. One is upstream (or backward) integration, where a company becomes its own supplier. For example, Delta Airlines "backward-integrated" when it bought a refinery to become its own supplier of jet fuel for its passenger planes. In another instance, the maker of Nutella—Ferrero—did the same when it bought a Turkish company that processes hazelnuts to supply the precious ingredient in the company's world-famous chocolate spread.

The second form of vertical integration is downstream (or forward) integration. This is the case when a company becomes its own customer. For example, Eileen Fisher, a maker of women's clothing, counts Nordstrom and Bloomingdale's as its customers, but the company also runs its own chain of shops. Exxon Mobile's gas stations are customers of its refinery business, which in turn is a customer of its exploration and production operations.

Vertical integration was common in the early part of last century. Companies sought security by moving upstream to control the means of production that supplied their main business, and swam downstream to ensure their path to market. For example, 100 years ago Ford owned rubber plantations, coal and iron ore mines, and even railways. And oil companies built their own network of gas stations to facilitate demand for their downstream (and upstream) products.

In the late 1960s and early '70s, vertical integration largely fell out of favor when conglomeration became fashionable. In fact, many industries underwent vertical disintegration. Today, for example, almost three-quarters of the parts going into American cars are sourced from third parties outside the United States. In the computer industry, companies once made the memory and processing chips and wrote the operating and applications software for the computers they manufactured and sold. Now, third-party specialists in chip making, software development, and hardware assembly dominate the industry. And although the largest energy companies still find oil in the deep sea, process it in their refineries, and sell it to Jane Doe at her corner gas station, the oil industry now has "pure play" companies in each stage of its value chain. For a while, it seemed as though vertical integration was a thing of the past.

Still, vertical integration is alive and well, including in Silicon Valley, where it's been given two new labels: the "full-stack business model" and "owning the value chain." Some tech companies are migrating upstream, like Netflix and Amazon, both entering the original programming business. Others are integrating downstream, such as BYD, the Chinese company that started out as a manufacturer of batteries and then moved downstream into electric car production to become Tesla's main competitor in China.

Some tech companies are vertically integrated in both directions, such as Apple, which owns and operates a retail chain to sell its own products and which also manufactures its own computer chips. In the same vein, Tesla integrated downstream through bypassing traditional third-party dealerships and setting up its own network of outlets to sell its cars directly to the consumer. It also integrated upstream by building battery plants to supply the energy source for its cars.

Many non-tech companies are also pursuing vertical integration. Here are some prominent examples:

- Disney integrated downstream when it cancelled its business with Netflix and set up its own streaming channel, Disney+.
- LEGO forward-integrated by setting up its own LEGO-branded stores to penetrate new markets like China and India, and also to mitigate the bankruptcy of retailer Toys "R" Us (a major seller of LEGO products).
- AT&T vertically integrated in the opposite direction (upstream) by

buying Time Warner (rechristened WarnerMedia and since sold off) to produce its own content for distribution through its cell phone, streaming, and satellite TV services.

- Likewise, Harry's, a U.S. company that sells men's razors and shaving cream by monthly subscription, acquired a factory in Germany to make its razor blades.
- Warby Parker, the eyewear company, did something similar by building a 34,000-square-foot optical lab to manufacture its own glasses instead of paying external manufacturers.
- Starbucks was described by Howard Schultz, its long-time CEO, as embracing "vertical integration to the extreme," because it buys and roasts all its own coffee and sells it through entirely company-owned stores.
- There's even a movement by some pension funds to bypass private equity firms and set up their own private equity operations.

Are all these modern forms of vertical integration *good* strategies? The answer is *yes* if both of two special conditions are met. The first is a "market failure" that is hurting a company's business. The most common types are supply risk, demand risk, and profiteering. The second condition is having the wherewithal to fix the market failure.

Netflix, for example, backward-integrated into programming, because its leaders felt that the cost per hour viewed is reduced significantly by producing its own series in-house, such as *House of Cards,* instead of licensing all its content from third parties. In effect, Netflix leaders determined that the content providers are overcharging.

Similarly, some pension managers who have set up their own private equity offices are forward-integrating to avoid what they consider to be excessive fees from private equity firms.

In short, Netflix and some pension managers are entering a new business that's in direct competition with those for whom that business is their focus. If their moves show sustained success, we will know that there really *was* profiteering going on. If they fail, they will learn that companies have to pay up for things that are not so easy to replicate on their own.[1]

Starbucks and Ferrero are examples of upstream integration to manage supply risk. Starbucks buys and roasts its own coffee because it does not trust suppliers to provide the quality it requires. Ferrero broke its long-standing refusal of M&A to buy a hazelnut producer because it feared a disruption in sourcing the essential ingredient in its most important product.

These two companies are among the world's biggest buyers of coffee and hazelnuts, respectively. Thus, they have the firepower to be their own suppliers of the core commodities they need to feed their main businesses. If they are right about their supply risk, their vertical integration will indeed be a critical ingredient to their continued success. But if they are wrong, it'll prove to be just an unnecessary complication of their business model.

The Apple and LEGO examples illustrate vertical integration to manage another kind of market failure: demand risk. Against the Apple board's initial reluctance, CEO Steve Jobs pushed the company into building its own stores, trying to get the message across that its computers are different than the generic Microsoft-based PCs and, later, attempting to ensure that all its products are displayed, sold, and supported in a manner consistent with Apple's brand values. Jobs simply didn't trust other retailers to do that.

Likewise, LEGO expanded its store chain to offset the loss of demand through Toys "R" Us and to build demand from a new set of customers in China and India.

Because their main businesses are so dominant, both Apple and LEGO can afford to forward-integrate into a very different business that's not all that profitable for the incumbents. But this strategy will become dangerously expensive if their main businesses were ever to lose their strongholds.

In a fascinating juxtaposition, BYD forward-integrated—from battery making to car production—in order to secure volume and margin for its original business. Tesla has done the opposite by backward integrating into battery production to mitigate perceived risk in the supply and cost of the most critical component in its products. (Interestingly, CEO Elon Musk has even suggested the idea that he might invest in lithium mining to guarantee a ready supply of the key ingredient in car batteries.)

Vertical integration is good strategy if it mitigates a market failure that really exists and if the company has sufficient weight and capabilities to enter its suppliers' or customers' business. But some companies vertically integrate where there is no market failure—where the market between suppliers and customers is highly competitive and the laws of demand and supply work efficiently. That's just diversification, which is fine if it's the result of a well-conceived multibusiness strategy (see chapters 3 and 47).

Sadly, vertical integration is often driven by an ill-conceived notion that a company could avoid the profit margin embedded in the price charged by its suppliers--or capture the margin earned by its customers--without having to earn a return on the capital and replicate the special capabilities that justify those margins. That's just bad strategy.

---

1   Judging by content dollars per Emmy won, the jury is decidedly out for Netflix. For example, according to VideoWeek and STATISTA, Netflix spends almost three times more per award-winning show than HBO Max. Meanwhile, Disney is learning that streaming is a difficult business and that its content-creation capabilities alone may not be enough to succeed in it.

49

What about horizontal integration?

Why be bigger and broader?

Horizontal integration consists of purchasing companies that serve the same customers or same kind of customers as the acquirer. There are two types of such integration. The first is corporate consolidation (sometimes referred to as a "roll-up" when it involves multiple acquisitions). This means buying or merging with a company that offers the same or similar products and services, such as Marriott International's purchasing of Starwood Hotels. Another example is Uber's attempt to buy Grubhub and combine it with Uber Eats in order to leapfrog DoorDash and become the biggest meal delivery service.

The second kind of horizontal integration is range expansion, meaning acquiring or combining with one or more companies that sell different products and services to the same or similar customers. Proctor & Gamble's 2005 acquisition of Gillette is an example. Both companies sell their products through grocery chains, convenience stores, pharmacy retailers, and the like. By acquiring Gillette, P&G materially expanded its range of products sold to those customers.

Many motives encourage horizontal integration and a lot of them lead to bad strategy. Perhaps the most common motive is to gain pricing power over customers or purchasing power over suppliers, or both. For example, the ride-hailing service Didi merged with Kuaidi, its domestic rival in China. It then engaged in a fierce price war with Uber to successfully force its American competitor out of the Chinese market. And soon thereafter, Didi exploited its dominant market position by reducing subsidies to drivers and riders.

Most leaders would love to have such power. But having it rarely benefits their companies for long. It can breed arrogance or complacency, bring costly regulatory scrutiny, and turn customers and suppliers into fair-weather friends eager for an alternative. These are no conditions for long-term success.

In open, market-based economies with level playing fields and well-functioning governments (I know…!), someone or something will eventually work to dilute a company's monopoly-like power. That could be government forcing companies like the original Standard Oil and AT&T to break up, and threatening to do the same with Facebook, Google, Amazon, and Apple.

Technology advancements can also loosen the grip of powerful incumbents. Personal computing upended IBM's dominance in computer manufacturing. Content streaming is currently eroding the power of cozy oligopolies in broadcast and cable TV. And ride-sharing services booked over the internet is fracturing local-taxi monopolies.

If government intervention or technological innovation don't do the trick, strategy innovations ultimately will. Decades ago, Nucor's mini-mills eviscerated the power of integrated steel makers. More recently, Harry's Shave Club's subscription service created cracks in Gillette's dominance (see chapter 63) while Warby Parker's approach to selling eyewear is doing the same to Lenscrafter and EssilorLuxoticca. In the airlines industry, Southwest Airlines' point-to-point innovation checks the pricing power of the dominant hub-and-spoke carriers—American, United, and Delta. And in China, upstarts from Meituan, Gaode Map, and Ctrip did to Didi what Didi did to Uber, by charging drivers less than half of Didi's commission and, in Gaode's case, nothing at all! In the end, Didi's power-driven corporate consolidation failed and did nothing for the sustainability of its business model. Meanwhile, new ride-hailing competitors are popping up in all of Uber's major markets—like Juno and Via in New York City—and chipping away at its pricing and purchasing power over passengers and drivers, respectively.

Didi and Uber are examples of what happens when leaders pursue strategies that depend on monopoly-like market power to be profitable. The profitability of their business models is crushed when that power is eventually taken away from them, either by the invisible hand of creative destruction or by the visible one of political intervention.

If the first misguided motivation for horizontal integration is to gain market power, the second one is to generate more revenue from existing customers. This spurred Sears' acquisition of both Coldwell Banker and Dean Witter Reynolds in 1981, as well as United Airline's purchase of Hertz in 1985. In each case, the idea was to cross-sell the acquired company's services to the acquiring company's existing customers, and vice versa.

This cross-sell motivation for horizontal integration effectively puts a company and its goals (of more revenue from existing customers) ahead of its customers and strategy. And it almost always leads to bad strategy (see chapters 31 and 46), which inevitably has to be fixed with horizontal *dis*integration.

Sure enough, Sears offloaded Coldwell and Dean Witter a decade after buying them, and a mere two years after United acquired Hertz, it sold the car rental company to Ford (which turned out to be yet another failed horizontal integration).

Clearly, cross-sell and market power are dangerous motivations for horizontal integration. This raises the question: is there any *good* motive for horizontal integration? The answer is *yes*, and it's this: *to get better for customers*. Both corporate consolidation and range expansion work best when they are the means to this end.

For example, from a standing start, Bob Walter made Cardinal Health a Fortune 50 company in about two decades, by rolling up local and regional drug distributors. When he started, the distribution of medicines was well established, but it was also highly fragmented geographically. This made the sourcing of prescription drugs exceedingly complex for nationalizing pharmacy retailers and regionalizing hospital groups.

Walter had a big idea to solve that problem. He called it the "prime vendor model," whereby Cardinal would aggregate the supply of drugs from the pharmaceutical manufacturers on behalf of a pharmacy retailer or hospital group. This brought much-needed rationalization of a fractured system and, most important of all, it supported a compelling proposition for both manufacturers and buyers of pharmaceuticals.

Corporate consolidation is good strategy when acquiring a company that provides the same product or service enables the acquirer to enhance its proposition—or its capabilities to market, sell, and live it. If customers don't benefit in some way, this form of horizontal integration won't work for long. The consolidated entity is just getting bigger, not better.

Something similar can be said about the other form of horizontal integration: range expansion. For this to be more than simply getting broader, it has to enhance the proposition a company already offers to its customers. For example, when IKEA acquired TaskRabbit, the handyman site, and Best Buy bought Geek Squad, the technical assistance firm, both organizations broadened their service offering in ways that materially enhanced the proposition of consumers visiting their stores and websites. Best Buy became a much more attractive place to buy sophisticated computer and other such products when its leaders horizontally integrated into the provision of technical assistance. Likewise, by adding a handyman service to its offering, IKEA's leaders mitigated a big negative—the hassle of assembling its products at home—for many people, thus making it a better place to go for home furnishings.

The drive to get bigger and broader through horizontal integration is a powerful one because leaders, boards, and shareholders alike want growth and the market power that comes with it. Still, customers don't care about a company's size or breadth unless it materially benefits them. Again, the best motivation for horizontal integration is *to get better for customers*. With that front and center, leaders will make better choices about horizontal integration, whether it's corporate consolidation or range expansion. Getting bigger and broader is the icing on the cake.

PART IX

Who Should Have What Role in Strategy?

There can be many cooks in the strategy kitchen, and that's a recipe for chaos.

50

What role should the corporate center have in strategy?

When "corporate" is worth more than its trouble

The "business unit" structure for organizational design gained momentum in the 1980s and is now used by most companies. Business units are organizational entities within a company, each of which has profit-and-loss responsibility. Organizing around business units gave rise to the idea of a "corporate center." This houses a range of staff functions that operate outside the business units, such as Finance, HR, IT, Legal, and M&A. It can also include operating functions like sales, marketing, R&D, manufacturing, and procurement that provide "shared services" to multiple business units.

The size and breadth of a company's corporate center—its number of people and range of activities—is a good barometer of how centralized or decentralized the company is. Berkshire Hathaway, a conglomerate with a multi-hundred-billion-dollar market value, is known to be highly decentralized (at least at the highest level of the company). Warren Buffett, its long-serving CEO, often boasts that Berkshire has only 25 people in its corporate headquarters. Other companies of similar scale might employ many thousands, often spread across multiple locations around a country, a continent, or the world.

A corporate center can fill many responsibilities, including the provision of services to business units, such as managing receivables, payables, reporting, and payroll; auditing the company's books; ensuring regulatory compliance; creating the company's quarterly and annual accounting statements; and much more. It might also be charged with running "strategic initiatives" that reflect enterprise-wide priorities—for example, to modernize its digital capabilities, adopt new techniques such as Lean Six Sigma and design thinking, or integrate a large acquisition.

Sadly, many business unit leaders love to loathe "corporate" (the corporate center) as a dead weight of unaccountable, administrative functionaries who tax the "real" engines of the company with onerous compliance requirements, excessive monitoring, redundant reporting, countless initiatives, endless meetings, intrusive staff, and bloated cost structures that are insulated from the disciplines of market competition.

Indeed, research conducted by Dominic Dodd, co-author of *The Three Tensions,* suggests that their skepticism is not so far off the mark: the rate of corporate centers that fail to justify their costs is over 55%. (See "Whole vs. Parts," chapter 4 of his book.) This high failure rate is explained by two problems. The first is lack of a compelling multibusiness strategy (see chapter 3); and the second is poor alignment of the corporate center's priorities, activities, and even attitude with such a strategy.

The acid test for a multibusiness company is whether its businesses are consistently outperforming in their respective markets primarily because the benefits they gain from being under that company's corporate roof exceed the costs (see chapter 15). The multibusiness strategy that leaders follow for their company should spell out what these benefits should be and which enterprise-level capabilities they should prioritize and actively nurture so they can be better than any other company at bringing those benefits to their individual businesses. The most important role of the corporate center, then, is to help company leaders implement that strategy.

To state the obvious, for the corporate center to play that role effectively, the company's leaders must pursue a multibusiness strategy that is clear to both the corporate center's leaders *and* their staff. To test this, I will often ask senior executives in the corporate center to write down their answers to three questions:

1. What is your company's approach to contributing to the success of its

individual businesses? In other words, exactly how does each business benefit from being part of your company?

2. What makes your company better than any others at its approach to contributing to your individual businesses?
3. How do you—the corporate center's leaders—help the company and its business units implement the answers to 1 and 2?

Readers of chapter 3 will recognize questions 1 and 2 as the first two of three essential questions that every multibusiness strategy must answer. Yet corporate center executives often struggle to answer them and, even if they do, their answers vary considerably from one person to the next. As a result, their answers to question 3 lack detail that is specific to their particular company. Instead, they default to generic answers. For example, here are some of the most common descriptions of the corporate center's role in strategy:

- Optimize the cost and quality of functions that are common to the business units.
- Create "revenue synergies" by coordinating sales, marketing, or pricing across business units.
- Spread "best practices" to the business units.
- Help the business units either develop their strategies or implement them, or both.
- Save the business units the time and trouble of dealing with investors, analysts, banks, and the like.

At first glance, this makes for a good and sufficient list. But most companies tend to overestimate the benefits of centralized services, revenue synergies, best practices, strategy assistance, and running interference with Wall Street. They also tend to underestimate the hidden costs of keeping these one step removed from the business units' markets. This is doubly so when their corporate centers lack crisp, enterprise-specific answers to questions 1 and 2 above. And that's when business unit leaders resent "corporate" and push back on its interventions, which, ironically, makes it even more difficult for the business units to benefit from being under their company's corporate roof. This explains why so many corporate centers (over 55%) struggle to justify their costs, and why so many multibusiness companies suffer from the so-called "conglomerate discount" (see chapter 3).

To be sure, corporate centers are busy with hundreds of day-to-day activities to keep the company train running smoothly down the track. They can easily lose sight of their most important responsibilities:

- To push their companies' leaders to have a clear, distinctive multibusiness strategy so the corporate center can set its own priorities
- To take the lead in incubating and nurturing their companies' leading capabilities
- To ensure that every business willingly—if not always enthusiastically—draws on those capabilities and contributes to them

These responsibilities should guide whether, and how, corporate centers implement shared services, coordinate business unit operations, spread best practices, help business units with their strategies, and do many other things. Otherwise, such activities have as good a chance of undermining the company's businesses as they do of helping those businesses succeed in their respective markets.

51

How should the strategy function contribute to strategy?

Three roles make the most difference.

Companies have a great many functions in their headquarters: finance; human resources; legal; marketing; IT; and more. In each case, the chief executive delegates a certain set of responsibilities and the authority to carry them out. Getting this right for each function—and keeping it so—is no small feat, especially for the strategy function.

Strategies are like children: people never love others' as much as their own. Leaders commit much more to a strategy when they have conceived, nurtured, and matured it for themselves. They shouldn't delegate the essential choices that a strategy comprises (see chapters 2 and 3) and should never hand off to others the responsibility for stretching and innovating their strategy when needed (see chapters 18 and 21). Nor should they let others do their creative thinking for them and be the "reviewers and approvers" of a strategy someone else has formulated on their behalf.

Leaders *can,* however, ask their strategy function to play three important roles: facilitation, observation, and inspiration. Done well, each role enhances the ability of leaders to work together on strategy, to anticipate when their strategy needs to change, and then to innovate their strategy when and where needed most. Let's take each of these three roles in turn.

Facilitation of high-quality strategy meetings is one of the strategy function's most important roles. Such meetings are the best mechanism that leaders have for making their strategies a collaborative effort (see chapter 22). The facilitator's job is to ensure that everyone leaves each strategy meeting feeling that he's been heard, that the group has made a consequential decision (or two or more) that is material to making progress on the company's strategy, and that the meeting took no longer than it had to. Consistently achieving this is no easy task.

For example, most teams are composed of a mix of people who tend to "overshare" and others whose thoughts run deep but silent. The facilitator may have to tamp down a verbose senior executive—even the CEO—and put a quiet one on the spot.

Moreover, good strategy discussions rarely proceed in a straight line. That's not always bad, as it can mean the creative juices are flowing. But random walks don't lead to consequential decisions. The facilitator has to know which decision (or decisions) the meeting is supposed to achieve and then help the group work toward it. At various points in the meeting, the facilitator should summarize the common ground and any material differences and suggest what should come next in the discussion and what should be sidelined for now. This offers a golden opportunity to both clarify and guide the group's strategic thinking.

Finally, meetings that chronically run over their time slot are meetings that no one wants to attend anymore. As a chief executive once said to me, "The facilitator has to keep us on topic and on time without pissing everyone off."

Another difference-making role of the strategy function is **observation.** Are leaders tackling the right challenges to their strategy? Have they zeroed in on the capabilities that make their company special? Are they actively investing time and energy in building those capabilities?

As important, has their strategy hit a growth ceiling? Has it lost its clarity or distinctiveness? Can it be stretched somehow to raise its growth ceiling? Is the strategy underpinned by a big idea that's still a big idea? Does it need new thinking and ideas? Are the assumptions and expectations of leaders that underpinned their strategy still valid?

More fundamentally, are the leaders operating with the same definition of strategy? Are they working with the same distinction between their strategy, business model, and plan…and between their strategy, vision, mission, and goals? Do they agree on what makes a strategy great and how to keep it great?

Sooner or later, one or more of these questions will uncover a fault line in the company's strategy. Executive turnover, evolving market conditions, and changing internal circumstances will ensure that. The strategy function can help leaders keep these questions top of mind and, by having their own keen observations, strategy staff can also help leaders be honest in answering them.

A third valuable role of the strategy function is **inspiration.** Every strategy needs innovation from time to time. And by looking at how strategy innovation happens in the real world (see chapter 21), we know that finding relevant innovations from the past—so-called "innovation precedents"—is the best way to inspire the new thinking and novel ideas it demands. But doing that well is not easy. It's labor-intensive and it can be messy, with a lot of wild-goose chases that produce very little. It's also a skill that gets better with practice and repetition.

Few leaders have the time *or* skill it takes to find the best possible set of innovation precedents for inspiring fresh ideas where a strategy needs innovation most. The strategy function is well-suited to building a trove of innovation precedents and putting them in front of the company's leaders. This is the most effective way to spark the leaders' creativity, to jolt them out of their everyday and business-as-usual executive-problem-solving mode, and thus to avoid the trap of corporate or industry orthodoxy. It also gives the strategy function a license to bring ideas that leaders might not otherwise consider.

Companies ask a great deal of their strategy functions, from orchestrating the annual planning process to running special projects, training new hires, monitoring market trends and competition, running cost programs, evaluating potential acquisitions, providing analytical support, supporting board meetings and business units…and many more. But as taxing as these roles are, their contributions pale in comparison to the value of the skillful and timely facilitation, observation, and inspiration that a strategy function can bring to leaders. When these three higher-order roles are blocked, whether overwhelmed by lower-value activities or simply not done well, the strategy function will lose its voice and power to influence. The organization's best people will sense this, making it difficult to recruit talented new blood into the function. And that will only dilute the strategy function's ability to facilitate, observe, and inspire.

It's no wonder, then, that many leaders of strategy functions voice frustration over not being regularly involved in strategy discussions and lacking a seat at the table when the real strategy choices are being discussed. According to a survey of 187 such leaders by Strategy& PwC, only 25% of respondents felt they were "very successful" at creating value for their company. And 65% thought their priorities weren't clear.

The solution is for the strategy function to use *every* activity as an opportunity to facilitate, observe, or inspire. For example, annual planning could be a chance to facilitate high-quality strategy meetings (see chapter 25); monitoring market trends and competition could yield observations about the current strategy's growth ceiling and opportunities to raise it (see chapter 18); and if the leaders' strategy needs innovation, the strategy function could volunteer to build a trove of innovation precedents that are relevant to where leaders need inspiration (see chapter 21). In other words, everything leaders ask of the strategy function provides an opportunity to help them make their strategy great—and keep it great—through facilitation, observation, or inspiration…or even all three.

52

How should directors be engaged in strategy?

Leaders get from their board what they put into it.

Some argue that when it comes to strategy, the buck stops with the CEO. They say that the most important role of boards is to choose CEOs, evaluate their performance, and make a change if necessary. Inserting the board into strategy muddies accountability.

But this is increasingly the minority view. For example, on its website, BlackRock—one of the world's largest, most powerful investors—demands that "boards have a critical role in providing input into…developing and implementing strategy." Moreover, leaders increasingly want their boards engaged in strategy, and most directors are more than willing.

This makes perfect sense. Boards have experience, contacts, knowledge, and perspective that can be tremendously helpful to guiding strategy. And they fill an unavoidable role in implementing it—for example, by reviewing and approving operating plans, waving through (or blocking) large capital expenditures, green- or red-lighting acquisitions and divestitures, making connections through their networks to help with business development and partnering, and so forth. As BlackRock says, being actively involved in strategy creates a "better context for key business decisions."

Yet I often encounter chief executives who are disappointed with their boards' contributions to strategy, and I talk with directors who feel unhappy with how they are (or are not) engaged in strategy. The reasons for this are many: dysfunctional differences within the board at one extreme or groupthink uniformity at the other extreme; dominant personalities or overly deferential ones; a shortage of information or too much of it; excessively regimented meetings or poorly disciplined ones; and more. The biggest problem, though, is that most boards and executive teams engage in ways that don't work very well for collaborating on strategy.

Take the usual planning process (see chapters 24 and 25). It typically ends with a formal request of the board to approve next year's budget and also to bless the long-term strategic plan. Directors are pummeled with detailed financials and dared to disagree with the proposed goal of "becoming the leading company" in this or that. Left implicit are the essential choices that every strategy must comprise (see chapters 2 and 3). It may be planning, but it's hardly strategy. And it leaves boards hard-pressed to genuinely contribute to strategy.

Perhaps realizing this, most companies have adopted strategy "off-sites." These meetings occur before the annual planning cycle starts. There's a roll call of presentations from various leaders; discussion of goals, market developments, competition, and performance; dialog on growth opportunities, M&A, and on and on; and sometimes there are guest speakers, videos, special events (even a safari!), and other bells and whistles to spice things up.

Directors appreciate these summits because they provide deeper information on the company's businesses, broader exposure to its leaders, fascinating things to discuss, often a bit of entertainment, and a chance to bond with one another and management.

But board directors need something other than the annual off-site and planning process to help them better contribute to strategy. There are two options. Each minimizes the chances that directors and leaders will end up with different views on a company's direction without knowing exactly why.

One of the two options is to carve out regular time—at least quarterly, if not monthly—to tackle issues and opportunities that have material, strategy-changing implications for the company to address now. Chapter 23 describes how this should work in practice. Not every issue or opportunity has to go through the board—only those that are most important to the company's economic health. The rest can be handled by the management team.

This first option operationalizes the practical reality that strategy is not a one-and-done thing—it's either dying or evolving, because there will always be a steady stream of challenges and developments. Moreover, important issues and opportunities can pop up at any time, such as a major competitor's move, a big loss (or gain) of business, or a disruptive change in technology or regulation. Leaders and directors can't always wait for the next planning cycle or off-site to roll around. Nor can they do full justice to the most important ones in an annual planning process, a once-a-year off-site, or a one-off meeting.

A second option is for the directors to play more of a collaborative, sounding-board role—one that's designed to help leaders test their own strategy thinking, as well as to keep it fresh and sharp. In such a role, the board helps leaders do the following:

- Challenge their essential strategy choices (see chapters 2 and 3) and weigh whether those choices remain sharply differentiating enough (see chapter 8).
- Explore various ways to stretch their strategy choices in order to raise the company's growth ceiling (see chapter 18).
- Reflect on whether and how their strategy choices are still the best ones for bringing the company's big idea to life (see chapter 9).
- Assess whether their company's "big idea" is still a big one (see chapter 16) and, if not, how to reinvigorate or replace it (see chapter 21).
- Detail how their strategy choices have evolved as a result of decisions they've taken on particular issues and opportunities.
- Show how their plans—or perhaps the company's business model, vision, mission, purpose, or goals (see chapters 4 and 5)—should change as a result of how their strategy choices have evolved.

Directors should bite off no more than one or two of these items at any one time. That's because each of them can benefit from its own, thorough "strategy discussion," and each should also produce a tangible decision on how to proceed. Rushing through all of them in a single session is a recipe for producing superficial results.

To be sure, making either of the two options work is challenging. There are non-trivial practical barriers to finding the time and space to make genuine strategy engagement work well. Board agendas are already packed with nondiscretionary items such as financial and operational reviews; attending various subcommittees; onboarding new directors; and signing off on audited financials, executive compensation, succession plans, M&A transactions, and new partnership agreements. Plus, directors tend to be busy people and they aren't always looking to volunteer more of their time to spend on a particular company's strategy.

Yet there's a more fundamental barrier as well. For leaders, it can feel burdensome and risky to set aside regular time for inviting the board to challenge their strategy. It can be uncomfortable to bring to the board issues and opportunities for which there are no obvious answers. In the school of management, we are taught never to present problems without a recommended solution—it's only human to jump to one and latch onto it.

Moreover, it's nerve-wracking to have smart, accomplished, and self-assured people scrutinize one's "strategy baby" and then to invite their critical thinking, disagreement, and creativity. Jeff Immelt, a 16-year CEO of General Electric, echoed this in his book, *Hot Seat: What I Learned Leading a Great American Company*, when he wrote, "There's a certain sense of vulnerability to saying I haven't figured this out yet." And yet he goes on to say that he wishes he had admitted "I don't know" more often. "There are a few times when that would've served me better."

Immelt is right. Leaders greatly increase their ability to keep their strategy great *and* to implement it by having directors actively contribute to strategy in a way that's not only deliberate, disciplined, and decisive but also open, dynamic, and creative.

On the flip side, most board directors prefer being genuinely involved in the real work of strategy rather than rubber-stamping visions, mission statements, plans, and detailed budgets. They value the commitment and understanding that come from actively engaging in strategy more than once a year. They recognize how it forces execution-sapping differences to the surface, fortifies subsequent decisions, and simplifies other governance matters such as compliance, compensation, risk, and succession. They discover that it creates trust and respect in cases when challenging management—and even each other—energizes the room. And they feel much more confident communicating, supporting, and soliciting shareholder feedback on their leaders' strategy.

An added bonus: Directors find their annual off-sites are much better because the board is so deep into strategy throughout the year. And they see more clearly the proper role of annual planning: to plan the implementation of strategy, not to create it (see chapter 25).

Perhaps most important of all, however, is the effect that a productively engaged board can have on a company's ability to innovate. Though new thinking and ideas can (and should) bubble up from below, *strategy* innovation is squarely in the realm of leaders' responsibility. It's only human for them to need active support—and sometimes a big push—to meet that responsibility. The two options described above offer the best way for directors to provide that support and push. This is especially crucial for large, established companies whose boards tend to take on a more ceremonial and administrative role, thus contributing yet another factor to why big companies struggle to innovate their strategies over time.

A final note: All the above presumes that leaders and their board have accepted a common definition of "strategy"; how it's different from a plan, business model, vision, mission, purpose, or set of goals; what makes a strategy great; and how to keep it great. Leaders should never take this for granted, especially when the composition of their executive team and board has changed in some material way.

53

How should employees be involved in strategy?

Staff can magnify the intel and brain power of leaders.

Leaders are responsible for building a growing, profitable, and loyal customer base. The choices they make for their strategy are deciding factors in how well they can meet that responsibility. Those choices must belong to leaders, and leaders must be accountable for the quality of their choices. The strategy buck stops with them.

This doesn't always sit well with those who feel that formulating strategy should involve everyone in an organization. The reasons given run the gamut, from matters of principle ("leaders shouldn't have a monopoly on something so important to the success of everyone") to the practical ("leaders don't have a monopoly on good ideas").

But strategy doesn't have to be democratized or crowdsourced for employees to have a valuable role in shaping it. For starters, staff can be a powerful radar for leaders. Interactions between employees and customers, suppliers, investors, or other stakeholders (see chapter 54) have the potential to uncover issues and opportunities for the company's strategy that leaders would not otherwise discover before it's too late and their options have overly narrowed.

For example, a strategy may call for focusing on a particular persona within a target enterprise customer, but the Sales team is learning that there is another persona that is more open to the company's offering (or worse, is a consistent blocker). Or the engineering group may see a new technology coming over the horizon that could accelerate (or eviscerate) one of the company's leading capabilities. Or the head of Investor Relations might hear something from a prominent industry analyst or lead shareholder that suggests a new issue or opportunity for the company's strategy (or that refutes a key assumption supporting it—see chapter 37).

These are all examples of how staff can magnify the intel of leaders to help them keep their strategy sharp. But beyond this, staff can play another important role in strategy, as well.

Leaders keep their strategy moving ahead by carving out regular time to work on particular issues and opportunities (see chapter 22) that either challenge the current strategy or offer attractive possibilities to stretch it (see chapter 18). Employees can play a vital role in helping leaders with this.

Let's take an example of a soft drinks company. The issue is *"Our products are increasingly stigmatized because of the obesity epidemic."* This has serious potential implications for the perceived value of the company's offering. It touches on product formulation, how the company markets its products, who can afford its products health-wise, and more. Responses could include changing the products themselves or how they are packaged (for example, smaller pack sizes). Other responses could be adding a social dimension to the offering (see chapter 34), leading with functional benefits when marketing the products, distributing through different channels that have more of a health halo, and adding nutritional research experts to the company's partnering capability.

Any one of these responses could mean a major reshaping of the *Who? Why?* or *What?* of leaders' current strategy (see chapter 2). Formulating the best response would benefit a great deal from the range of domain expertise that different employees can bring, such as the science of ingredients, manufacturing and packaging technology, social media, distribution, and more. A team of such employees could act as strategy advisors to leaders by helping to imagine alternative responses to the issue, evaluate those alternatives, and analyze how to course-correct the current strategy based on the chosen response. This effectively increases the brain power of leaders to tackle additional issues and seize fresh opportunities with more rigor than they could on their own. (And not for nothing, it also gives employees real-world experience with the art and practice of strategy before they become responsible for strategy themselves.)

These two roles—intel and brain power—magnify the ability of leaders to keep their strategy fresh and responsive to an ever-changing landscape. Yet for employees to play these roles effectively, they must have and maintain a proper understanding of the strategy their leaders have chosen for the company. And the best way to ensure this is with a rolling series of "strategy roundtables."

These are organized into groups of eight or so people each. Each roundtable is facilitated by a member of the leadership team. If there are 10 members and if each of them takes responsibility for leading three to four roundtables every six months, all of the top managers and high-potential future leaders ("HIPOs") can be covered at least once annually, even in the largest company.

A typical roundtable runs for an hour and is organized around four standard questions:

1. What is our strategy as you see it today (see chapters 2 and 3) and our plan for implementing it (see chapter 4)?
2. From your interactions with colleagues and other stakeholders (customers, suppliers, investors, and so on), what issues and opportunities do you see for our strategy or for how we are implementing it?
3. How can we improve the strategy or its implementation?
4. What is your role in implementing our strategy?

The main objective is for participants to walk away from each roundtable with the confidence that "I know how I fit into our strategy because I know what it is and how it's being implemented." The other objective is for leaders to assess how well their organization truly understands their strategy so they can then plan for implementing it. In this regard, employees' answers to questions 2–4 can be just as revealing as their answers to question 1.

Conducting strategy roundtables with the company's top managers and HIPOs may seem like a big investment (roughly 6 to 8 hours per leader per year for the largest company), but it's not when compared to the return it can produce. To begin with, the roundtables are always an eye-opener for leaders. They see first-hand that not everyone can speak with one voice about the company's strategy, yet everyone really has something to say about how to improve it or its implementation. This provides an opportunity for leaders to clarify where there is confusion or misinterpretation, and thus to fortify and disseminate throughout the organization a deeper understanding of the strategy choices leaders have made *and* why. This gives employees the necessary context to be effective implementers of strategy, and then to be helpful advisors when they are recruited to help leaders address a particular issue or opportunity that could demand that strategy evolve.

As important, the roundtables consist of effective ways to activate the intelligence role of the company's HIPOs by gaining insight from what they are seeing, hearing, and experiencing in their interactions with each other—and from the company's stakeholders. This will always suggest issues and opportunities that could rise to the top of the agenda, which in turn guides the work that leaders should be doing together on their strategy (chapter 22).

Of course, strategy roundtables with staff are not a magic bullet. But when they're done well and consistently, leaders will find that their key managers and future leaders become a powerful radar system and a useful cohort of strategy advisors. Moreover, employees will be given a better shot at knowing their part in implementing the company's strategy, what their own priorities should be, whom they should be working with, and who should be working with them (see chapter 28). Even if the strategy buck stops with leaders, these are reasons enough for them to invest their precious time in engaging their staff in strategy, in the ways suggested here.

54

What role should other stakeholders have in strategy?

There's a lot to gain if they are asked the right questions.

Great strategies comprise sharply differentiating choices that are powered by a big idea and co-created by the leaders who retain ultimate responsibility for the success of their enterprise (see chapters 8–10). The more inspired their choices, the better their strategy will be. And one source of inspiration is so-called stakeholders.

Two types of stakeholders are internal to the company: directors and employees. We tackled them in chapters 52 and 53, respectively. In this chapter, we explore the role of three external stakeholders: customers, suppliers, and investors. Proponents of "stakeholder value" and "stakeholder capitalism" include other constituencies such as local communities, governments, and society at large (see chapter 36 and appendix 1). But we focus here on the stakeholders that are most engaged with a company on a day-to-day basis.

As with staff and the board, leaders have much to gain by engaging customers, suppliers, and investors in strategy. As external stakeholders looking in, they can be good sources of new thinking and ideas. But leaders have to be very careful about how they tap into these sources. They cannot be as transparent with outsiders. Thus, there is an inherent asymmetry in information and knowledge that can distort what leaders hear from a customer, supplier, or investor. Moreover, successful stakeholders have productive, symbiotic, and ultimately self-interested relationships with companies. Even if they had perfect information and knowledge, they might "curate" what they have to say in order to keep the relationship on a positive footing and best serve their own interests.

Subject to these caveats, stakeholders can play a unique, even an irreplaceable role in helping leaders keep their strategy great. But to activate that role, leaders have to ask the right questions. And those questions are different for each type of stakeholder. That's because stakeholders in each category—customer, supplier, or investor—can see things that stakeholders in the other two categories cannot. For example, customers have firsthand experience with the offerings of both the company and its competitors; suppliers have direct exposure to the company's capabilities and to the capabilities of its competitors, as well; and investors have finely tuned antennae to evaluate a strategy's growth, profitability, and execution challenges. Thus, the questions leaders ask should be tailored to the unique vantage point each type of stakeholder has. Here's what that means in practical terms:

Customers: This group includes end users or consumers as well as intermediaries such as retailers, resellers, aggregators, wholesalers, and distributors. Seeking answers to the following questions will help leaders gain the most from engaging customers in a dialog about strategy:

- Why do you choose a product (or service) offering such as ours, and how?
- What is the problem we help you solve with our offering, and what is the novelty of our solution?
- What alternatives to our solution—other than direct competitors'—do you consider, if any?
- What do you think about the value of our offering in terms of benefits versus costs, tangible and otherwise?
- How could we create more or different value by evolving our offering or how we work together?
- What would make us better at marketing, selling, or realizing the value we promise?

Readers of chapters 2 and 9 will see the source of these questions. They are framed to help leaders gain real-world perspective on the *Who? Why?* and *What?* of their strategy, as well as on the big idea that powers them. In the process, leaders will gain privileged insight on their customers that traditional market research, focus groups, and other such things never produce. Plus, an important side-benefit is the opportunity to educate customers on the real value of the company's offerings.

It's worth noting here that the questions above are *not* aimed at getting feedback on the relationship and experience customers have with the company per se, though that will surely come out one way or another. A second caveat: the "customer" in the questions above depends on the type of business (for example, consumer vs. enterprise business) and on who is being asked the questions (for example, the end user/consumer, or an intermediary entity such as a retailer).

Suppliers: These include contractors for things like manufacturing, research, software engineering, and fulfillment/distribution; providers of materials, components, and other such supplies; and purveyors of services such as management consulting, public relations, and marketing and communications. The more that suppliers like these serve other companies with the same or similar target market, the more they have to offer. But the questions to ask them are different than those for customers:

- Compared to the companies you serve that have similar customers to our own, how strong is our offering and the value it promises?
- Compared to those companies, what would make us better at marketing, selling, or realizing the value we promise with our offering?
- How could we create more or different value for our customers in how you and we work together?

Leaders will need to read between the lines of what they hear, for suppliers will understandably be extremely careful about how open and frank they can be at this point. But this kind of engagement is a golden opportunity to benefit from the eyes, ears, and experience of those who serve direct or indirect competitors. It will also help suppliers see their role in making their customer's strategy a success. And there's a cherry on top: leaders will be surprised by how energizing being engaged this way can be for their suppliers.

Investors: This constituency comprises those who hold the company's equity and debt securities. These can range from hedge, mutual, and venture funds to private equity and debt funds; so-called activist investors; wealthy individuals; home offices; traditional bank lenders; and more. This group also includes those who provide research and analysis to investors.

Such stakeholders are most interested in the earnings prospects of the strategy that leaders have adopted for their company, and in the leaders' ability to implement that strategy. So, they will have the most to say about these questions:

- What is our strategy as you see it today?
- How is our strategy different? How do its differences fuel (or hinder) our future earnings power?
- What challenges or barriers do you see to implementing our strategy?
- Do you see ways to stretch our strategy for more growth potential (see chapter 18)?
- Do you see the big idea behind our strategy (see chapter 9), and do you understand the competitive moat we have dug to protect it (see chapter 16)?

Invariably, when engaging investors on these questions, one or both of two scenarios will play out. In the first, leaders hear responses that convince them they are missing a major issue (and opportunity) for their strategy that could make a big difference to their company's future earnings power. This is an essential insight that will help leaders in their work together to keep their strategy great (see chapter 22).

In scenario two, leaders learn that investors are missing something fundamental about the strategy, or about how it's being implemented, or both. In effect, scenario two is the reverse of scenario one, and it presents a precious opportunity to set the record straight. This empowers investors to be more effective partners in helping leaders keep their strategy moving forward and to fully realize its execution power. Plus, there's an added benefit for public companies: when leaders and investors are on the same page, the company's stock price is more likely to match its intrinsic value, thus minimizing the dysfunction and headaches that a mismatch—in either direction—can create for everyone.

Here's a table that summarizes the best way to engage each type of stake-holder in strategy:

Customers	Suppliers	Investors
• Why do you choose a product (or service) offering such as ours, and how? • What is the problem we help you solve with our offering, and what is the novelty of our solution? • What alternatives to our solution—other than direct competitors'—do you consider, if any? • What do you think about the value of our offering in terms of benefits versus costs, tangible and otherwise? • How could we create more or different value by evolving our offering or how we work together? • What would make us better at marketing, selling, or realizing the value we promise?	• Compared to the companies you serve that have similar customers to our own, how differentiated is our offering and the value it promises? • Compared to those companies, what would make us better at marketing, selling, or realizing the value we promise with our offering? • How could we create more or different value for our customers in how you and we work together?	• What is our strategy as you see it today? • How is our strategy different from competitors, and how do its differences fuel (or hinder) our future earnings power? • What challenges or barriers do you see to implementing our strategy? • Do you see ways to stretch our strategy for greater growth potential (see chapter 18)? • Do you see the big idea behind our strategy (see chapter 9) and the competitive moat we have dug to protect it (see chapter 16)?

Taken together, these stakeholder groups can play a crucial role in helping leaders address their own blind spots, see issues and opportunities hiding in plain sight, and course-correct their strategy before it's too late. And by actively helping stakeholders play that role, leaders will motivate, inspire, and cultivate stronger relationships with their customers, suppliers, and investors alike. That alone can be worth the effort it takes to genuinely engage stakeholders in strategy.

55

What role should CEOs have in business unit strategies?

How to avoid the extremes of abdication and appropriation

The typical large company is organized around a set of business units with leaders who report to the chief executive officer. Each leader is charged by the CEO to grow a profitable and loyal customer base. Thus, like the leader of any business, business unit leaders must come up with strategies that they are enthusiastically committed to implementing. This puts their CEOs in a tricky position. Here's why.

The more latitude and authority business unit leaders have to develop their own strategies, the stronger their commitment to implementing those strategies. This implies that CEOs should take a hands-off approach to their business units' strategies. However, a CEO is clearly accountable for the company's performance, and the quality of any company's business unit strategies surely has an outsized impact on its performance. Moreover, business units operate within the context of a CEO's multibusiness strategy for the company at large (see chapter 3). They are not only the beneficiaries of that strategy, they also have a crucial role in living it, and their strategies play a big part in that role. So, shouldn't CEOs have a big say in their business units' strategies?

All this is to say that there are strong arguments for CEOs to take a *hands-off* approach to their business units' strategies, and there are equally strong arguments for them to take a *hands-on* one. So where on the spectrum between abdication (granting strategy autonomy to the business units) and appropriation (taking over business unit strategies) should CEOs operate?

The answer lies in recognizing that making business unit leaders responsible for their own strategies is an act of delegation to which the rules of effective delegation must apply.

The first rule is to delegate with control points. These are times when the delegator and the delegatee periodically check in with each other to evaluate progress, raise issues, answer questions, and generally ensure that things remain on track. Delegation without control points is really just abdication, while delegation with excessive control points is appropriation.

In delegating business unit strategy, the CEO gives the business unit leaders the freedom to drive their own strategy, but regularly checks in with two queries:

1. Are the *Who? Why?* and *What?* of the business unit's strategy clear (see chapter 2)? Are they compelling (see chapters 8 and 9)? Do they adequately reflect and amplify the company's vision, mission, purpose, and goals (see chapters 5, 31, and 33)? Has anything changed that would call for the strategy to change?

2. Does the business unit's strategy both fortify and benefit from the company's multibusiness strategy (see chapter 3)? Has anything changed in the latter that could (or should) require a change to the former?

As long as the CEO is satisfied with the answers to these questions, there's no need for more active intervention. But if CEOs don't like what they are hearing or seeing, they must intervene.

The second rule of effective delegation is to have the right frequency of control points. This depends on a number of factors:

- **How experienced is the business unit leader?** The less experienced a business unit leader, the more she and her strategy will benefit from the CEO's engagement. That argues for a more-frequent cadence of control points.

- **How new to the company is the business unit leader?** She may be a very experienced executive, but if she's new to the company, she won't yet have internalized the CEO's strategy for the company overall. Thus, she'll benefit from more-frequent engagement with the CEO, to ensure that her strategy adequately reflects and reinforces the CEO's strategy for the company overall (see chapter 3).
- **How important is the business unit?** All else being equal, the more important a business unit, the more engaged the CEO should be in its strategy. A business unit could be important because it's an enormous profit contributor (for example, ESPN at The Walt Disney Company); or it's a deliberately disruptive play that is small now but could become the company's future profit engine (like AWS—Amazon's cloud-computing business—was to its parent company in its early days); or it's a chronic money loser that is sapping the company's wherewithal (akin to an auto company's small-car and EV businesses); or it has become a source of bad press (such as Bud Light for AB InBev). Neither the CEO nor the company can afford to have an important business unit's strategy go off the rails. If that is happening, it calls for a relatively heavy dose of ongoing engagement from the CEO to prevent that from happening, rather than having to clean up the mess after the fact.

CEOs should use these questions to guide their degree of engagement in each business unit's strategy. For units with more-experienced, tenured leaders, CEOs can be relatively hands-off. But CEOs need to be more hands-on with freshly minted business leaders, especially if they are new to the company or in charge of its most important business units.

In addition to the three factors above, there are two others that CEOs should consider:

- **How new to the company is the CEO?** Those CEOs who have been brought in from the outside will obviously have little experience with the company and its businesses. They must engage frequently with each business unit leader on strategy, both to learn their companies' businesses and to inform their own strategies. This is doubly so for CEOs who are new to the industries in which they now operate.

- **Has the CEO's overall strategy materially changed?** This could be related to a big acquisition, merger, or divestiture; or be sparked by a technological breakthrough; or be instigated by the board or activist investors. Whatever the reason, a change in strategy at the corporate level may require an enormous amount of engagement by the CEO with the business units to ensure that their strategies complement and benefit from that CEO's new strategy for the company overall.

These two factors, if present, would apply to every business unit in a company, but they naturally fade over time as the CEO and his or her multibusiness strategy settle in. This is when the three factors farther above come to the fore. They provide CEOs with a rubric for avoiding the extremes of abdication and appropriation, and they typically lead to different degrees of engagement across the business units.

All the above presumes a direct reporting relationship between the CEOs and the business unit leaders. That's not always the case in very large companies. They often have a layer of executives between the CEO and business units. This layer acts as a "span breaker" to make more manageable the number of direct reports to the CEO. But it can inadvertently create a barrier—a "layer of clay"—that CEOs have to break through in order to engage properly in their business units' strategies; and it can stoke tension or sow confusion with the span-breaking executives (SBEs) if their role in business unit strategy is not clear.

CEOs have four options to solve this problem:

1. **SBE as CEO deputy:** The SBE stands in for the CEO to oversee the strategy for each business unit in his purview. He uses the rubric described above to determine how engaged to be in each of his business units' strategy. This may feel like the cleanest option, but it's also the riskiest because it inevitably reduces the visibility that CEOs have into their business units' strategies. For this option to work, a CEO must gain absolute trust in the SBE's ability and motivation to act on the CEO's behalf.

2. **SBE as strategy partner:** The SBE partners with the CEO in overseeing the strategies for each of his respective business units. He's in the room with the CEO and integral to the strategy

decision-making for each of his business units. This can lead to messy meetings if the SBE fundamentally disagrees with the CEO on a business unit's strategy, but it also creates the means to see and resolve any disagreements, rather than letting them fester in the background.

3. **SBE as operating partner:** The SBE is delegated the responsibility for acting on behalf of the CEO on all matters except for business unit strategy. His role is akin to that of an operating partner in a large private equity firm. He's in the strategy room with the CEO, but only to listen and learn in order to gain a full understanding of the strategy context within which he plays her role. The intention is not to muzzle the SBE, though he may feel that way if his role as an operating partner is unclear.

4. **SBE as selective strategy partner:** The SBE is a strategy partner to the CEO on the most important business units and the CEO's deputy for the rest. This gives CEOs visibility into the business unit strategies that matter most, without having to consume precious time on other business units that don't matter as much.

These options are not mutually exclusive. Option 1 could be appropriate for one SBE, while option 2, 3, or 4 could be appropriate for another. The best option for each SBE depends on his or her own experience, expertise, tenure, and business unit portfolios, and also on the company's leadership succession plans.

Finally, for any of these options to work well—especially option 1—the SBEs must gain a firm grasp of the CEO's multibusiness strategy and be on the same page as to what "good" looks like for a business unit strategy. Sadly, this is often not the case, which is yet another reason for why the "conglomerate discount" is so prevalent at multibusiness companies (see chapters 3, 15, and 50).

....

PART X

What About Strategy for Different Types of Enterprises?

What can leaders learn from entities with less maturity, or that have different ownership structures, or whose objectives don't include making a profit?

56

How is strategy different for startups?

They're just beginning—does that make a difference?

Great execution requires a sharply differentiating strategy that is clear and tangible to a company's people and teams (see chapters 8 and 28). Creating such a strategy can often be deceptively difficult for leaders of a startup. Let's explore why that is.

Founders of startups typically have a big idea for a solution to a problem. The more innovative their solution, the more foreign their novel products and services will be to the status quo, and the less certain they can be about the essential strategy choices that they should make.

Figuring out those choices before it's too late is one of the great challenges of turning a fledgling startup into a successfully scaled business.

There are two ways to address the challenge. One is to stick to a broad vision and use it to guide the new company's direction and day-to-day efforts. Leaders adopt this approach because they feel they don't know enough yet and don't want to be boxed in by having a more-specific strategy.

The problem is, the broader the vision for a startup, the more likely it is that *any* priority will fit under its umbrella, thus giving leaders the license to do whatever feels important in the moment. This almost always leads to everyone else in their organization feeling whipsawed by priorities that seem to change daily. And that creates a general feeling of randomness in the company's direction, along with an uncomfortable lack of certainty for what everyone should be doing to support it. This is not exactly a recipe for seamless, right-first-time execution.

The broad-vision approach also has a problem concerning a startup's funding. Although some investors may sign up for a world-changing vision with few specifics behind it (WeWork and Masayoshi Son, anyone?), many will not. They want to see a decisive and deliberate strategy for how the fledgling company will build a thriving, loyal base of paying customers that ultimately results in a profitable company.

The good news, though, is that preserving a startup's flexibility does not have to come at the cost of being deliberately decisive about its strategy. The trick is to distinguish between "stated" and "working" choices.

"Stated" choices are fully communicated to employees, investors, and even customers and other stakeholders. For example: "This is our 'bullseye' *Who?*— our target customer. This is our *Why?*—why our target customers should choose us. And these are our *What?*—the handful of capabilities that we are prioritizing and nurturing to make us better than anyone else at marketing, selling, and making good on our *Why?*" (See chapters 12–14 for more on each of these.)

"Working" choices are different than stated choices. They are provisional responses to open issues and opportunities that could lead to a material change of the founder's current strategy choices, such as a new target customer, new value proposition, or new capability. Working choices are meant for leaders to deliberate privately or to test in real-world settings before they commit to a change in their stated strategy.

By operating with this distinction between stated and working choices, leaders can act decisively and flexibly at the same time: decisively, with regard to the company's direction and the proposition to new investors who may shy away from broad visions without tangible strategies; and flexibly, with regard to exploring and discovering what the optimal strategy is while the leaders are building their business with their current strategy.

One example of this way of managing strategy is RJ Scaringe, who founded Rivian Automotive in 2009. His strategy was decisive: to offer a better electric truck than Tesla's. His plan was to launch his vehicle in 2020. But amid coronavirus lockdowns, its debut was delayed. In response, Scaringe floated the idea of using the "skateboard" that underpins his electric truck as a platform for other battery-business solutions. Shortly thereafter, he struck a deal with Amazon to build some 100,000 electric vans using Rivian's skateboard. Scaringe started his company with a clear idea, a target market, and an attractive customer proposition, and then he revisited all three when circumstances called for it.

To be sure, it's not easy for the leaders of a startup to decisively state their strategy choices at the same time they're still learning what those should be. But the best way to accelerate their learning is to take a stab at their strategy choices, see what works and doesn't work in the real world, and then evolve accordingly. Otherwise, every opportunity will seem to be a good one, thus sending leaders and their teams down different paths in response to whatever appears on the horizon. When that happens, they will waste a lot of precious capital and time that could have been used more wisely. Perhaps worse, not being decisive—if only conditionally—prevents leaders from prioritizing where to look for the best opportunities.

Sometimes leaders of startups resist stating a decisive strategy because they fear losing the flexibility to change their mind—and the company's direction—if warranted by new developments or fresh learning. The solution is to push for clarity:

- on the most important choices that will guide their company's priorities, decisions, and actions,
- *and* on the issues and opportunities that leaders should be tackling to keep their strategies apace with an ever-changing situation.

With this understanding, the company's leaders are anticipating and responding to how their strategy should evolve in a deliberate way. That's how you get the benefits of having adopted a decisive and flexible strategy to turn a startup's big idea into a successfully scaled business.

Amazon is another example of the stated-versus-working-choices approach to strategy. In the beginning, Jeff Bezos, the company's founder and CEO, was clear about his *Who?* (buyers of books), *Why?* (broadest range, easily searchable, securely purchased, delivered quickly), and *What?* (such as sourcing inventory, warehousing and retrieval, and delivery logistics and partnering). But he always had his company constantly working on refining and stretching those choices—for example, in his original e-retail business, by expanding his *Who?* beyond buyers of books to buyers of anything; enhancing his *Why?* with one-click functionality, two-day delivery, and Prime membership; and fortifying Amazon's *What?* by investing in AI and drone-based delivery. He also added to Amazon's business portfolio by creating Amazon Web Services—its cloud-computing business—as well as a third-party e-retailing platform. To this day, Amazon has both the laser-like focus of having a nailed-down strategy and the restlessness of constantly working on it.

There is something wise in this example for leaders of mature companies, too. Unlike many startups, leaders of established companies (or their predecessors) have obviously found successful strategies for commercializing and scaling the big ideas that got them going in the first place. Their particular challenge is different: mitigating the risk of having their strategy choices become stuck in whatever they've been doing all along, regardless of inevitable changes happening all around them. This is both the effect and the cause of a kind of corporate myopia wherein opportunities and imperatives to innovate strategy are missed. It's also a form of corporate drift in which the company's essential strategy choices passively evolve without forethought and adequate deliberation.

The myopia makes a company fall behind in an ever-changing world, while the drift produces a lack of clarity in the organization that undermines execution (see chapter 28). Together, the myopia and the drift produce stasis and irrelevance, often followed by a long, mostly invisible, excruciating decline during which profitable growth becomes ever more elusive, financial engineering the default, and execution an exercise of running harder to stay in the same place. Having a combination of stated and working choices solves this problem, because the former forces subconscious strategy to the surface while the latter shines a light on the issues and opportunities that require strategy innovation (see chapter 21).

The stated-versus-working-choices approach helps founders keep their strategies from being too fluid. But it also helps leaders of established companies avoid their strategies becoming too static.

57

Is strategy different for private companies?

They don't have publicly traded shares—does that matter?

About 30 years ago, the academic Michael C. Jensen wrote a now-famous article for *Harvard Business Review* in which he predicted that private companies would overtake public ones as the predominant form of corporate ownership. Since then, the number of public companies in the United States has fallen by more than half from its peak in 2000. Meanwhile companies owned by private equity firms (which buy and sell companies on behalf of pension funds, college endowments, and other such investors) has risen twenty-fold in the U.S. Moreover, new companies are waiting longer than ever before they make the leap to public ownership.

Jensen's argument was that being privately owned was a superior form of corporate ownership, because it made leaders focus more single-mindedly on "value creation." Yet leaders rarely express their rationale for going (or staying) private in that particular way. Here are the top four reasons I've heard from leaders over the years:

1. To make the changes we need outside of the public eye
2. To focus more on the long term and get off (or stay off) the quarterly earnings treadmill
3. To avoid the red tape, hassle, and costs of being a public company

4. To realize the enterprise value that our current stock price fails
    to reflect

These cover most of the justifications that companies use when they go private. Take Dell Technologies, the PC-maker founded by Michael Dell in 1984 with a "build to order" manufacturing model and a "direct to companies" sales model. Some 25 years after taking the company public in 1988, Mr. Dell and his buyout partner, Silver Lake Partners, paid about $24 billion to purchase all the company's shares in the largest leveraged buyout since the Great Financial Crisis of 2008.

According to reports,[1] Michael Dell had become frustrated with the mutual funds and retail investors who discounted his efforts to reinvent the company from a PC business to a diversified technology group that could go head-to-head with IBM, Microsoft, Hewlett-Packard, Cisco, and the like. After his company's stock fell from around $30 in late 2007 to less than $10 five years later, Mr. Dell and Silver Lake concluded that the company was in fact undervalued, and offered $14 per share to take it private.

Dell himself celebrated the deal by saying the company now had "the freedom to invest in a future that lies beyond the next quarter" as well as "the flexibility...to pursue organic and inorganic investment without the scrutiny, quarterly targets, and other limitations of operating as a public company." On the company's website the transaction was described as enabling the company "to continue the execution of its long-term strategy...to focus on bringing best-in-class solutions to customers...[and to] be even more flexible and entrepreneurial, allowing it...to serve our customers with a single-minded purpose and drive the innovations that will help them achieve their goals."

The website also said that going private "better positioned [Dell] to shape the forces of cloud, big data, mobile, and security that are changing the way people live, businesses operate, and the world works, just as we did when we helped revolutionize the power of the PC almost 30 years ago." Subsequently, Dell cut costs, tightened operations, offloaded divisions, and paid the princely sum of $67 billion for EMC, the dominant player in data storage that also happened to own VMware, which in turn had pioneered "virtualization" (where software applications don't have to reside on individual machines).

The "future" and the "long-term strategy" in which Michael Dell and his team wanted the "freedom" to invest was essentially a shift from low-margin hardware toward higher-margin systems and services for corporate customers. This is eerily similar to the strategy change that Lou Gerstner successfully made at IBM in the early 1990s (see chapter 5), who had done that all under the intense glare of being a highly visible, iconic public company.

So, here are some questions one might ask:

- Why did Dell have to take his company private for it to be more flexible, entrepreneurial, innovative, and customer-focused?
- After "revolutionizing the power of the PC" as a public company, why did it have to be private in order "to shape the forces of cloud, big data, mobile, and security"?
- Public companies cut costs, tighten operations, offload divisions, and make big acquisitions all the time. Why did Dell's company have to be private in order to do what many public companies do all the time?

The point is, corporate boards and executives alike want to go (or stay) private for many reasons, such as those in the numbered list near the beginning of this chapter; but the essential choices that constitute a strategy (see chapters 2 and 3) don't depend on whether a company is private or public. Leaders may think that being private offers them more freedoms and fewer limitations, but when it comes to strategy, that doesn't matter.

There's no difference in what makes a strategy great, or how to *keep* it great, for a private company versus a public one (see chapters 8–10). Moreover, the right scope of strategy, guideposts for that strategy, and engagement of various stakeholders in the strategy are the same, whether a company is private or public (see the range of chapters 29–55).

When leaders are considering whether to change from one form of ownership to another (public-to-private, or vice versa), they should always challenge themselves by asking: "Would any of our businesses change their *Who? Why?* or *What?*—and if so, how would customers benefit from those changes? For the company overall, would we alter how we contribute to the success of our businesses or change the capabilities we prioritize to enable that contribution? If we did, then how would our businesses benefit from such changes, and would it affect the types of businesses we should own? And finally, why, exactly, can we make these changes only by converting the company to a new form of ownership?"

At a minimum, this will help leaders fully realize whatever advantages they see in transforming their ownership structure. As important, it will help them better communicate and implement their strategy choices, even if they don't undertake such a big existential change in their form of ownership. And perhaps it would also lead them to conclude that changing their ownership isn't necessary if the only reason for doing so is to…uh, "change their strategy." To be sure, there are many potential advantages to being a private company, but the ability to change strategy is not one of them.

---

1   For example, see "Dell: the tricky maths of a reverse merger," *Financial Times*, December 9, 2018.

58

What makes strategy different for family firms?

Their owners are related to each other— what difference does that make?

Family enterprises have a lot going for them. They don't have to worry about the quarterly reporting grind of public companies. Their close familial relationships—if positive—can help them respond quickly to new-market opportunities and threats. And if they have their name on the front door or their family reputation and legacy on the line, they have a strong incentive to ensure the quality and integrity of their company's products, services, labor relations, local community presence, and more.

Yet most family firms fail to survive beyond a single generation. According to the Family Firm Institute, fewer than a third of family businesses survive into the second generation; 12% make it to the third; and a mere 3% to the fourth.

In "The Special Role of Strategic Planning for Family Businesses," the author J. L. Ward concluded that strategies at family-owned companies are less aggressive than in other private companies. By "less aggressive" Ward meant that they tend to forego attractive growth opportunities and they underinvest in innovation. If true, that's a recipe for shortening the half-life of any enterprise. And it suggests that while strategy should be the same for a family company as it is for any other, in practice, it often isn't. The question is: Why? What's different about being family-owned that would change the substance or practice of strategy?

Family companies have two key differences. One is that family owners aren't as free to walk away if they don't like their company's direction. Owners of a public company—its shareholders—can more easily "vote with their feet," based on their confidence in its leaders' strategy and ability to pull it off, and also on their own particular investment criteria (see chapter 37). Family owners don't have this kind of freedom.

A second difference concerns the governing responsibility of a company's leaders. In most cases, leaders are primarily responsible both for growing their company's earnings power and for reinvesting an appropriate portion of current profits to achieve that. But that's not always the case for family-owned businesses. They can often be asked to serve a range of family interests, such as creating liquidity for retirement, education, health crises, or wealth diversification; minimizing estate taxes; funding a philanthropic foundation; providing career opportunities for the next generation; or creating spin-off business opportunities for members of the current generation.

All these interests can greatly influence the strategy choices that leaders make for a family-owned company. For example, they might choose to enter a new business in order to create a leadership opportunity for a family member; or they might sell a business to create liquidity for the family's financial needs. They might add a digital technology department to provide a career path for a newly minted computer science graduate in the family; or, at the other extreme, they could forego any investment in digital capabilities to preserve current profits for the family's immediate financial needs. These examples show how family interests can complicate strategy choices and thus affect the company's earnings power.

To sort through this complexity, leaders of a family firm need to add a second dimension to their strategy. The first dimension is *business strategy*, which is the same as it is for any other company (see table below). The second is *family strategy*.

A family strategy comprises three essential choices. The most important of these is to spell out the "lead family members": those whose interests the company should prioritize. Are these people the current generation or the next one? Or members of a particular line of the family? Or perhaps family members who are active in the company, or who have no operating roles at all?

Of course, different family members can have a different set of interests. Clearly prioritizing some over others is no easy task. But not doing so will put the company in a near-impossible situation, where it's gets pulled in so many different directions—or its freedom of action is so limited—that it's not commercially viable for the long term.

The second most important choice for a family strategy is to prioritize the interests of lead family members that the company must serve. These could be supporting a social purpose or mission; offering job guarantees to employees; providing personal development opportunities for their offspring; pledging to make the company "greener"; enhancing the family name, reputation, and legacy; funding a lifestyle or a charity; or even offering generous perks to the company's staff.

For example, the family owners of Deichmann SE have their company support an employee relief fund for personal hardships like severe illness. They even offer its staff the option of spending a week-long "health holiday" in Switzerland. Likewise, at EBSCO, a family-owned information services company, a percentage of operating profit is allocated to matching employees' charitable giving and also to an employee savings trust.

Leaders and lead family members must also agree on the costs of providing the benefits they are willing for the company to bear. This could involve constraining its ability to reinvest current profits, or declaring out of bounds certain businesses that family members want to steer away from, no matter how successful they could be under the family's corporate roof.

Finally, a family strategy can be deemed complete when leaders and lead family members agree on the capabilities their company must have to meet the family's priorities. This might include a professional development capability to prepare future generations; a governance capability (including board composition, roles, and allocation of voting rights) to manage trade-offs between the company's business strategy and family priorities; or an innovation capability that engages family members in finding novel solutions to any conflicts between business reinvestment needs and family commitments.

Here's a table summarizing the essential elements of a business and family strategy, respectively:

Business strategy choices*	Family strategy choices
Who is our ideal customer?	Who are the lead family members whose interests should be prioritized?
Why should the ideal customer choose us?	Which interests—needs, wants, goals, commitments, etc.—of lead family members will we serve, and what costs will we bear to serve them?
What capabilities will make us the best at marketing, selling, and living our *Why*? with minimal trade-offs for our family strategy?	Which capabilities will make us the best at meeting the interests of lead family members, with minimal trade-offs for our business strategy?
* See chapter 2. Note, if the company has multiple businesses, leaders also need to have a multibusiness strategy (see chapter 3).	

Since both the company's business context (market conditions, competitor moves, technology advancements) and family situations (death, divorce, marriage, graduation, births, finances) will continually evolve, leaders need to find a time-effective way to actively collaborate with family owners, help them regularly confirm their business and family strategies, and reinvigorate those strategies when needed. This should make as transparent as possible any trade-offs between serving the lead family members' interests and fortifying the company's future earnings power. And it should help leaders figure out how to optimize the business strategy so as to minimize those trade-offs.

All this goes to say that running a family-owned enterprise can be deceivingly complicated. The governing responsibility of leaders is usually split between building the company's earnings power and serving the family's priorities. That doubles the always-difficult strategy choices they have to make (see table above) and complicates their implementation and execution challenge. Moreover, as one generation follows the next, the number of family members multiplies, compounding the already-difficult task of keeping everyone on the same page and course-correcting the company's direction as its circumstances inevitably change. Perhaps that's why so few family firms survive the first generation.

The framework offered above can also be used for any complicated owner situation. For example, if there's a particular shareholder group that controls a public company—like the Hershey Trust at Hershey Corporation, or the scions of Fritz Henkel who own the majority of shares in his 144-year-old namesake company—and if that shareholder group has other priorities (such as a social mission), the leaders of that company could benefit from adopting an explicit "controlling owner" strategy. Or if the majority owner of a private company has priorities other than bolstering its earnings power, the leaders of the company might want to spell out a "majority owner" strategy.

In both cases, the choices are very similar to the "family strategy choices" in the table above. And by having such a strategy, leaders give themselves a tool to navigate the complexity of managing through situations where owners with outsized influence have noncommercial objectives and priorities.

(59)

What is strategy for nonprofits?

They have no customers, investors, and profits— what difference does that make?

Many nonprofit leaders think that "strategy" is only for profit-seeking businesses, not their mission-oriented enterprises. But consider this series of mission statements:

• Giving underserved children the skills and support they need to be successful.	• Advance sexual and reproductive autonomy, choices, and improve health worldwide.
• Expand global access to health care.	• Create lasting solutions to poverty, hunger, and social injustice.
• Give people the power to build community and bring the world closer together.	• Bring clean, safe water to people around the world.
• Refresh the world in mind, body, and spirit, and inspire moments of optimism and happiness.	• Develop innovative, principled, and insightful leaders who change the world.
• Empower every person and every organization on the planet to achieve more.	• Inspire lifelong learning, advance knowledge, and strengthen our communities.
• Expand access to quality education and opportunity for people who are left behind.	• Spread ideas.
• Advance sustainable economic growth and financial opportunity.	• Improve mental health and well-being through counseling, education, support, and advocacy.
• Inspire and nurture the human spirit.	• Change lives. Change organizations. Change the world.

Can you tell which column has the mission statements of for-profit companies? The first one. The point is, businesses can be every bit as mission-oriented as nonprofits. Nonprofits have to compete as hard as businesses to achieve their missions and, like businesses, they need a strategy to do so.

Here's a comparison of the strategy choices for each type of enterprise:

Strategy choices	For-profits	Nonprofits
Big idea	A novel solution to a material problem, unmet need, or unsatisfied want that makes its mission uniquely possible and compelling	A novel solution to a material problem, unmet need, or unsatisfied want that makes its mission uniquely possible and compelling
Who	Customers: those who generate a company's revenue by buying its products and services Other stakeholders: those who gain from a company's achieving its mission, e.g., staff, investors, communities	Supporters: those who generate a nonprofit's funding by contributing to its programs and initiatives, e.g., donors, government agencies Other stakeholders: those who gain from a nonprofit's achieving its mission, e.g., target beneficiaries, staff, communities
Why	The balance of benefits and costs customers experience by buying and using (or consuming) a company's products and services—what motivates customers to buy	The balance of benefits and costs supporters experience by contributing to a nonprofit's programs and initiatives—what motivates supporters to contribute
What	The handful of capabilities that makes a company better than anyone else at marketing, selling, and living its *Why?*	The handful of capabilities that makes a nonprofit better than anyone else at marketing, selling, and living its *Why?*

Based on these differences, a nonprofit strategy must answer four essential questions:

- What is the big idea behind our mission?
- Who are the ideal supporters of our mission?
- Why should our ideal supporters choose us over their alternatives?
- What handful of capabilities should we prioritize and nurture, not merely to achieve our mission, but to be the best at finding, attracting, and serving our ideal supporters?

When a nonprofit's leaders can answer these four questions with one voice, they have a clear strategy. And the more compelling and distinctive their answers are, the better that strategy will be.

Still, that's easier said than done, especially because the questions are interdependent. The answer to each depends on how leaders answer the other three. Leaders have to iterate between all four questions to find answers that reinforce one another, their mission, and their current and essential strengths.

Moreover, each question is challenging in its own right. For example, one of the most important factors that makes a strategy great is exactly the same for both nonprofits and for-profits: it stands on the shoulders of a big idea—a superior solution to an important problem, need, or want.

Kathleen Colson is the founder of The BOMA Project, a breakthrough nonprofit that runs an innovative "poverty graduation" program in seven African countries (and counting). To date, BOMA has helped more than 700,000 women (and counting) start businesses and form savings groups. To share her experience, Colson held a seminar for nonprofit leaders, called the Big Idea Seminar (her firm is even named "Big Idea Consulting"). She found that "not one...could clearly state the problem they are trying to solve."

That's too bad. A "big idea" makes a nonprofit's mission uniquely possible and compelling. No amount of strategizing, planning, or execution can make up for lacking one. Moreover, big ideas keep nonprofits out of zero-sum games where their success can only come at others' expense (see chapter 9). And strategies that stand on big ideas offer many more opportunities for extending a nonprofit's mission than those with nothing novel behind them to offer the world (see chapter 20).

The *Who?* question is not easy, either. The range of potential financial supporters depends a lot on a nonprofit's particular mission and stage of development (startup, scale-up, mature). And identifying and dealing with these factors can be mind-bogglingly complex, from individual and corporate donors to family and other foundations, NGOs and government entities, corporate or other advertisers, and even volunteers who donate their time. Plus, financial support can come from a nonprofit's target beneficiaries, such as a university's students who pay tuition or a museum's visitors who purchase entry tickets, thus muddling two of its most important constituents: target beneficiaries and financial supporters (see table left).

The *Why?* question is tricky, too. Compelling propositions for nonprofits start with having well-defined missions and uniquely powerful approaches to achieving them. For example, if the mission for a nonprofit is to cure or prevent cancer, does it have either a novel way of finding cures for the disease or a uniquely effective approach to preventing it? If so, the nonprofit has the makings of a very powerful proposition. If not, good luck!

A nonprofit's pitch usually has to contain more than just a bold statement of its mission and approach. It also has to include benefits that are personal or specific to its priority supporters, such as:

- A good fit with a supporter's own mission or bequest
- The status, name recognition, or reputational value of being associated with a nonprofit (for example, an elite university or museum) or its particular cause (education or the fine arts)
- A salutary effect on an externality or social ill that a supporter really cares about—such as cleaning up water or air, defeating a particular disease, defending the rights of disenfranchised people, or addressing a shortage of technical or financial skills

Most financial supporters don't explicitly expect something in return for their altruism, or articulate it even if they do. Moreover, what compels one supporter can be very different from what compels another, and it can change over time. Nevertheless, nonprofit leaders have to be crystal clear on the *Why?* that hits the bullseye for each type of *Who?* they are targeting.

As for the fourth question—the one about capabilities—nonprofit leaders are typically all over the map. This is often because they're hazy on their big idea, their *Who?* and their *Why?* and thus they can't be specific enough on what they need to be better at than anyone else. It's also because "capabilities" can be slippery. Each is a mix of know-how, procedures, tools, technology, and assets that often cut across an organization's internal boundaries (see chapter 14). For nonprofits, these could fall into—or across—the following key areas:

- Articulating a particular mission in a tangible, compelling way and making it well understood—by staff, directors, partners, financial supporters, and so on
- Defining, realizing, measuring, marketing, and selling the impact of achieving a particular mission
- Keeping overheads within the now-established norm of 15%–25% while also creating and maintaining the ability to invest in critical infrastructure, such as data and analytics, financial systems, the latest technologies, new staff, and professional development
- Sourcing unrestricted funds for inventing, testing, and scaling new or different approaches
- Replacing financial supporters when the nonprofit's independence policy calls for a pause in or even termination of their funding
- Partnering with national and local government agencies, global and local NGOs, other nonprofits, and companies that are critical to realizing a particular mission

Simply coming to agreement on the right handful of truly distinctive, mission-specific capabilities in such areas is hard enough, but establishing and maintaining sharp accountability for nurturing them is a great leadership challenge. All the more reason to be crystal clear on what they should be. Otherwise, a nonprofit's strategy is just a pipe dream.

Most nonprofits can articulate their missions and plans, but many fall short on strategy because they can't answer the four questions listed above in a clear, compelling manner that is well understood by all the most important financial supporters and other stakeholders. That's a missed opportunity. A nonprofit's strategy forms a powerful trio with its mission and plan:

- Missions define the heart and soul of what nonprofits do, and why they exist.
- Strategies prescribe how the nonprofits can win financial supporters for their missions.
- Plans set out how they will achieve their missions and implement their strategies.

Each part of the trio makes the other two stronger, and each is weakened if one or the other is missing in action.

None of the above is to say that nonprofits should be run like for-profit businesses. But most nonprofits do indeed have to compete for financial supporters, much like businesses need to compete for customers. Thus, the tool of strategy has an important role to play in making a nonprofit's mission possible to achieve. The focus of strategy (financial supporters) may be different than for a for-profit business (customers), but the essential choices—*Who? Why? What?*—are essentially the same.

There's something in all this for leaders of for-profits, as well. For example, should their promise to financial supporters—a.k.a., their investors—go beyond providing attractive financial returns and include benefits associated with achieving their company's particular mission (see chapter 33)? Should such benefits be included in what they offer to their customers (see chapter 34)? Should they target investors (or customers) who would be most attracted to their mission? Should they raise capital from investors for individual programs or initiatives? Questions like these can help for-profit leaders distinguish their strategy—and then devise ways to implement it.

PART XI

What About Strategy for Different Types of Industries?

Leaders can learn a lot from the acute strategy challenges faced by companies in other domains.

Note to readers

The industries included here make the cut only because I have some first-hand experience with each of them. Thus, I feel somewhat qualified to opine on some of the more pressing strategy challenges they face and on what leaders from any industry can learn from those challenges.

🐠 60

Health Care

When meeting a customer need is not enough

I once worked with a company that invented a digestible sensor which could be embedded in a pill and turn an analogue drug into a digital medicine. When patients swallow it, the sensor inside records the dose and time of ingestion. This is a novel solution to an enormously expensive problem known as "nonadherence," where people don't take their medicines as prescribed. Thus, an expensive resource (therapeutic drugs) is wasted and, worse, patients suffer even costlier health complications down the road, adding expense to the entire health care system.

Like any big idea, this one needed a strategy to fully realize its tremendous potential value—both health and economic—to society. And that required the company's leaders to choose their *Who? Why?* and *What?* (see chapter 2). So far, so simple.

Yet things got complicated very quickly. Take the first strategy choice the company's leaders had to confront: *Who* the target customer should be. Common sense would suggest it's whoever pays. In this case, that would be hospital systems that pay for the information produced by the company's digital medicines and also pharma company partners who pay for the service to embed the technology in their pills. But common sense would also suggest that private and public insurers are forking over real money to reimburse for the use and consumption of the company's offerings, that doctors must at least "buy into" the product before they'll prescribe it (even if they don't pay for it), and that nurses have a big influence on treatment protocols and decisions. And what about employers who pay for the insurance plans that cover the cost of using digital medicines? Or patients—won't they incur at least some of the cost with their co-pay and, more important, don't they always come first?

All these actors had to change their practices, routines, and expectations for this company to succeed. And that wouldn't happen unless each of them saw a compelling reason—a *Why?*—for doing so. This means the *Who?* was a hydra, so fully realizing the potential of the company's big idea demanded a strategy with a compelling *Why?* for each of the hydra's many heads.

Leaders who operate in the health care industry are all too familiar with this challenge of corralling a complicated web of players to build a thriving enterprise. But it's actually a fairly common challenge in many arenas. Take the typical college: its "customers" include parents, students, high school counselors, and even employers—all four parties must have a compelling *Why?* to choose a college over their many alternatives. Or consider the situation where a business is selling a service—such as software implementation or management consulting—to another business: in many cases, the executives choosing, using, implementing, and paying for the service provider are different people, and each of them requires a *Why?* that addresses their particular needs. A third, more prosaic, example is breakfast cereal: grocery chains buy the sugary stuff from cereal makers; parents purchase it from the supermarket; and their kids devour it at home. All three parties—grocery chains, parents, and children—must have a compelling *Why?* to purchase (or demand its purchase of) its product rather than someone else's cereal or breakfast choice.

The point is that companies in most industries have to appeal to multiple parties to generate revenue. Leaders' choice of who should be the ideal customer has to include more than the people or entities that fund its revenues. And the *Why?* of strategy must address each party who influences whether a company's offering is bought.

Returning to the digital medicine company, the need was clear: greater adherence to a drug treatment leading to better patient outcomes and lower lifetime cost-of-care. The value of meeting this need should be self-evident, so the industry should be falling all over the company's solution for meeting it. Right?

But it turned out that the company's offering added a great deal of extra work on overworked doctors to read and act on adherence data reports. It required patients to wear a patch that receives the digital medicine's signal and to change their behavior that was leading to the lack of adherence in the first place. Hospital systems had to modify their systems, processes, and treatment protocols. And the company's leaders learned that Big Pharma didn't always want payors to know more about actual usage or regulators to have too much new data from a clinical trial—such as on non-compliers versus non-responders—as that might undermine their case for the efficacy of a new drug and thus affect their profits. Moreover, the company's Big Pharma partners had to switch to selling an outcome (greater adherence) through a product-as-a-service (medicines that produce real-time data and analytics on adherence) that could result in reduced product revenues for them (due to less wastage of their drugs) and that at a minimum requires them to change their business model in a fairly fundamental way. In other words, the company's product imposed a number of changes, costs, and perceived risks on those who could make or break its big idea.

As a result, despite the promise of better patient outcomes and lower costs across the entire health care system, doctors balked at the extra work it required. Hospital systems struggled to coordinate all the moving parts involved in implementing the company's solution and feared the financial risk to their razor-thin margins. Most patients didn't always want the uncertain prospect of better health enough to change their deeply engrained behaviors or face higher co-pays (in this case, from taking their full prescription rather than skipping doses). And Big Pharma struggled with the prospect of potentially awkward data, additional burdens, discomforting uncertainties, and creating a business where medicines are sold as a service rather than a product.

A convincing pitch for this company had to demonstrate that meeting the adherence need with its solution would produce meaningful and unique benefits for everyone—all six or seven heads of the hydra! And those benefits had to more than justify all the real and perceived costs the various parties would experience in buying, implementing, and using the solution. These benefits could include a new revenue opportunity for doctors and hospital systems; reduction of payors' medical costs that exceed any premium reductions from lowering such costs; peace of mind for patients' families; and a way for Big Pharma partners to extend the life of drugs nearing patent expiration. As for the cost side, the company's offering could include a service model that absorbs much of the extra work from doctors; simplifies the implementation of operational changes required of hospital systems; and offers Big Pharma partners a proven playbook for commercializing medicines-as-a-service.

This example shows that meeting an unmet need is not enough to have a compelling *Why?* Leaders have to spell out the benefits—both hard monetary ones and soft nonfinancial ones—that customers will experience by buying and using the company's offering to meet an unmet need. And leaders must explicitly anticipate—and then justify or mitigate—*all* such costs that customers will incur by going with a company's offering versus taking their next best alternative, ranging from the obvious financial and other tangible costs to the intangibles like the perceived hassle or risk of going with something new.

Going back to the other examples: Which benefit–cost equation for each of a school's prospective parents, students, high school counselors, and employers will compel them to prioritize it over the many other universities they could choose? For an enterprise service provider, which value equation for each of the buyer, users, implementers, and payer in a prospective account will propel them to select it over their perceived alternatives? For the cereal maker, what's in it for the grocery chains, parents, and their children to, respectively, stock, purchase, and consume a particular cereal brand? And which costs—such as shelf space or health impact—do any of these parties see that need to be justified or mitigated? Answering questions likes these, and not relying on simply stating the need (or want) that a company's offering is supposed to meet, is the key to unlocking a compelling *Why?* for any company operating in any industry, not just health care.

61

Life Sciences

When "thinking globally and acting locally" is only half the battle

Leaders in the life sciences industry face many challenges in creating, sustaining, and implementing great strategies. But two really stand out. One comes from the inherent uncertainty and long lead times associated with discovering new medicines. It can take over a decade—longer than the tenure of most leaders—for successful discoveries to become revenue-generating medicines.

Moreover, many discovery efforts produce surprising outcomes, such as a novel drug for a disease area no one was expecting. For example, AstraZeneca's Farxiga drug started off as a treatment for diabetes; then it was found to also be effective in treating chronic kidney disease; and recent studies even showed that it helps patients with heart failure. These outcomes were neither intended nor predicted by the company's leaders, and yet they led to the discovery of a versatile, multi-billion-dollar drug, the creation of a new business to market the drug, and a significant change in the company's multibusiness strategy.

Another example comes from Novo Nordisk. For decades, the drugmaker's sole focus on one therapeutic area—diabetes—has been unique in its industry. As part of that effort, it developed Ozempic, only to discover that it's also highly effective in treating weight loss. Novo's discovery thrust the company into an enormous new business—the treatment of obesity—that it had never intended to enter, thus changing a decades-old strategy seemingly overnight.

In an industry with such long lead times and unpredictable outcomes, how do leaders create a robust strategy? A great example comes from Franz Humer, the CEO of Roche Holding AG from 1998 to 2008. He was an early pioneer of a strategy called "personalized medicine." (Yes, it's somewhat cliché these days, but it was new 30 years ago.)

Diagnostics and drugs became the twin pillars of Humer's multibusiness strategy because he judged that being in *both* businesses was critical to being great at personalized medicine. And that led him to make a daring multi-billion-dollar investment in a company almost six thousand miles away from his headquarters in Basel, Switzerland: the Northern California company Genentech, which led the way in developing novel medicines and diagnostics geared toward addressing genetic differences across the human population.

Humer's strategy also led him to make several other moves against the grain in his industry at that time, including the decision to exit over-the-counter consumer products, divest vitamins, and avoid the generic medicines sector. Moreover, "personalized medicine" became a common mission of the company's R&D efforts and of its investments in enterprise capabilities, like genomics. All this was novel in the early 2000s, and it turned Roche from a struggling, middling pharma company into a global powerhouse. Moreover, Humer's strategy survived and has thrived beyond his tenure.

Leaders in the life sciences industry are not alone in facing long, uncertain investment horizons. And the strategy solution they often seek is similar to the one Humer found for Roche. For example, a big cost of doing business in the oil-&-gas industry is the risk of drilling many "dry holes" before striking oil or gas. Moreover, it can take over a decade to turn a new gusher into a robust revenue stream. Back in the late 1980s and early 1990s, John Browne (now Lord Browne) tackled this challenge by inventing his "elephant fields" strategy when he ran the exploration business for BP, the U.K.-based energy company. He made BP the leader in finding new fields with enormous reservoirs of oil-&-gas, and also in turning existing fields into elephants by swapping wells with—or acquiring them from—other oil companies operating in those fields. This effectively increased the return on investing in exploration, because the total cost per delivered barrel from elephant fields is far lower than from more-fragmented fields.

The car industry offers another example. In the time it takes to design, engineer, and set up factories for volume production of a new model, many factors that will make or break its success—such as consumer preferences, economic conditions, and even the company's leaders—can change in material and unpredictable ways. BMW, the German auto manufacturer, found a solution with "the ultimate driving machine." This was originally just a slogan introduced during the 1970s by Bob Lutz, who was leading global sales and marketing at the time. But it's become a durable customer proposition that is common to every BMW model as well as a standard of design and engineering for its new-model pipeline. This reduces uncertainty in the company's R&D by cutting BMW's exposure to consumer shifts, economic cycles, and leadership turnover that can make new models obsolete before they hit the market.

If uncertain R&D with long lead times is the first strategy challenge that stands out for the life sciences industry, the second is global–local complexity. Leaders of pharma companies must respond to the unique health care system in every market they face and, at the same time, must operate to take advantage of their global scale and scope.

Leaders of multinational businesses in *any* industry have this challenge. And they have two basic options for tackling it: they can choose to have a global proposition with localized offerings, or the reverse. BMW is a prime example of the first. As noted above, its pitch—"the ultimate driving machine"—is the same everywhere in the world. But its product line-up is specific to individual markets, such as a relatively richer mix of SUVs in the United States and a higher proportion of top-end luxury and sporting models in Germany. To make this work, BMW's main operating units are global functions: design, engineering, manufacturing, sales, marketing, and leasing and lending services. They respond to demand and input from country and regional operations so as to implement the company's global strategy.

Starbucks offers an example of the second approach: a global product set with local propositions. Its offerings—the roasts and recipes used in its menu of coffee drinks—are nearly identical from market to market. But its broader proposition varies around the world, with more of a fast-food feel and drive-in format in the United States, a high-end café atmosphere in Germany, and so on. The leaders in each market drive their own local strategy—that is, the *Who? Why?* and *What?* for their particular market. The company's global functions—such as coffee-bean sourcing and roasting, new drinks development, IT, and more—support local leaders with high-quality ingredients, menu innovations, digital capabilities, and more.

To complicate matters, a life sciences company has to operate somewhere in between the BMW and Starbucks models. This is because—as noted above—their leaders need a global strategy that accommodates high-risk R&D with long lead times. And that usually leads to a proposition that is common across all markets, such as the Humer-Roche example of "personalized medicine." This would suggest the BMW model, where a global strategy gets customized locally. But, just as with Starbucks and its range of coffee drinks, a typical life-science company's product portfolio is essentially the same in every market. And because health care systems vary a great deal from country to country, the relative influence of actors—from patients to doctors, nurse practitioners, physician assistants, providers, private payors, government payors, and so on—and the pitch that appeals to each of them will vary a lot around the world (see chapter 60).

For example, private and public payor definitions of "value" are not the same from country to country, and thus product development and clinical research must produce evidence that can appeal to each country. This suggests the Starbucks model, where local strategies get supported by global operations—R&D, manufacturing, regulatory affairs, and the like.

Global-Local Strategy Options for Multinational Businesses

	Option 1	Option 2	Option 3
Proposition	Global	Local	Global and Local
Product/Service Mix	Local	Global	Global and Local
Example	BMW	Starbucks	Life Sciences Companies

The oft-used prescription for multinational companies is "think globally and act locally." But that doesn't quite capture what leaders of global life-science companies are up against. They have to create organizations that can think and act both global *and* locally. This requires them to master both of the strategy models exemplified by BMW and Starbucks, respectively, whereby leaders of their global functions as well as their local operations simultaneously lead and support *both* a global strategy for the company overall *and* a local strategy for every market. This must be why leading a global life sciences company is called "work"!

62

Retailing

When "retail is detail" doesn't cut it

Retailers provide places for people to buy the products they need and want. The places typically include physical stores, online websites, and catalogs, while the products range from own brands to third-party brands. Moreover, they can feature "shops-within-a-shop" (like Disney and Sephora shops in JC Penney) and can provide ancillary services, such as installation, repair, and even credit; classes on interior design, photography, and wine; and fitness studios, spas, and barber shops. To attract shoppers, many retailers also offer entertainment—including live music, Santa Claus, play areas, video game lounges, and on and on—as well as refreshment, like a coffee bar or a restaurant.

All these variables can make or break a retailer's success—its foot and online traffic, transaction volume and size, inventory management, margin realization, average spend per store or website visit, and more. That's why leaders spend mountains of time on getting all these variables right. This is where the mantra "retail is detail" comes from.

But getting the details right—as important as that is—won't make up for the lack of what powers outsized success for any business: a distinctive strategy based on a big idea that's still a big one. And, thanks to the rise of online retailing and the decline of malls, that's a huge challenge for traditional retailers.

When Amazon.com was founded in 1997, it was impossible to see what's clear today: that online retail is creating an existential challenge for incumbent retailers. Malls are losing both stores and shoppers, and main streets everywhere are pocked with retail closures, including even Fifth Avenue in midtown Manhattan.

In the U.S. alone, retailers have closed more than 100 million square feet of space *per year since 2016*. While a lot of this is due to a cyclical correction of overzealous building for the last few decades, the bigger reason is "Amageddon" and its corollary, "Mallfall." These are directly or indirectly effecting a profound restructuring of the retail landscape, including the liquidation of Toys "R" Us, Payless ShoeSource, and Gymboree; the bankruptcy of Barney's, Pier 1 Imports, Debenham, and House of Fraser; the mass store closures of Family Dollar, Forever 21, Sears, and Kmart; and the proposed-then-rescinded split of Old Navy from Gap, Inc.

If the seismic forces of Amageddon and Mallfall were registering 6 or 7 on the Richter scale before the Covid-19 pandemic, they are surely registering 8 or 9 now. Even retailers that seemed to be doing all the right things before the pandemic weren't getting much for their efforts.

Take Nordstrom. Its leaders invested early and heavily in e-commerce. They largely avoided over-expanding its store network, and the company has far fewer outlets than Macy's, JC Penney, and other retailers who have been closing hundreds of locations. They moved quickly to introduce services that brought together e-commerce and physical stores, such as same-day shipping for online orders pulled from local stores. They rewarded employees for both store and online sales. They were quick to experiment with new formats, such as HauteLook, the flash-sale website, and with TrunkClub, an online clothing subscription service. They even poached employees from Amazon, whose Seattle's headquarters are only six blocks away from Nordstrom's head office.

All of this may prove to be enough in the end, but judging by Nordstrom's valuation, probably not. Its stock market value has dropped from $15 billion in 2015 to less than $3 billion more recently.

Here's what is going on: Nordstrom made it big with two big ideas. The first was to be a category killer in men's shoes when "category killer" wasn't a thing yet. Before Nordstrom, no one had seen any store carry as much inventory in men's shoes as it did. On the back of that, Nordstrom developed its second big idea: epic customer service based on highly personal relationship-building between sales-floor staff and shoppers, and a then-unique, almost heretical policy of "no-questions-asked-no-receipts-necessary" for merchandise returns. That idea stretched well (see chapter 20) into a broader offering that became its full-line department store where shoes are still important but now take up only a fraction of Nordstrom's floor space.

Today, however, Nordstrom's original big ideas are not strong enough to counter the heavy headwinds buffeting the company and its industry. It's hard to see what makes the brand stand out anymore. That's why "doing all the right things" isn't always enough, and why Nordstrom has lost over 80% of its value.

Walmart is a radically different story. In 2015 I published a piece for *Forbes. com* (see appendix 2) in which I wrote, "Now is the time to innovate the company's strategy," because the big idea that drove nearly 50 years of the chain's massive success was no longer big enough to drive its future. And while Walmart's leaders were doing a lot of good things—selling off underperforming foreign businesses, updating stores, improving product mix—they needed a new big idea.

In that same article, I offered three possibilities: repurpose its 4,000 superstores as fulfillment centers serving an online retailing business (much in the way that Amazon's 100+ fulfillment centers serve its original e-commerce business); adopt a membership program (similar to the Costco or the Amazon Prime models); or group its superstores into different "clusters" and build from the ground up a workable format for each cluster that's customized to its particular type of customer base (like suburban vs. rural) and also to its mix of competitors (such as discount chains, category killers, middle-income department stores, or mall-based retailers).

Since I wrote that piece, Walmart leaders have effectively chosen the first two of these options. They rolled out same-day delivery and buy-online-collect-in-store services at all of its 4,000 superstores in the United States. And they unveiled a new subscription service called "Walmart+" that offers similar benefits to those of Amazon Prime, including same-day delivery of groceries.

Walmart's leaders are effectively turning an albatross of aging assets on the verge of obsolescence into something that even Amazon can't match: some 4,000 same-day delivery fulfillment centers and pick-up locations within 10 miles of 90% of the U.S population. This is especially powerful in fresh groceries, where the "last-mile" delivery problem is particularly acute. Grocery is one of the most important parts of Walmart and a business that Amazon has struggled mightily to crack (which is why Amazon is experimenting with acquiring and building its own grocery outlets).

To be clear, Walmart initially did what many incumbents do when their industry feels overwhelmed by innovative upstarts: they launch imitation and acquisition countermeasures (see chapters 63–64). They created Walmart.com to mimic Amazon.com and scooped up the e-commerce sites Jet.com (a startup created to underprice Amazon), ModCloth (women's apparel), Bonobos (men's apparel), and Moosejaw (outdoor products). None of it worked to revitalize the company. Jet.com cut staff and was folded into the rest of Walmart, Bonobos laid off workers, and ModCloth was sold.

Still, it seems that the idea of repurposing Walmart's superstores as fulfillment centers for an online grocery business has done the trick. And more important, Walmart's leaders are turning that idea into an even bigger one: borrowing from Walt Disney's original concept of using its film studio to feed other businesses, such as television, comics, toys, and theme parks (see chapter 3). Walmart intends to put supercenter stores at the heart of a web of next-gen businesses such as one for selling shopper data, for display advertising space, to get targeted coupons, and to find sponsored search results to its suppliers; another for providing warehousing-and-delivery-as-a-service to e-retailers; a third called Walmart GoLocal that will serve the "last-mile" delivery needs of local and national retailers; and a fourth that will offer "edge-computing" infrastructure in each store for local businesses or autonomous vehicles that need fast data processing. Plus, in early 2021 Walmart announced a partnership with Ribbit Capital to create a new fintech that will take advantage of the 1500 Walmart MoneyCenters (twice the number of Citibank branches!) in its store network.

Investors, at least, are buying all this as a "very big idea" that no one else can replicate. That's why Walmart's valuation tripled since 2015 after stagnating for 15 years before that. Such a stunning reversal for a company of Walmart's size and vintage can only happen when its leaders find a new big idea that is even bigger than the one that made it great in the first place (see chapters 16, 20, and 21).

To be sure, others are trying versions of Walmart's big idea. But they can't, and that's why it's such a powerful idea. For example, Home Depot—the home improvement chain—is offering free two-day delivery and installing automated lockers across its nearly 2,300 outlets for quicker pick-up of customer orders.

This certainly enhances Home Depot's overall offering, but it doesn't solve a big problem like the "last mile" one in grocery.

Kohl's is another example. The department store lets customers take any items they buy from Amazon to any of its 1,100 outlets and Kohl's will pack and ship them back to the internet retailer for free. The idea is to bring potential shoppers to Kohl's, but it's not clear how making it the dumping ground for unwanted merchandise bought from Amazon enhances what Kohl's already sells. That's most likely why Kohl's stock market value took an even steeper nose-dive than Nordstrom's.

The changes in retailing wrought by "Amageddon" and "Mallfall" are here to stay. Each retailer must find its own new big idea to survive those changes and thrive again. Nordstrom hasn't found one. Walmart has. Maybe Waterstones'— the U.K. bookseller—has found one, too, with its concept of the anti-chain format for its bookstores. Instead of the traditional pile-'em-high-in-look-alike-stores-with-centralized-buying, the company's idea is to create a series of one-off stores, each with a boutique, upmarket, and localized feel and inventory. In its Bradford, U.K. store that means carrying a lot of books on poetry and mathematics; the store in Yarm—a rural community—is redolent of books on animals; and the branch in London's Piccadilly market turns its basement floor into an event space for rabid fans of *Harry Potter*. It's a kind of back-to-the-future idea to revive the notion of local bookstores, and it's working so far.

Of course, retail is not the only industry to be rocked by seismic change. For example, the mainframe computer sector was shaken to its knees by the personal computer, which itself is now being challenged by smartphones. Dissemination of news, sports, entertainment, and advertising over the internet has decimated traditional cinema, music, magazines, newspapers, and media agencies. Animal farming and meat processing are both being upended by plant-based meat, which itself could be overrun by cell-based meat in the not-too-distant future. Traditional consumer products are getting trounced by the wave of insurgent brands offering better ingredients, more transparency, sharper pricing, and greater social responsibility, value, or purpose (see chapter 63). And "fintech" continues to create turmoil in the financial services industry (see chapter 64), while virtually hundreds of "edtech" companies are challenging deeply embedded models of teaching, learning, and professional development.

Incumbent leaders in any industry who are facing big changes like these can learn a great deal from closely watching the divergent paths of retailers: should they double-down on the Nordstrom approach to incremental innovation and optimization of their strategies, or should they instead take the Walmart path and challenge themselves to find a new, even bigger idea that replaces the one that made their companies great in the first place?

63

Consumer Products

When upstarts force leaders to innovate their strategies

Companies in the consumer product goods industry—often referred to as "CPGs"—produce branded products for people to buy. They distribute their products through retailers and, increasingly, sell directly to consumers via websites.

Like many industries, this one is being challenged by a proliferation of upstarts that are eating into the growth of its incumbents. And its eating into the growth of CPGs. Despite hundreds of acquisitions over the last few years, the combined global market share of the top 50 CPGs has waned.

Whereas retailing is under siege from online retailing (see chapter 62), consumer product giants are suffering from something different: a proliferation of upstart brands from new companies across almost every category, ranging from food and beverages to personal care, health, wellness, beauty, and more. These next-gen brands promise better ingredients, more transparency, fairer pricing, and greater social status, responsibility, value, or purpose. They are sucking up precious shelf space, growth, and margins from the billion-dollar "power brands" that are the bread and butter of traditional CPGs.

To understand what's going on, consider two iconic power brands: the battery-maker Duracell and an iconic maker of blades and razors, Gillette. Duracell ranks in the 98th percentile of all major brands in the strength of relationship consumers have with its brand. This comes from BERA Brand

Management, which continuously collects consumer perceptions of over 2,000 U.S. brands that collectively account for at least 75% of sales in more than 200 categories.

Consumers *love* Duracell, much more than its main rival, Eveready, whose brand strength ranks in the 66th percentile among BERA's 2,000 brands. That's why Duracell commands a price for its double-A battery bought through Amazon.com that's about 50% higher than Eveready's.

Gillette currently ranks just below the 90th percentile—still very high, but much less than it used to be, and materially lower than Duracell's score. Critically, Gillette's Uniqueness score—an essential factor in BERA's overall brand-equity metric—is in the mid-70s. Duracell's is in the high-80s. Imagine that: a brand of old-tech batteries is significantly more differentiated in consumers' eyes than a brand of highly sophisticated razors and blades!

This is explained by the entry of innovative brands such as Harry's Shave Club, Dollar Shave Club, and MicroTouch Solo. They promote a compelling proposition for a very large subset of the shaving population: good-enough quality at a much lower price with a subscription model that makes it easy to keep a ready supply on hand. This has severely crimped Gillette's trajectory and challenged its incremental innovation model, which has worked well for decades: simply adding ever more blades to its cartridges, then charging higher and higher prices for them.

To revive Gillette's brand, its leaders have to go back to their business strategy and rethink everything about it. For example, should they embrace or reject the type of customer that is attracted to shave clubs? Can Gillette leaders differentiate their offering of benefits in ways other than greater and greater shave quality, which seems to have hit the point of diminishing returns? Should they build a capability that enables Gillette to manage a portfolio of multiple shave brands, each having a different *Why?* for a particular type of *Who?* Gillette needs breakthrough answers to such questions, not simply more product innovation, to overcome the headwinds acting against its brand in blades and razors.

While the consumer battery category has escaped the insurgent-brand phenomenon so far, a lot of others have not—like snacking (Kind, Verba Energy, etc.); beverages (for example, Sierra Nevada beer, REBBL energy drink, and Neat vodka), skincare (COOLA, Sun Bum, Moon Juice, etc.), and even household cleaning products (such as from The Honest Company).

Companies offering big power brands in categories like these have three options for how they respond: imitation; acquisition; and innovation. The first two seem sensible, and a lot easier than the third. Still, they won't fortify the relationship consumers have with the power brands they already own.

Take option 1, *imitation*—copying a startup's innovations and using one's incumbent advantages, like scale and scope of distribution, to overwhelm the fledgling competitor. The problem is, the stronger an incumbent brand's heritage, the more it stands for something significant in consumers' eyes. And the more successful a novel, new brand (like White Claw, the alcoholic seltzer), the more it means something different from what the incumbent brand represents. The incumbent brand risks diluting its strengths by simply mimicking the new entry. That's because consumers are savvy—they can spot the difference between genuine improvements to a brand's proposition and a cynical attempt to blunt another brand's innovation. For example, keep an eye on Bud Light Seltzer, AB InBev's recent imitation of White Claw. Will this be a successful stretch of the Bud Light brand, or merely an expensive imitation that falls flat (so to speak)? Will consumers see the logic of downing an alcoholic seltzer with a light-beer brand attached to it, or regard it as just a desperate move to make up for Bud Light's loss of growth to a new category?

As noted earlier, most of the consumer giants have tried option 2, *acquisition*. And they've had some real success in growing the small brands they acquire into larger ones. For example, Kellogg's bought the healthy cereal maker Kashi and turned it into a mainstream brand; the Coca-Cola Company did the same with Vitamin Water, a "health beverage"; while P&G turned Native natural deodorant into a power brand after buying it. But none of these acquisitions changed the growth trajectory of Kellogg's traditional cereal brands, Coca-Cola's original namesake products, or P&G's personal care power brands.

Option 3—*strategy innovation*—calls for leaders of an incumbent power brand either to reinvent their *Who? Why?* and *What?* or to find a new big idea, or both. For example, leaders of Dove, the personal care brand, innovated their *Why?* by adopting a social purpose (see chapters 13 and 33): "to educate and inspire girls on a wider definition of beauty." Another example is Pabst Blue

Ribbon whose leaders resuscitated this old, traditional, Midwest beer with an innovative change in their primary customer—one that zeroed in on counter-cultural types like bike messengers and snowboarders to make "PBR" cool with the non-corporate, non-pretentious, unglamorous, hipster crowd (see chapter 12).

Of the three options, strategy innovation may seem the more challenging one, but it's often the best one to revitalize an incumbent brand that has been commoditized, cheapened, or turned old-fashioned by new-wave brands, or has been outed for "greedflation," or is associated with some social ill.

There's an important takeaway in all this for leaders working in other industries: When leaders measure and monitor the strength of their brand equity, they give themselves a powerful tool for evaluating the health of their strategies, detecting when those strategies need innovation, and understanding what kind of strategy innovation they need. That's because their brand and business are two sides of the same coin. Brand strength reflects the health and wellness of the business strategy behind it, and vice versa.

That's why Gillette's declining brand equity in blades and razors is a strong signal that its strategy has indeed lost some of its edge. In contrast, the leaders of airline Southwest have found one of the most meaningfully differentiated strategies in its industry, at least for now (see chapter 8). It's no coincidence that no other major airline comes close to Southwest's brand equity. Its differentiation is 70% stronger than Delta's and more than twice the brand differentiation of United and American Airlines.

64

Financial Services

When partnering trumps imitation and acquisition

The Financial Services (FS) industry accounts for 15% to 20% of the entire global economy. And the traditional companies in this industry all share a common threat and opportunity: the "fintechs."

These are digital-first companies that make use of computer technology to improve and automate financial services for enterprises and consumers. New fintechs are born every day. They leverage digital technology to keep costs low; they benefit from the increasing acceptance of taking financial services online; and above all, they are exploiting the reality that many people feel dissatisfied with traditional providers of financial services, especially the big banks.

According to *Knowledge@Wharton*, "fintechs are growing rapidly…[because] they target pain points [that customers] experience with traditional banks." For example, Affirm—founded in 2012 by PayPal cofounder Max Levchin—finances purchases with point-of-sale loans at much lower interest rates than consumers pay on their credit cards. The company uses personal data from social media to evaluate credit risk and then to offer interest rates and repayment terms tailored to individual borrowers.

Likewise, the payments specialist TransferWise offers low-cost international money transfers by using a peer-to-peer model that matches the transfer requests of various customers. And a student loan company called PYT Funds—PYT stands for "pay your tuition"—helps banks transform their "turndown pool" of student loan applicants into profitable customers by assisting the applicants in crowdsourcing the collateral required for bank approval.

Armed with next-generation capabilities in areas such as big data, social media listening, cloud-based computing, and AI, fintechs promise customers lower prices, greater convenience, and highly customized offerings. And, unlike the traditional players, they are not encumbered by legacy IT systems. They can build platforms that are faster, are way more efficient, and have greater flexibility than incumbents' systems that are buried in layers of last-century technology.

The typical response of incumbents has been to imitate or acquire the upstarts (see chapter 63), or set up "accelerators" that run competitions to find the most-promising startups, or even start a venture fund in Silicon Valley, and so on. Some of these efforts may succeed in their own right, but few have so far; and they won't produce the fundamental innovation that traditional incumbents need for the 21st century. Instead, leaders of these companies should see fintech as potential partners that can help them reinvent their incumbent strategies and business models for the digital age.

Happily, incumbents have a lot to offer fintechs in return. Their systems and platforms may not be cutting edge, yet incumbents have the controls, audit trails, balance sheet, and fail-safe features required for large-scale financial services. And as fintech grow, they'll need organizations, processes, and systems for managing frauds, claims, collections, and anti-money-laundering. Again, major FS companies can do all this.

The aforementioned Levchin once said to me, "Fintechs have what many FS [financial services] companies need: superior access to troves of big data, modern and relevant front ends aligned to customer expectations and preferences, and software architecture that has been developed from the ground up based on modern technologies and principles…but [as they scale, they] will soon be subsumed with the same things they were trying to solve."

He acknowledges that fintechs can't keep growing larger without developing many of the resources of a traditional financial institution. And as they scale up, fintechs will attract greater scrutiny from regulators and will need full-fledged compliance capabilities—the charters, licenses, and systems required to meet regulatory requirements and to operate within industry guardrails that FS companies have refined over generations.

Levchin believes fintechs would be willing to share their distinctive capabilities with FS companies in exchange for taking on traditional functions for which the fintechs have no real aptitude or affinity. He foresees that FS companies might become the gatekeepers to the guardrails for regulatory compliance, funds transfer, and other traditional capabilities, and could eventually take a fee for the business that comes into their "ecosystem" from the fintechs. He thinks fintechs and traditional FS companies would consider this a fair trade.

Indeed, setting up partnerships with fintechs, rather than buying or imitating them, is increasingly gaining traction. Revenues from such partnerships are approaching $100 billion annually. And anecdotal evidence from *Strategy+Business* suggests that banks that partner with fintechs generate more than twice the average profitability of their industry.

Meanwhile, incumbents are learning just how expensive fintechs are to acquire; how difficult it can be to integrate them into the more-staid cultures of decades-old FS companies; and how frustrating it is to see founders and key staff leave after lock-ups end, and then to watch innovation dwindle. The incumbents are also learning that they aren't cut out to be venture capitalists or incubators or accelerators, nor able to recruit younger tech talent fast enough, given the firms' enormous overhang of very mature workforces.

At the same time, fintechs are changing their tune as well. As Olivier Khayat, co-CEO of the western European commercial banking at UniCredit, said to *Financial Times*, "Most fintechs are not here to disrupt or replace banks, but to act as partners and suppliers. That is working extremely well."

The partnership between BankMobile and Customer Bank could be a model of what Khayat means. BankMobile is a mobile-first bank, and Customer Bank is a traditional bank in Phoenixville, Arizona. BankMobile effectively operates as the digital banking arm of Customer Bank, helping it acquire customers at much higher volume and lower costs, and thereby making it possible to pay higher interest on customer deposits than do Customer Bank's traditional peers.

Other examples include Nimbla, Paytm, and Microf. Nimbla has teamed with Barclays to offer invoice insurance to the U.K. bank's small-business customers; in India, Paytm has partnered with Citigroup on a Paytm First Visa card for the extraordinary number of 300 million urban and emerging-affluent customers within Paytm's payments system; and Microf joined forces with

SunTrust, a U.S. regional bank, to offer lease-to-own loans to the bank's retail customers to help them buy HVAC systems.

Even Big Tech is open to collaboration with Big Banking. For example, Google is offering a mobile bank account called Plex that will be managed by a traditional bank, starting with Citibank and 10 other banks and credit unions in the United States. And Amazon is offering working-capital loans from Goldman Sachs to its U.S. merchant customers.

Collaborations such as these can work in any industry where new players are using leading-edge technologies to bring new propositions, capabilities, or customers into a traditional industry. For example, in consumer products, P&G struck a deal with W. M. Barr & Co. Inc. to work together on launching a surface-area, bacteria-killing disinfectant that relies on Barr's technology.

In industrials, Caterpillar and Uptake, a Chicago-based data analytics firm, have a partnership through which the younger firm is helping the century-old giant compile, organize, and analyze sensor information from its bulldozers, backhoes, and other construction machinery. Likewise, John Deere, the tractor manufacturer, has a deal with Hello Tractor, a Nigerian startup that enables farmers to hail tractors just with an app. The idea is to connect small-scale farmers, who cannot afford the outlay for a tractor, with the vehicles' owners.

And in the health care industry, the new company Carena and several large hospital groups are partnering to provide a low-cost telemedicine service, while Otsuka, the Japanese pharmaceutical company, partnered with Proteus Digital Health to digitize therapeutic drugs for mental health.

To succeed at such collaborations, incumbent leaders must prioritize the business lines, customer segments, offerings, and capabilities that most need reinvention—wholesale, "big-bang" change is usually a bad idea. They should seek out tech players that operate in areas closest to those parts of their business that most need strategy innovation, as these are the most likely candidates for profitable collaboration. And incumbent leaders need to decide what sharing of assets and capabilities will govern the collaboration. For example, in financial services, it could be sharing their balance sheet or customer base in exchange for access to a fintech's back-end technology or its front-end customer interface.

Collaborating with innovative, tech-savvy newbies gives companies a powerful option for getting ahead of changes roiling an industry. But it won't work unless leaders are clear on where, exactly, innovation is more important than continuity in their strategy (see chapter 40), as well as whether collaboration with the upstarts is the best means for innovating their strategy where it's needed most (see chapter 41).

(65)

Banking

When suppliers are the product

Banking is an enormous sector within the much bigger financial services industry. It comprises two essential services. One is giving people and enterprises a safe and secure place to hold and manage cash deposits, and the other is lending that money to borrowers. By law, a bank must have a charter to accept deposits. This distinguishes a bank from every other kind of financial services company (see chapter 64).

A banking business makes money by charging a higher rate of interest on its loans than the rate it pays on deposits. Its customers are borrowers—people or enterprises who pay interest and fees for the money they borrow. Its suppliers are depositors—those who supply the raw material (that is, funds) that it needs to be able to lend to its borrowers.

A distinguishing feature of banking is that its suppliers and customers are often the same people (or entities). Many—if not most—of a bank's borrowers are often its depositors; and many of its depositors are often its borrowers. This sets up an important challenge for a bank's leaders: What should be the *Who?* and *Why?* for their strategy to build the most profitable base of customers (borrowers) and suppliers (depositors) at the same time? The more distinctive their answer, the more differentiated their strategy (and the more differentiated their strategy, the better their execution—see chapter 26).

Two companies offer compelling examples of such strategies. One is USAA, a San Antonio, Texas-based company that was founded in 1922 as a life insurance company. It has a uniquely defined priority customer: current and former members of the military and their families. Its customer proposition is differentiated by a reputation for understanding the financial needs of such people with great empathy, as well as by a manifest will and ability to serve those needs better than anyone else. On average, USAA's customers are *four* times more willing to recommend USAA than any other bank's customers are willing to recommend it. The affinity that USAA's customers have for the company is practically unheard of in an industry that tends to rank ahead of only law and consulting in popularity.

USAA's depositors are its most likely borrowers, and vice versa. Moreover, 80% of its customers are willing to acquire another financial product from the company, such as a mutual fund, credit card, insurance policy, or IRA. That's the highest among banks by a wide margin—and compares to less than 50% for Wells Fargo's customers (see chapter 46).

The intense loyalty of USAA's customers—as well as their willingness to put most of their financial lives into the company's hands—greatly reduces the company's cost of acquiring, serving, and keeping them. That's a big deal, because such costs account for half of a typical bank's operating costs. And that's why USAA has been one of the most profitable banks for decades, despite offering some of the lowest interest rates and sticking to a highly conservative risk profile. It's also why USAA not only escaped the need for bailout money during the 2008 financial crisis, when it subsequently grew while most banks retrenched.

Silicon Valley Bank (SVB), in California, offers a second example of how to build a profitable base of borrowers and depositors with a distinctive *Who?* and *Why?* It opened its doors in 1983. Technology companies were flowering in the area now called "Silicon Valley" because of its fertile mix of stellar academic institutions, free-wheeling culture, and bountiful sunshine. But these companies needed capital to get off the ground, and they didn't have much access to traditional equity investors or to debt lenders who simply didn't understand the complexities of funding technology entrepreneurs.

Two Wells Fargo bankers, Roger Smith and Bill Biggerstaff, and a Stanford professor, Robert Medearis, saw the problem and decided to do something about it. They started SVB by raising money from 100 technology "founders" who would not only invest in the bank but would also make deposits and refer their peers to it. They became experts in understanding the financial needs—and risks—of technology companies and the venture capital firms ("VCs") that invested in them, from hardware (such as semiconductors, data storage, and electronics) to software and internet infrastructure, health care (like biotechnology and medical devices), and, more recently, cryptocurrency companies. One venture capitalist described SVB's value as "breathing, eating, and drinking the [technology-investing] Kool-Aid every day."

Before its implosion in 2023 (see end note in chapter 26), SVB served almost two-thirds of all existing startups and over 600 VCs. Its startup and VC customers were loyal depositors as well as borrowers whose stability gave them a strong foundation for stretching their strategy on both sides of their business—for example, into money market accounts, certificates of deposit, and commercial paper on the deposits side; also into later-stage commercial and syndicated lending on the borrowing side; and, again on both sides, into financial services such as foreign exchange and cash management.

Despite determined and encroaching competition from Wall Street, SVB sustained well-above-average profitability even though it carried an even higher level of expensive liquidity—as measured by the amount of deposits held compared to loans outstanding—to protect it from the inevitable shocks of operating in the cyclical, highly volatile technology sector (again, see end note to chapter 26 on the implosion of SVB in 2023).

The examples of USAA and SVB demonstrate that employing a sharply differentiated strategy is quite possible in an industry dominated by look-alikes. But are they the exception to some rule that says it's almost impossible for bigger financial institutions to differentiate their banking businesses? For example, can anyone see a difference that matters between the banking businesses of Wells Fargo, JP Morgan Chase, Citigroup, or Bank of America? Consumers can't: the big-four banks have an average brand differentiation score that puts them in the bottom 20% of all brands. Out of 200 categories, banking is in the bottom 3% on differentiation, ahead of only light beer and prepaid mobile providers. Perhaps traditional bank leaders have given up on strategy and replaced it with cross-selling, diversifying, retrenching, expanding, contracting, and endless financial engineering. And maybe that's why they are regularly outperformed by the likes of USAA.

There are lessons in all this for leaders who run so-called "two-sided" businesses. For example, consider the following table:

Business	Suppliers ("the product")	Customers (of "the product")
Traditional media	Readers, viewers	Advertisers
Social media	Users	Advertisers
Ride hailing (e.g., Lyft)	Drivers	Passengers
DNA testing (e.g., 23andMe)	DNA kit buyers	Health researchers
Fitness gyms	Trainers	Members
Recruiting websites	Job seekers	Employers

For companies like these, the suppliers are effectively the product that customers pay for. The more attractive these suppliers are to a company's priority customers, the stronger its value proposition to those customers. And the more distinctive a company's customer target, the sharper leaders can be about whom they want in their supplier base. Thus, as in banking, having a great strategy and outstanding execution in a two-sided business depends a lot on having a distinctive *Who?*, a meaningfully unique *Why?*, and a handful of leading capabilities that apply to both sides of the business.

A final word

If in this book I have appeared to say that there's only one way for leaders to define "strategy" and it's my way, I would like to correct that appearance here. I am really saying two things. First, the leaders of a business should agree on what they mean by that term. Though that may seem obvious, it's not the case in most companies (see chapter 1). If leaders don't agree on what strategy is, how can they possibly create a great one and keep it great? This mortally damages the power of strategy to support great execution.

The second thing I am saying is that for a business to be a wild success, its leaders must have distinctive choices for their *Who? Why?* and *What?* I also say that this is nearly impossible unless those choices are inspired by a big idea that solves an important problem, an unmet need, or an unrequited want with a better solution. And I say that fantastic execution is impossible without distinctive choices for *Who? Why?* and *What?* that are powered by a big idea. Finally, I say it doesn't really matter how leaders define "strategy" *if* they have a big idea *and* a distinctive *Who? Why?* and *What?*

So, no—it's not my way or the highway when it comes to defining what strategy is.

Now, if leaders were to ask me how they *should* define strategy, I would point them to chapters 2 and 3. The definition of *strategy* in those chapters has unique benefits. For starters, it's the best way to distinguish between a strategy and a business model and plan…and a vision, mission, purpose, and goal…and financial engineering…and implementation and execution…and tactics. That matters because when leaders conflate these things, their odds of ending up with a winning strategy become tragically short, and that will always hurt execution.

As important, thinking of strategy as recommended in chapters 2 and 3 gives leaders a simple, powerful tool to shape their thinking, decisions, and actions on a wide range of questions that bedevil the running of any business well. Readers of the chapters that follow chapters 2 and 3 will have experienced many examples of such questions. For answering them, I have yet to find any single definition of strategy that provides a framework as effective as the one recommended in chapters 2 and 3 (if I am wrong, please do let me know at *act2advice@gmail.com*.)

Finally, readers of Part X of this book will have explored what leaders of any company can learn from other kinds of enterprises—whether those just starting out, or those in private hands, or those with a nonprofit objective. And readers who dipped into Part XI will have found examples of the insight and inspiration that leaders in any industry can gain from looking at the acute strategy challenges in other industries. If I was able to convey these parts with clarity and insight, it was only because I had chapters 2 and 3 firmly in mind. No other definition of strategy could guide my thinking as well as those two chapters.

So, while many leading lights of strategy offer a bewildering array of competing definitions of strategy, I do humbly recommend that leaders use the small number of choices framed in chapters 2 and 3 to define theirs.

I close by thanking you for opening this book! I hope you found something in it that will help you be a better leader or strategist or student of strategy. And I invite you to join me in the mission to help leaders reclaim strategy as the powerful leadership tool it deserves to be.

APPENDIX 1

How to navigate the great shareholder– stakeholder debate

And find your own solution to a perpetual issue with more heat than light

Is a company accountable to its shareholders or to its stakeholders? Is shareholder or stakeholder value its primary responsibility? Should shareholder or stakeholder capitalism define our economic system? These questions spark other questions, too, including: What is a company's social responsibility? What is the purpose of a corporation? And what is a company's governing objective? Questions like these have been debated for decades and will continue to be debated for decades more. The arguments they spark create a loud, even bewildering backdrop for leaders who want to have and hold great strategies. In this appendix, leaders will find a framework and some advice to help them find their way through the noise and confusion. But first we have to understand how we got here.

The invention of public companies created a separation of ownership from management and sparked the fear that such companies were accountable to no one. The solution was to make management accountable to shareholders. The principle was to equate the rights of shareholders to the property rights of owners. And the thinking was that shareholders bore the risks and rewards of the company's failure and success, and so they had corresponding rights to control it. Today, this is often referred to as "shareholder capitalism."

But, whether right or wrong, this solution has never been wholly satisfactory because there are so many other constituencies—like customers, employees, communities, and society at large—that have a "stake" in a company's actions and impact. This gave rise to an alternative solution widely known as "stakeholder capitalism."

Perhaps no one is more associated with stakeholder capitalism than the German economist Klaus Schwab. In 1971 he convened the first meeting of what would become the World Economic Forum in Davos, Switzerland. Schwab wanted business executives, government officials, and nonprofit leaders alike to discuss the notion of stakeholder capitalism. The idea caught on and, decades later, the language of stakeholder capitalism permeates politics, economics, and business. Thus was born the great shareholder–stakeholder debate.

But unfortunately for business leaders, the debate continues to generate a lot more political heat than practical light. This is because two versions of both "shareholder capitalism" and "stakeholder capitalism" are floating around. Each version suggests fundamentally different goalposts and guideposts for corporate governance and decision-making. And protagonists in the debate are often unclear about which version they are arguing for or against. This makes it exceedingly difficult for business leaders to pin down exactly what they are hearing.

So, what are these competing versions? Let's start with the term "shareholder capitalism." In its first version, "shareholder value" is defined as the value today of all cash flows that a business is likely to generate *for the rest of its life*. Finance professors call this "net present value," while Warren Buffett, the longtime chairman and CEO of Berkshire Hathaway, calls it "intrinsic value." By this definition, shareholder value is essentially a measure of the company's future earnings power, net of its ongoing investment needs and opportunities. It is also a proxy or synonym for the company's economic health—both today and for the long haul.

Under this definition of shareholder value, "maximizing shareholder value" means consistently choosing those strategies that are most likely to yield the greatest future earnings power after accounting for any investment they require. It also means that leaders can never stop looking for better strategies, because they can never know with absolute certainty if there are higher-value ones than those they've considered so far.

This version of maximizing shareholder value does not tolerate two kinds of "ism's." The first is "short-termism," as in cutting productive research-and-development (R&D) or buying back shares to hit an earnings-per-share target. The other problem is the opposite of short-termism, and it's just as deadly: "long-termism." This is the tolerance of luxurious investment, lax overhead, and low-balled targets. These behaviors put a company's health at risk because they sap the profits that are needed today to invest for the future.

Finally, this version of maximizing shareholder value calls for companies to, as Wayne Peacock, the CEO of USAA, said, "…do the right thing because it's the right thing for shareholders. [This means]…to take care of employees and truly create the environment in which they can feel welcome and that they belong…to support communities where we work and live…and to act in a socially responsible way."

There is, however, a second, quite different definition of shareholder capitalism. It treats "shareholder value" as a synonym for today's stock price and considers "maximizing" it to mean putting short-term profits and current shareholders first. This is the version that Jack Welch, the former CEO of General Electric, had in mind when he defined it as "setting a stock price goal" and went on to famously call it "the dumbest idea ever." It's also the version that Paul Collier describes in *The Future of Capitalism*, when he writes, "[it's] a sole focus on the bottom line…[where] companies no longer feel responsible to their employees or the communities where they operate." And the same for Roger Martin in his book *Fixing the Game*, where he calls it "tracking the company's stock price on screens," "distracting CEOs with stock-based compensation," "spinning lines to shareholders," and "trading long-term…value for temporary gains."

The table below summarizes how very different these two versions of shareholder capitalism are.

Two Versions of Shareholder Capitalism

	Version 1	Version 2
Shareholder value	The value today of all future earnings that a business is likely to generate *for the rest of its life*, net of its ongoing investment needs and opportunities.	Today's stock price.
Maximizing shareholder value	Creating and making choices that are most likely to yield the greatest future earnings power, net of investment those choices require.	Maximizing short-term profits.
Serving stakeholder interests	Essential to a company's shareholder value—*and* a consequence of maximizing it (see chapter 35).	Subordinated to *current* shareholders' *current* interests.
A corporation's social responsibility	To profitably solve problems with solutions that provide more benefits than costs to society, including externalities.	To make money regardless of the costs to society.
Leaders' decision time frame	Short-term and long-term.	Short-term.
Corporate behavioral boundaries	Legal, ethical, and moral norms of communities in which a business operates.	"All's fair in love and war," and "business is war."
Directors' primary responsibility	Care and loyalty to the company's long-term economic health as a whole, independent of any particular constituency.	Current shareholders and their interests ("shareholder primacy").

To further complicate matters, two versions of stakeholder capitalism are often bandied about, as well. An example of the first version (Version A in the table below) was adopted in 2006 by the U.K. Companies Act with the following guidance: "Corporate leaders are urged to pay close attention to how stakeholder factors affect long-term value maximization." This is sometimes referred to as "Instrumental Stakeholderism."[1] In his 2021 letter to CEOs, BlackRock's Larry Fink described it as, "[a] company…delivering value to its customers, employees, and communities…to deliver long-term, durable profits for shareholders."

The other version of stakeholder capitalism (Version B in the table below) is expressed as follows: "Directors have a plurality of independent constituencies and must balance a plurality of autonomous ends." This is known as "Classic" or "Beneficial" or "Structural" Stakeholderism. It calls for companies to serve the interests of non-shareholders and to take the lead in addressing large-scale societal problems and inequities even if it doesn't contribute to shareholder value.

The table below compares these two versions.

Two Versions of Stakeholder Capitalism		
	Version A	Version B
Stakeholder value	The benefits a company generates for stakeholders, net of any costs, including externalities.	The benefits a company generates for stakeholders, net of any costs, including externalities.
Creating stakeholder value	Essential to a company's shareholder value—and a consequence of maximizing it (see chapter 35).	An end in itself, with each stakeholder having equal (or unspecified) importance as every other stakeholder.
Creating shareholder value	Inevitable outcome of creating stakeholder value in ways that fortify the company's future earnings power.	To be "balanced" against serving the interests of other stakeholders.
A corporation's social responsibility	To profitably solve problems with solutions that provide more benefits than costs to society, including externalities.	To take the lead in solving society's problems.*
Leaders' decision time frame	Short-term and long-term.	Short-term and long-term.
Corporate behavioral boundaries	Legal, ethical, and moral norms of communities in which a company operates.	Meeting the interests of all stakeholders.
Directors' primary responsibility	Care and loyalty to the company's long-term economic health as a whole, independent of any particular constituency.	Care and loyalty to the interests of all multiple constituencies.

* Examples are illiteracy, infant mortality, inequality, aging populations, carbon emissions, water scarcity, land degradation, climate change in general, and diversity and inclusion.

For business leaders, the shareholder–stakeholder debate can be confusing, because the debaters rarely make clear which version of "shareholder" and "stakeholder" capitalism they are invoking in the two tables above. For example, in July 2020, Presidential candidate Joe Biden said, "It's way past time we put an end to the era of shareholder capitalism. [Companies] have responsibility to their workers, their community, to their country." Was he railing about Version

1 or 2 of shareholder capitalism in the first table farther above? Another example comes from the World Economic Forum. In January 2020 it came out with a manifesto urging companies to move to stakeholder capitalism. Is it advocating Version A or B in the table just above?

The good news is that if business leaders put what they hear from those advocating a particular form of capitalism through the screen of the two tables above, they'll be better able to separate noise from signal and wheat from chaff. For example, consider the Business Roundtable (BRT). In August 2019, it published with great fanfare a proclamation on "The Purpose of a Corporation." It was signed by no fewer than 181 CEOs whose companies represented over one-third of the total market capitalization in the U.S. equity markets. Its key statement read "We share a fundamental commitment to all of our stakeholders," which they list as "customers, employees, suppliers, communities, and shareholders."

Note the order. Because shareholders come *last,* pundits loudly pronounced BRT's proclamation to be "ending shareholder primacy" (as *Fortune* described it) and "abandoning the shareholder-first mantra" (*Financial Times*). Or, in other words, "shareholder capitalism" is dead and "stakeholder capitalism" is to take its place. But consider the following facts:

Fact 1: Jamie Dimon of JP Morgan Chase and Alex Gorsky of Johnson & Johnson (J&J) signed the BRT statement when they were not only the CEO of their respective companies, but chairman as well. Moreover, Dimon chaired the BRT and Gorsky led its Corporate Governance Committee at the time BRT's statement was issued. Yet JP Morgan's own corporate governance guidelines state very clearly that "the Board as a whole is responsible for the oversight of management on behalf of the Firm's shareholders." Likewise, J&J's governance guidelines demand that "the business judgment of the Board must be exercised… in the…interests of our shareholders."

Fact 2: All the 100 or so companies who updated their corporate governance guidelines after putting their names to BRT's proclamation still have guidelines that explicitly align the duties of directors with the interests of shareholders.

Fact 3: In an article for the *Wall Street Journal,* authors Lucian Bebchuk and Roberto Tallarita wrote, "Shareholders submitted more than 40 proposals to [the BRT's] signatory companies on how to implement the [BRT's] statement…. The companies all opposed these proposals." Moreover, no company's compensation practices or guidelines link director compensation with stakeholder interests. Instead, there remains a strong alignment of director pay with stock price.

Fact 4: The Business Roundtable claims that the views expressed in its 2019 statement are "consistent with existing corporate law and [do] not require any change to companies' bylaws and governance guidelines." Yet researchers from the Harvard Law School's Program on Corporate Governance say that leaving these documents unchanged means directors can *only* "consider stakeholder interests whenever doing so would serve long-term shareholder value."

Fact 5: In a previous proclamation, published in 1997, the BRT endorsed "maximizing shareholder value" as the governing objective of public companies. In that proclamation the BRT said, "It is in the long-term interests of stock-holders…to treat its employees well, to serve its customers well, to encourage its suppliers to continue to supply it, to honor its debts, and to have a reputation for civic responsibility." Now compare that to the list of five "commitments" included in the BRT's August 2019 statement: "delivering value to customers, investing in employees, dealing fairly and ethically with suppliers, supporting the communities in which a company operates, and generating long-term value for shareholders." Are these really different? Perhaps that is why the BRT claims that neither changes in corporate law nor alterations in company bylaws and governance guidelines are necessary (see Fact 4 above).

Fact 6: In an interview with the *New York Times*, the BRT's president, Joshua Bolten, said, "[Our proclamation] was not a demotion of…long-term sharehold-ers, because, in our view, the interests of all stakeholders align in the long-run."

Fact 7: The consulting firm McKinsey & Company is a signatory company. In June 2020—*after* signing BRT's proclamation—it published an article in which the authors advised business leaders that "maximizing a company's value to its shareholders, now and in the future" is a better objective than "simply maximizing today's share price." In October 2022 it *republished* a 2015 article with the headline "Shareholder-oriented capitalism is still the best path to broad economic prosperity." The piece ends by stating, "the shareholder model…is the best at bridging the broad and varied interests of shareholders and stakeholders alike." Also that same month it published an article titled "Five ways that ESG creates value" that included a statement that "businesses…need to satisfy the needs of their customers, employees, and communities…in order to maximize value creation."

Based on these seven facts, one has to wonder: which versions of shareholder and stakeholder capitalism are the BRT and its signatories really advocating? Leaders can form their own view, but they can safely assume that the BRT's August 2019 proclamation is at the very least a rejection of Version 2 of shareholder capitalism (see first table above), with its sharp emphasis on short-term profits, current stock price, and "putting shareholders first." Leaders should reject that version, too. To whom is it not obvious that making as much money as fast as possible while ignoring your staff, customers, and community won't ensure that a company can flourish?

Those same facts also tell us that the Business Roundtable probably doesn't think Version B of stakeholder capitalism is the answer, either. Leaders should reject it, as well, as it creates an impossible standard. Business leaders are endlessly confronted with tough decisions that involve unavoidable trade-offs between competing interests of different stakeholders. By supporting Version B, they make those decisions intractable and guarantee that they will politically shoot themselves in the foot sooner or later.

For example, consider Marc Benioff, chief executive of Salesforce. To celebrate his quarterly earnings report in August 2020, he proclaimed, "This is a victory for stakeholder capitalism." The very next day, in the midst of the Covid-19 pandemic, Salesforce informed 1,000 staff that their jobs were gone! When called out by the *New York Times*, all Benioff could muster in response was that "[Stakeholder capitalism] has to be viewed as both capturing an evolution and expressing an aspiration." Huh?

Having rejected Version 2 of shareholder capitalism and most likely Version B of stakeholder capitalism, we are left with Versions 1 and A as the best characterization of the BRT's position. The keen reader will notice that they are mirror images of each other. Two sides of the same coin. Ying and yang. Neither shareholder nor stakeholder capitalism. Just "smart, responsible, competitive capitalism." The kind that has lifted mankind out of the primordial soup. The kind that Warren Buffet describes in one of his annual shareholder letters:

"Berkshire is a Delaware corporation, and our directors must follow the state's laws. Among them is a requirement that board members must act in the best interest of the corporation and its stockholders. Our directors embrace that doctrine. In addition, of course, Berkshire directors want the company to delight its customers, to develop and reward the talents of its 360,000 associates, to behave honorably with lenders and to be regarded as a good citizen of the many cities and states in which we operate. We value these four important constituencies. None of these groups, however, have a vote in determining such matters as dividends, strategic direction, CEO selection, or acquisitions and divestitures. Responsibilities like those fall solely on Berkshire's directors, who must faithfully represent the long-term interests of the corporation and its owners."

To be sure, *all* companies are under pressure to be more responsive to their workers, communities, and the environment, and "maximizing shareholder value" often comes under fire when it's associated with being the opposite of that. Sadly, if leaders want to rile certain politicians, journalists, academics, lawyers, or business leaders, all they have to do is say that companies should maximize shareholder value. As Rajan Raghuram, a former governor of the Reserve Bank of India, said, "It sounds sinister—even if it may be the right thing to do... ." Or as the late Supreme Court Justice Antonin Scalia joked about constitutional originalism, "It's viewed as a weird affliction that seizes some people—'When did you first start eating human flesh?'" In many quarters, shareholder value is viewed the same way.

No, the great shareholder–stakeholder debate will never end as long as there is a short term and a long term, a separation of ownership from management, and stakeholders—ranging from investment managers, stock analysts, customers, board directors, and executives to middle managers, frontline staff, unions, suppliers, governments, citizens, local communities, and society at large—who all want their interests to come first, ahead of all other stakeholders.

Nor will the debate be over as long as there are those who invoke Version 2 of shareholder capitalism in order to demonize it, such as Martin Wolf who in his book *The Crisis of Democratic Capitalism* writes, "[Shareholder capitalism] prioritizes, above all else, efforts to maximize the (short-term) price of a company's stock—all other purposes (including what the firm actually does) be damned."

Wolf and other demonizers like him know that no leader of sound mind and judgment thinks that any business can be consistently "successful"—however it's defined—without paying due attention to its so-called "stakeholders." Good leaders know they have to provide meaningful value to all stakeholders—to offer competitive pay, benefits, and work environments to their people; to set prices that entice customers to buy not only once, but multiple times; to constantly improve the value of their offerings to justify those prices; and to find innovative solutions that minimize, if not eliminate, inevitable conflicts of interests between stakeholders.

Good leaders also know that corporations should not act as the arbiters of sociopolitical progress, but rather should be guided by a government of, for, and by the people to achieve such progress. They recognize that business is valuable socially because it solves problems in ways that generate wealth. They do not apologize for that. Nor do they let themselves be cowed into abandoning Version 1 of shareholder capitalism by being beaten over the head with Version 2. Instead, they use language to fight back—language that is right for their own companies and circumstances, like the language Peacock found for USAA and Buffett for Berkshire Hathaway.

---

1   See "What Does 'Stakeholder Capitalism' Mean to You," Lynn S. Paine, *Harvard Business Review*, September–October 2023.

APPENDIX 2

Decades of writing on strategy

This book began with many dozens of pieces I published in *Harvard Business Review*, *Forbes.com*, and especially *Strategy+Business*. Readers can find a complete listing in this and the following pages.

HARVARD BUSINESS REVIEW

How Brand Building and Performance Marketing Can Work Together, May/June 2023 (with Jim Stengel and Cait Lamberton)

Creating an Organic Growth Machine, May 2012 (with David Meer and Samrat Sharma)

Five Rules for Retailing in a Recession, April 2009 (with Tim Romberger and David Meer)

Managing the Right Tension, December 2006 (with Dominic Dodd)

HBR.ORG

Don't Draft a Digital Strategy Just Because Everyone Else Is, March 16, 2016

A Brief History of the Ways Companies Compete, April 22, 2015

Defining Strategy, Implementation, and Execution, March 31, 2015

Long-Termism Is Just as Bad as Short-Termism, September 25, 2014

Reinvent Your Company by Reassessing Its Strengths, May 30, 2014

Should GE Be Scrapped for Parts? May 16, 2007

FORBES.COM

Three Strategy Pivots to Make Wal-Mart a Great Investment Again
Dec. 14, 2015

Why Wal-Mart Needs Strategic Innovation to Become a Great Investment Again
Nov. 29, 2015

The Investment Opportunity in Killing Alcoa's Faux Strategy
Nov. 11, 2015

With Alcoa's Split, a Faux Strategy Bites the Dust
Oct. 9, 2015

Wondering Where the Alpha Will Be from Alphabet (nee Google)
Sept. 27, 2015

Still Searching for the Strategy in Alphabet (nee Google)
Sept. 7, 2015

ESPN: The Exception to Disney's Strategy
Aug. 17, 2015

Why Long-Term Investors Can Bet on Disney
Aug. 4, 2015

STRATEGY+BUSINESS

Does shareholder value still have a place in strategy?
NOVEMBER 12, 2019

What's the link between strategy and "doing good"?
SEPTEMBER 3, 2019

How is strategy differing for nonprofits?
JUNE 18, 2019

How long should a long-term strategy be?
MARCH 21, 2019

How can you help your leaders get more creative?
FEBRUARY 6, 2019

What's the right mix of organic growth and acquisitions?
OCTOBER 2, 2018

Can strategy be decisive and flexible?
MARCH 15, 2018

Can Best Buy Thwart the Grim Reaper?
MAY 13, 2013

We're from Corporate and We're Here to Help
APRIL 8, 2013

The Right Ideas in All the Wrong Places
MARCH 11, 2013

Sourcing Growth
FEBRUARY 26, 2013

How Leaders Mistake Execution for Strategy (and Why That Damages Both)
FEBRUARY 11, 2013

Strategy or Execution: Which Is More Important?
JUNE 1, 2012

Strategy: An Executive's Definition
MAY 29, 2012

The Two Levels of Strategy
APRIL 27, 2012

Total Shareholder Returns
MARCH 21, 2011

MIT SLOAN MANAGEMENT REVIEW

Favaro, Ken, and Manish Jhunjhunwala. "Why Teams Should Record Individual Expectations." *MIT Sloan Management Review*, vol. 60, no. 2, 2019, pp. 89–90.

Favaro, Ken. "What Is Your Strategy's Big Idea?" *MIT Sloan Management Review*, 2016-sloanreview.mit.edu/article/what-is-your-strategys-big-idea.

FEI: FINANCIAL EXECUTIVES INTERNATIONAL

The Great Shareholder-Stakeholder Debate
March 23, 2021

Acknowledgments

Just as it takes a village to raise a child, it also takes one to produce a book. And, oh, what a village I had to help me with this book!

Writing can be a lonely endeavor. You think you have something clever to say about a topic or question…until you write it down, read what you wrote, and realize, "Uh-oh, that's really not very good." So, you roll up your sleeves, sweat bullets, and iterate until you have something that's not totally embarrassing. Even then, you are unsure. So, you ask people you trust to be your sounding board. I had two, John Favaro and Greg Rotz.

John, one of my five siblings, is the Da Vinci in my Italian-American family. In addition to being a world-class software engineer, manager, and consultant, he's a great writer. Greg, a mentee-turned-mentor from my checkered past, is a world-leading management consultant. I tortured both of them with every word I wrote for this book. They never hesitated to give me the feedback I needed to hear and some suggestions for acting on their feedback.

If this book is worth the paper and bits it consumes, it's because of the questions that headline its chapters and the quality of answers found in those chapters. I owe a lot to the many people who, over the years, challenged me with those questions and taught me so much about how to answer them. There are just too many to list here, but I would like to call out some of them. They fall into two camps.

Former and current colleagues are in the first camp. These include Bill Alberts, Jim McTaggart, Peter Kontes, Ron Langford, Paul Favaro (another sibling!), and Dominic Dodd (Marakon Associates); Shumeet Banerji and Cesare Menardi (Booz & Company); Nadim Yacteen (Recombinators); Bill Duggan (Columbia Business School); and Stefanos Zenios (Stanford Graduate School of Business).

The second camp includes the many CEOs, senior executives, and board directors who allowed me to cross their threshold, and from whom I gained much wisdom (and not a few gray hairs). They come from some of the world's largest public companies as well as startups, private companies, and nonprofits. The most influential of these include Lord Blyth, David Thompson, and Martin Bryant (Boots UK Ltd.); Sir Brian Pitman (Lloyds Bank); Lord Browne and John Buchanan (BP plc); Sir John Sunderland (Cadbury Schweppes plc); Franz Humer (Roche); Norm Bobbins (LaSalle Bank); Bob Walter (Cardinal Health); Peter Kahn and Rich Zannino (Dow Jones & Company); Sir Jon Symonds, Andrew Thompson, and George Savage (Proteus Digital Health); Frank Fischer (NeuroPace); Glenn Hubbard (Columbia Business School); Ryan Barker (BERA); Nan Wei Gong (Figur8); Kathleen Colsen (BOMA); Kelly Blanchard (Ibis); and John Svoboda (Svoboda Capital).

Everyone in both camps flashed before my eyes more than once while I was slaving over this book. My memories of working with them helped me to write honestly and, I hope, with more than a modicum of insight and humility.

I am indebted to *Harvard Business Review, Forbes.com, Strategy+Business,* and many other journals for allowing me to rehearse my thinking on their unsuspecting readers. Much of what was market-tested in those publications found its way into *Real Strategy.*

Writing a book is hard enough. Publishing one is no piece of cake, either. It involves mind-numbing details: copy editing; cover and interior design; page layouts; proofing, proofing, proofing; ISBN numbers; registration of book and publishing imprint—the list goes on. As my wife knows, I'm not a particularly good details person (she means "not an unimportant-details person"). So, I couldn't have published *Real Strategy* without the meticulous, well-organized, and strong-backboned support of Holly Brady, Publishing Strategist at Brady New Media Publishing; the diligent, fun-hearted, and eagle-eyed copy editing of Mark at Mark Woodworth Editorial Services, who suffered through my raw writing to help me bang it into serviceable shape; and the beautiful design work of Vicky Vaughn Shea from Ponderosa Pine Design.

No acknowledgments would be complete with a shout-out to one's family. In my case, that goes to my wife and emotional-support blanket, Lisa. She deserves my immense, heartfelt gratitude for (almost) never balking about leaving her alone on so many weekend mornings while I chipped away at the rock pile of writing this book. I wish I could honestly tell her that it won't happen again, but a little white lie will have to suffice for now.

So, a village, indeed! Sounding boards, devil's advocates, clients, colleagues, fellow travelers, publishers, and family—I thank them all.

About the Author

Ken Favaro specializes in working with business leaders—CEOs, executive teams, and boards—in three areas: strategy, innovation, and organization. To each of these three areas he brings a skeptical, clear-eyed perspective that has been sharpened and honed from decades of fruitful and painful learning about how to separate the wheat from the chaff. He prides himself on having a keen detector of B.S. (including his own, he hopes) to help leaders optimize their productivity and efficacy.

After graduating from Stanford University with Bachelor of Science in Engineering and Master of Business Administration degrees, Ken cut his teeth at Bain & Company and then spent the bulk of his consulting career—25 years—at Marakon Associates, during which he served as CEO for six years. After Marakon, Ken joined Booz & Company (now Strategy& PwC) to lead its global strategy practice for six years.

At Booz, Ken co-developed a new approach to strategy and innovation that he now calls "Precedents Thinking." He has co-taught that approach and its variants to MBAs, Executive MBAs, and executives as a guest instructor at both Columbia Business School and Stanford Graduate School of Business.

Ken is no more a professional writer than he is a professional golfer. But he loves to write about business almost as much as he loves to play golf. He is co-author of *The Three Tensions* (Jossey-Bass, 2007), four feature articles in *Harvard Business Review*, and countless pieces for other publications.

Ken currently lives in Bronxville, New York, with his wife, Lisa. They have three grown children—Nic, Alex, and Cristina—and wonderfully extended families on both sides of their marriage.